Women Writing in America

Women Writing in America:
Voices in Collage

Blanche H. Gelfant

PUBLISHED FOR DARTMOUTH COLLEGE

 BY UNIVERSITY PRESS OF NEW ENGLAND
HANOVER AND LONDON

Text and photograph credits appear on page vi.

Copyright 1984 by Trustees of Dartmouth College
Second printing 1985
Printed in the United States of America

LIBRARY OF CONGRESS CATALOGING IN PUBLICATION DATA

Gelfant, Blanche H., 1922–
    Women writing in America.

    Bibliography: p.
    Includes index.
    1. American literature—Women authors—History and criticism—
Addresses, essays, lectures.   2. Canadian literature—Women authors—
History and criticism—Addresses, essays, lectures.   I. Dartmouth Col-
lege.   II. Title.
PS147.G4   1984   810'.9'9287   84-40298
ISBN 0-87451-307-3
ISBN 0-87451-308-1 (pbk.)

For Nina and Alan

CREDITS

Contents

Acknowledgments

The Rockefeller Foundation for the Humanities provided a precious commodity—time—for the reading and writing that produced several of the pieces in this critical collage.

Like most writing, all these pieces have benefited from the comments of colleagues. Seldom intended as specific criticism, such comments were often made in the course of conversations for which I am grateful.

I am grateful also to Deborah Hodges, who helped me meet many deadlines. Her skill in typing was matched only by her reliability and her patience with endless revisions.

For the gift of sympathy, and for specific suggestions, I am indebted to one person who has over the years read various pieces closely and by her comments encouraged their completion. At one time a colleague, and at all times a friend, Dr. Arlene Heyman has helped me with her editorial comments, her incisive questions, informed by her experience as a writer and a psychoanalyst, and her intolerance of obscurity, pretentiousness, and jargon. Writing of the need for exemplary figures, I seem to have found one in my friend Arlene. She is what the heroines of modern novels often wish to be—a complete and self-possessed person who can fulfill, without loss or fragmentation, the demands of her multiple roles as wife, mother, public citizen, and professional woman. She is also fun.

Women Writing in America:

An Introduction

An Introduction

This volume gathers together a number of critical pieces that focus in different ways upon American women writers. Their diversity—extreme between figures like Ann Beattie and Meridel Le Sueur, or Willa Cather and Margaret Mitchell, or Anzia Yezierska and Jean Stafford—has been for me part of their appeal. I have enjoyed listening to highly distinctive voices and hearing them sound, singly and contrapuntally, certain themes common to American writers, and particularly, to women. Seeing these essays grouped together, I realize that I too pursue certain themes. They became most evident to me in the essay on Ethel Wilson, a Canadian writer to whose work I had been asked to bring an "American" perspective. When I compared Wilson with American male writers like Ernest Hemingway and Theodore Dreiser, I saw how pervasively I deal, as a critic, with violence, uncertainty, and nihilistic visions of life, and with the writer's quest for a language consonant with an American landscape that is always being discovered or created, that is always new. When I compared Wilson with American women writers like Willa Cather, I realized how precariously I balance idealism against bleak disillusionment in discussing the literary treatment of such ordinary events as courtship, marriage, family gatherings—events that usually shape women's lives. American motifs and women's experience—their confluence is the general theme of this volume.

In all the works these essays discuss, I find evidences of violence which, like the "hidden mines" of Ethel Wilson, American women writers plant in their fiction and then conceal by various narrative strategies: by "forgetting" in Willa Cather, by deflecting attention to trivia in Ann Beattie, by disguising violence as accident in Jean Stafford, or, as in Wilson, by eliding its consequences. Another diversionary tactic is, simply, beauty of style. For the writers' sentences arrest one by their rhythm, fluidity, and sound, by language that is highly individualized and poetically resonant, often haunting. Almost always, however, a

1

beautiful verbal surface contains—holds and withholds—an awesome violence that suddenly erupts from hidden depths. A child is raped, a wife is murdered, a woman's body discovered mutilated. Then the sentences resume their fluid movement, the story's surface closes over its terrible gap, and life goes on, though the reader may never again be the same.

The essay on *Gone With The Wind* notes how a language of clichés, which makes individuality of voice impossible, both reveals and attenuates the violence of racism and rape, so that the novel satisfies simultaneously the reader's wish for superiority, for prurient pleasure, and, through the attenuation, for a sense of moral rectitude. This essay raises the issue of popularity, a sexually complicated issue, since women's success as novelists has often been viewed as failure by their "fellow" writers and by critics. Both, we know, have denigrated the lady "scribbler." Not unexpectedly, then, *Gone With The Wind* has been attacked as clamorously as it has been acclaimed. Indeed, its popularity has been attributed to the execrableness of public taste; the common (woman) reader, it seems, admires writing that is aesthetically and morally defective. In pursuing the secret of *Gone With The Wind*'s extraordinary popularity, I do not deny the novel's weaknesses. Rather, I find them edifying as they revealed a cultural and literary matrix from which "great" American novels also spring. Thus, I use *Gone With The Wind* as an exemplary text, seeking in it—even in its clichés, stereotypes, and distorted representations of rape and race—the secret of an appeal that novels of complex vision and art possess but make obscure. For as "great" novels develop themes and images that *Gone With The Wind* simplifies, they disguise and subvert them, and leave them ultimately inexplicable. Inexhaustible mystery may be a secret of "great" novels; popular fiction, however, must seem accessible. Traditionally, popular women writers have made their work accessible to the common woman reader in recognition of a shared purpose: that the reader wishes to learn, and the writer, to teach. The lesson of *Gone With The Wind*, as Margaret Mitchell clearly knew, was survival—a motif that runs through the diverse works I discuss. For all her faults, Scarlett O'Hara knows the secret of survival, and in this respect she is, like prototypical popular heroines, an exemplary figure presented for the reader to emulate. Moreover, though she is childishly selfish,

Scarlett becomes capable of caring for others—for her father, her sisters, her impoverished aunt, for the broken Ashley Wilkes. Her driving obsession is not, as she believes, romantic love, but the desire to reestablish a devastated home; and however devious her means, which include a ludicrous attempt to sell herself to Rhett Butler, she manages to restore her beloved Tara. She is thus at once a protector of home and, in her pursuit of Ashley, its destroyer. Making Tara rise from its ashes, she is a creation goddess and also the goddess of strife who creates havoc in Atlanta; a scarlet woman and a savior; flirtatious schemer and fool; victim and survivor. Her relationships with her father and her husband are impossibly complex, since she is to each inseparably mother, daughter, and wife. No role defeats Scarlett, and all demonstrate her strength, her will to survive— or, simply, her will. I am, of course, not advocating Scarlett's conduct, but rather describing her function as the heroine of a popular novel. This means setting her, with all her faults, in the long tradition of women characters who purport to teach the reader how to live.

Only as I was completing a description of the city's "hungry" heroines did I realize how urgently I was pursuing images of survival, how much I wished to find in American writers and their characters salient examples of women who were not mad, suicidal, starving, raging, or sinking into inanition. Like the heroines I was delineating, I wanted to hear the sound of voices strong enough to have shattered women's well-known "silence." Perhaps that desire has motivated all these pieces, for as a critic I seem to have been gathering assurances of the strength of American women writers. I liked knowing that some as diverse in age as Le Sueur and Beattie are writing prolifically, and that they have succeeded others as accomplished and intelligent, and as different, as Willa Cather, Mary Austin, and Katherine Anne Porter. However, the ability of such writers to develop a distinctive voice does not allow for easy optimism. That, clearly, is impermissible, given the massive literature we now have on women's victimization. Moreover, none of the writers I discuss has escaped the exigencies of a woman's life—not even, as various essays point out, Willa Cather. All of them were spent in ways peculiar to their sex; but all seem to have learned a secret of recovery. Tillie Olsen's novella "Requa" enacts this secret as its young protagonist regains his life and the writer her voice. Scarlett O'Hara embodies the secret as she recuperates from endless losses—the loss of her romantic hopes and the loss of her home, her mother, her child, her entire world. In Le Sueur's *Rites of Ancient Ripening*, "woman" recovers the songs, along with the history, of Native Americans so that her timeless voice may sing with a politically persuasive passion. Thinking back on the novels, I am sorry that Molly Fawcett in Stafford's *The Mountain Lion* could not live long enough to recover from the humiliation and self-hatred she was being conditioned to feel. Though she is one of the few characters under discussion who dies, I argue that today she would have found a place in the world to live. For in her intelligence and rebelliousness, she is a sister to the "sisters of Faust," those "hungry" heroines whose generic characteristic is survival. Inimical as the contemporary world may still be to these unbeautiful and unconventional young women, it cannot absolutely deny them their place. This may be the least that one can say, but at least it is more than could be said for the old mythic West that drove Molly from its territory.

In discussing works like *The Mountain Lion, My Ántonia, Rites of Ancient Ripening,* and a variety of urban novels, I have looked for the intersection of American motifs with themes pertinent to women: female patterns of development, mother-daughter relationships, romance and marriage, conflicts between caring for others and the self, response to a demand for passivity, and (disguised) forms of rebellion. Points of intersection between setting and sex have become, I believe, the nexus of subversions appealing to women writing in America. For here, in a new land that has mythologized the possibilities for a new life, writers could show characters refusing to submit to old traditions. They could show them also in the process of discovering and exploring, actions particularly suitable to immigrant heroines, some of whom have openly identified themselves with Columbus. This identification focalizes the essay on urban fiction, in which I see the city's adventurous women as perennial immigrants. The essay itself tends to subvert an expectation that urban violence must crush the novel's heroine, if not physically, then by the weight of a materialism that turns her into a voracious consumer or a product to be consumed. American urban fiction imagines other possibilities: a chance for a woman to feel free and move about in the city, to locate in its multitudinous neighborhoods a room of her own, and to relocate the object of her desire. Instead of love, certain urban heroines "hunger" for knowledge, for they come to believe that love and marriage constrain, while knowledge permits one to possess and transform the self. For a woman, even the desire for self-creation is implicitly an act of social subversion.

I have been arrested by the many instances of subversion to be found in apparently traditional American women writers, some of whom, like Cather, Stafford, and Porter, resented adjectival labeling; each wanted to be known only as a writer. In *My Ántonia*, once Cather identified an immigrant woman with the land she helped transform, she had to subvert the traditional story of seduction and abandonment she seemed to be telling. Thus, she allowed Ántonia to bear her illegitimate child, and both mother and daughter to live—in the end, happily. She could not do otherwise, since she had made Ántonia's fate as girl and woman a synecdoche for America. The plot of female development thus became inseparable from the history of a nation which, like an inchoate girl, changed as it matured and fulfilled its destiny. But Ántonia did not simply figure forth the incandescent changes in the American landscape. As a pioneer woman imbued by Cather with mythical metamorphosing power, she effected change by transforming a desolate prairie into rich farm fields and orchards. She also brought life to a barren land, populating it with sons and daughters. Cather thus gave her women enormous social responsibilities, and did this, I believe, while taking enormous risks; for she would place her heroines in traditional "women's" plots and then rescue them from their trivial designs. Even Marion Forrester of *A Lost Lady* is rescued as memory transforms her from a fallen woman into an indelible image of promise—perhaps the same promise, the perennial promise, that America had originally offered and then, as this novel would have it, betrayed. Cather thus enlarged the lostness of her "lost lady" by conflating it with losses she believed America had suffered during a historic period of decline. She was adumbrating, unknowingly of course, a serious loss to her art when this decline would become for her absolute and she would have to sever the synecdochic relationship between women and land. In *Lucy Gayheart*, a late novel set in a late period, America is irrevocably changed, and so is the role of woman. Instead of playing the central part in an inspiring historic drama, she has become, like Lucy, merely an accompanist. Nevertheless, *Lucy Gayheart* also seems to me a subversive novel, since in it both writer and heroine refuse to meet the expectations of the romantic love story that Cather was using as her literary pre-text.

The essay on Meridel Le Sueur, a writer once considered (by McCarthy) dangerously subversive, notes the problems produced by the conflation of Native American history with a quest for "feminine" form. This thematic conflation seems to me neither personal nor fortuitous, since it has appeared also in Mary Austin, a polemically feminist writer. The essay analyzing the story of her literary life alludes to Austin's importance in recovering Native American songs, but does not state the importance she found in them as a generative force. Austin asserted that native rhythms had shaped traditional American poetry and, more startlingly, that they were rhythms to which human life was biologically bound. Like Le Sueur, she was imputing to Native Americans a timeless and perennial wisdom which they shared with women (her ideal of women) along with a shared minority status. In rendering native traditions, Austin and Le Sueur valorized "otherness," defining alienation as an opportunity to think and speak for one's self. Accordingly, alienation, the underlying theme of modern American male fiction, must be placed within a semantic code that defines the meanings that key thematic terms have for women. Among these terms are enclosure or confinement and renunciation which, like alien-ness, need not necessarily signify loss in American women writers. On the contrary, through solitariness and renunciation women characters often find for themselves, especially in urban fiction, a private space in which to maintain a necessary inviolability. Even as seemingly unrebellious a figure as Lucy Gayheart refuses love and marriage, preferring the solitude and confinement of her little room in Chicago. There she feels protected against the violations she fears from her handsome suitor and from the world.

In Le Sueur, alienation affirms the value of difference. Le Sueur believes that cultural and sexual difference, merged in the persona of her Indian woman, produces a life force that may counteract male drives she finds oppressive and death-ridden.

In recuperating an American past dominated by men, Le Sueur's "Indian" poems describe a drama alarmingly different from Cather's heroic romance. The central historic fact of this drama is genocide, a metaphor for all forms of destruction—destruction of the land, of community, and of an empathetic way of seeing and singing. The woman who sings in Le Sueur's poems, a universal "I," promises the return of ancient life-renewing rites, for she believes in a pattern of eternal circularity that is mythic, religious, and Le Sueur adds, immutably biological. Another conflation thus takes place in the poems as the languages of different codes express a single encompassing vision that includes all forms of life and all time. This vision of universal community, Le Sueur declares, is primordially female.

In describing literary works as polemical as *Rites of Ancient Ripening,* as romantic as *Lucy Gayheart,* or as poignant as "Requa," I have tried to maintain an appropriate critical distance without claiming a disinterested objectivity that I think any critic would have difficulty in demonstrating. I may not always have discerned the personal involvement that guided the choice of works I have found interesting. Sometimes, the choice seemed a matter of chance. Sometimes, indeed, I wrote about works I had literally *found*—like Le Sueur's writings, which I discovered in the most desultory way on a shelf in a bookstore on a street in San Jose to which I had been led by chance, a wrong turn in the road. Nevertheless, I knew what I was looking for when I picked up the slender paperbacks, and knew what I had "found" when I read them. I am looking always, of course, for aesthetic pleasure, but I find it enhanced by the encounter of American motifs with women's lives, the thematic nexus that I believe gives these disparate critical pieces coherence.

Disparity and coherence are, of course, the essence of collage—a form created from "found," fragmented, and often discarded pieces. If I imply an analogy between this volume and a collage, it is to suggest a preference for criticism that is open-ended, capable of surprise, and subversive of traditional standards and forms. In these respects, it seems to me congenial to a feminist inquiry. For the analogy valorizes a continuously open canon, since collage is an open form. These critical pieces include non-canonical works; but though they refer to writings about Black women, Chinese, Native Americans, immigrant

Jews, they are neither comprehensive nor fully representative.[1] Still, as a "collage of voices" *Women Writing in America* is perennially open to other authors, those already "found" by critics and those yet to be discovered, perhaps among the discarded, overlooked, or undervalued. As in a collage, material usually considered "junk" (like women's popular fiction) may assume value when recovered and placed in a new context or seen from a new perspective. Juxtaposition of disparate pieces allows for new ways of seeing, for re-vision, the activity central to feminist criticism.

As it challenges traditional aesthetic criteria, collage is inevitably subversive. By using "found" objects, rather than those "given" by tradition, it questions the material of art; it may ask, for example, why marble and bronze are suitable for sculpture, but not rusted iron; and yet by visibly incorporating in its art society's "junked" pieces, it questions an economic system that systematically produces waste. Olsen's "Requa," set in a junkyard, seems to me a verbal collage, composed as it is of fragments of experience as well as sentences, of truncated poems and phrases, of disparate typographies. This form suits the theme of broken lives, which in the novella are being pieced together and given coherence. Meanwhile, the characters themselves care for discarded things, making them useful as they recover them from the junkpile. In the same way, the writer is making society's discarded characters luminous. In Olsen's fiction, as in Le Sueur's, distinctions between the ugly and the beautiful, the useless and useful, the forgettable and the recoverable, become blurred—as they do in collage. For once disparate pieces are placed side by side on a common ground, whether a canvas or a story, they assume equal aesthetic value. In socially oriented criticism, differences between popular and high art may blur. I am not suggesting that *Gone With The Wind* or the popular novels I have discussed here are indistinguishable as art from works of imaginative and stylistic complexity; but I believe that denying them "greatness" (attributable to comparatively few American novels) should not mean depriving them of cultural or even literary importance. Clearly, collage values judgment, though it questions, rearranges, and upsets a value system. The essay on women's literary lives judges Cather's novel *The Song of the Lark* superior as art to Austin's *A Woman of*

Genius, while it finds the latter more valuable to readers concerned with women's struggles to express their genius.

I begin this volume with a piece on Grace Paley called "Fragments for a Portrait in Collage." In it I try to find the secret of wholeness for women whose lives are fragmented into multiple and conflicting roles and into discontinuous stages. That seemed to me the secret that Paley has discovered, for she is indelibly, indisputably, her own self, while she is a wife, mother, teacher, activist and public figure, exemplary woman, and writer. She may be the emblematic figure in this collage. Her voice is inimitable—as are the voices of all the American women writers gathered here. This volume invites the reader to listen.

Grace Paley:

Fragments for a Portrait in Collage

Grace Paley

ON GRACE PALEY

The only time I ever belonged to an underground was when I joined the coterie of Grace Paley fans who admired her stories before they became widely known. Her first collection, The Little Disturbances of Man, *was passed to me under the table, as it were, as a test of initiation. If I became ecstatic over the strange elliptical snappy funny stories I would be* in. *How could I resist when Paley spoke a wise-cracking smart lingo that to me was native speech? Those of us in the Paley underground in the sixties waited with proverbial bated breath for the next story, the new collection. When it arrived,* Enormous Changes at the Last Minute *showed that in Paley's fiction, and in life, there is continuity rather than final ending. The apocalyptic last minute, when possibilities are closed and hope dies, has never occurred for Paley, though it has for others of her generation who have come to believe that the world will never change and their fruitless attempts to change it must cease. This is not to say that Paley is a vapid optimist, as no one could think after reading "Samuel" and "The Little Girl," stories in which mere children gratuitously die. Paley knows about death, and about drugs, human loneliness, disappointment, violence, rape; but she has learned the secret of how to survive the knowledge as a writer and a woman in the public world. Her ever-increasing visibility makes her an exemplary figure to other women, a burden that she should find light to bear since all she need do is be her self. This "portrait" is based upon real encounters with Paley and fantasies.*

Settings and Encounters, Real and Imagined:

In Hanover, New Hampshire, you meet your best friends—and your enemies—at the Co-op Food Market on the Lebanon Road. Waiting at the meat counter, you tell about your children, off to school or coming home, your latest trip, skiing, maybe, or backpacking, or cruising the Greek Isles, the gossip—how terrible that so-and-so is separating or permutating, or sick, or drinking again. You leave the Co-op quickened. You have your freshly cut meat, natural bread, a wedge of Vermont cheese, and a sense of daily life, ordinary repetitive happenings that tell of the little disturbances of man.

One day in the summer of 1975, a short, pleasant, homey-looking woman was wandering down the cookie aisle of the Co-op. She looked familiar to me, as people do in small-town places. Suddenly, I recalled other times and other settings, occasions that her presence inspired: a party in a loggy country house in Erieville, New York, given in her honor by the English Department of Syracuse University; and not long afterwards, a cocktail gathering in a Manhattan hotel room crowded with professors talking to her volubly (and probably meanly) about the Modern Language Association meeting they were attending. She wore, on that wintry evening, long black boots, a woolen plaid poncho that seemed to me then bohemian, and loose, comfortable clothes which were like her manner, easy but city-wise. Her hair was held back in a bun that carelessly let little wisps escape and fall about her face. Everything about her seemed casual, plainly and naturally there, set outside of time at a time when women teased and sprayed their hair into wires and wore glossy clothes. I see now that she had the deceptively simple style of her stories, but as with the stories, the style aroused interest and curiosity. You might be missing something in that casual put-togetherness, of her clothes or her words, in that easy surface beneath which, you will discover, lies coiled an intent to arrest, an insight into disturbance, a relentless intelligence alert to life and its enormous changes.

Pushing my shopping cart, I ran to her in the cookie aisle. I had just published a review of her new book of stories, *Enormous Changes at the Last Minute*, and I had something to offer her: my adulation—but since that was intangible, I proposed instead a

13

cup of coffee, and we talked. We were to talk again various times over the next few years, and to me our conversations were always as elliptical as the form of her stories: something was being left out, the secret, a wonderful secret, I thought, that should be shared because it was rare and precious, and someday I was going to ask it directly of this elusively mysterious woman.

"Huh," I imagine her saying, "Me mysterious! What's mysterious about me?"

"Oh, ho," I would answer. "What isn't? You tell me. What were you doing in the cookie aisle of the Co-op? How come you're living a village life in Thetford, Vermont—your boots and poncho now a country style? You, a city-people person! Look at you and the Bronx, and you and Brooklyn and Coney Island, and all the city people in your stories. How could you leave them, even for a summer, when they're still sitting on the stoop steps eating ice cream, or setting up their orange crates to squat in front of the house for the day, watching the world go by—your world? The city streets need you to watch the women who are sitting by the windows watching the streets. You're the one who knows them, how they yell down at the kids and throw them apples and nickels for candy. How can you stay away," I would say, "even for a year, from the Northeast Playground where your women get together and carry on playground politics that's not so different from life? What about the city parks, where you put Faith up a tree? You can't go away to the country and leave Faith behind, the way Goodman Brown did [I thought a high-class literary touch would flatter and persuade]. And the city tenements where Faith's kitchen is a world with love and death and desertion going on, and children growing up. You're the one who made Faith tell her son Richard about the city, a setting she asked him, and you asked us, to love. Where else could Richard go to school with Jews, Presbyterians, and bohemians, and a smart Chinese like Arnold Lee? Faith said. In what other setting?"

FAITH TO RICHARD:

"Now Richard, listen to me, Arnold's an interesting boy; you wouldn't meet a kid like him anywhere but here or Hong Kong. So use some of these advantages I've given you. I could be living in the country, which I love, but I know how hard that is on children—I stay here in this creepy slum. I dwell in soot and slime just so you can meet kids like Arnold Lee and live on this wonderful block with all the Irish and Puerto Ricans, although God knows why there aren't any Negro children for you to play with . . . (original ellipsis)

("Faith in a Tree")

Naturally, the Critic Now Appears:

Out of context, Faith's words may seem ironical—"tough and cheery" in the Paley manner, and cleverly inverted—so unaccustomed are we to praise of the city as a place to live, let alone bring up children. But in the story, Faith means what she says. She likes all kinds of kids, as Richard jealously complains. She likes the polyglot faces and personalities that tumble about her in the city's parks, playgrounds, and housing projects, in the subways and the streets. She really regrets that her son has no black children to play with, tough little boys like Samuel who, in the short story "Samuel," jiggles and hops on subway platforms, where accidentally he is killed. Samuel turns out to be irreplaceable, as is every person to someone of Paley's sensibility and profession. She sees herself as a kind of catcher in the rye, saving the heedless running children of the streets—and the adults—from falling over the cliff of time into oblivion. Rescue is the writer's responsibility, explains the narrator of "Debts," who is, like Paley, a storyteller: "It was possible that I did owe something to my family and the families of my friends. That is, to tell their stories as simply as possible, in order, you might say, to save a few lives." (Start by trying to save a few lives on paper, and you might end a pacifist like Paley, protesting the waste of lives in the Vietnam War.) Samuel dies in the subway—and the runaway in "The Little Girl" dies in an appalling way the writer cannot allow—but the stories of their death memorialize them and assert the unique value of each living boy and girl. Soon after her son's death, Samuel's mother has another child, but "immediately she saw that this baby wasn't Samuel. She and her husband together have had other children, but never again will a boy exactly like Samuel be known."

This sense of the value of life—of every individual life and of life as process and change—may be exactly what we mean by faith; and Paley's heroine, who pops in and out of her stories, growing older and treasuring both past and future, is well named. Faith believes in the possibilities of personal change, and she is not frightened or appalled by social change, the transition of neighborhoods in the city, for instance, from white to black. Jolted by a seemingly gratuitous encounter—like running into an ex-husband on the library steps or a neighborhood cop in the park—Paley's heroine will change her hairdo, her job, her "style of living and telling." Faith comes down from the tree and enters the world where there are peace marchers against the Vietnam War, and policemen who won't permit them, and children like Richard who scream and stamp their feet, strapped dangerously in skates, and protest against repression. Her son's fury transforms Faith (wise mother to be led by a child) into a woman who thinks "more and more and every day about the world."

In the story "The Long-Distance Runner" (like all Paley stories, comic and convincing though incredible, unimaginable by anyone else and yet about anyone and everyone), Faith runs backwards to her past as she revisits "the old neighborhood" to see what is new in the world: the future. Black children swarm "the houses and streets where her childhood happened," and there, "as though she was still a child," she "learns" as she lives for three weeks in the apartment where she grew up, held willing prisoner by the black lady Mrs. Luddy, whose stories and son and person she comes to love. Love makes life continuous, a process in which change does not destroy but rather conserves and carries on essential meanings and relationships: another family in the Brooklyn apartment, another race, another color, but still mother and son and an exchange of life-giving stories, still a baby crawling around in diapers, still life and death, and humor. Still, also, the staccatto city-talk of people, combination of cliché, wisecrack, and insult: fresh, as in *fresh kid* and as vigorous, new, and immediately alive.

MRS. LUDDY AND FAITH:

The next morning Mrs. Luddy woke me up.

Time to go, she said.

What?

Home.

What? I said.

Well, don't you think your little spoiled boys crying for you? Where's Mama? They standing in the window. Time to go lady. This ain't Free Vacation Farm. Time we was by ourself a little.

Oh Ma, said Donald, she ain't a lot of trouble. Go on, get Eloise, she hollering. And button up your lip.

She didn't offer me coffee. She looked at me strictly all the time. I tried to look strictly back, but I failed because I loved the sight of her.

("The Long-Distance Runner")

The Critic Continues:

I find in such passages not irony, but sentiment. Expressed differently, the feelings might seem cloying or cute, but the hardboiled elliptical style controls the emotions it exposes. In a comic outlandish way, the story evokes a sense of love, hope, faith, and interest—plain old-fashioned interest in life and its idiosyncratic open-ended twists and turns. You never know where a Paley story is heading, though you know the conventions that should rule literary events, especially the convention that stories must have an end. Belief in the possibilities of change clashes with the literary convention of closure. "She can change," insists the narrator about the heroine of the story she tells in "A Conversation with My Father." Describing his daughter as a writer, the father enumerates Paley's qualities: "Number One: You have a nice sense of humor. Number Two: I see you can't tell a plain story." The father, who knows what stories should be, having read Chekhov and de Maupassant, demands "tragedy. The end of a person": "Tragedy! Plain tragedy! Historical tragedy! No hope. The end." But though she wants to please her father, the storytelling daughter feels a responsiblity to the woman she has invented: she wants to rescue her from the inexorability of plot, that "absolute line between two points . . . [which] takes all hope away." Conventional plots bring stories to a predetermined end, but the hopeful writer who believes in the possibilities of change—and so looks for ways to skew the straight line of destiny—will try to save her characters, even those who die, from an unalterable fate. If oblivion seems an ineluctable end for the ordinary women, men, and children who scramble briefly on our city streets, then remembering them in stories becomes an act of human defiance as well as of rescue. Caring for those who would otherwise be forgotten, the storyteller shields her characters and her readers from a dark nihilistic vision of emptiness, the ultimate end that makes life a meaningless drama and its actors not tragic but simply null. "Everyone, real or invented, deserves the open destiny of life," the daughter tells her father, a man of eighty-six, bedridden with rubbery legs, and approaching death. Even so, he wants to hear stories, and though he demands from them tragic denouements, stories save him from a tragic end: he cannot worm one out of his daughter, nor can he ever be extirpated from the invented "conversation" in which he exists, one that by its open-ended form fixes him forever into a context of hope. "With you, it's all a joke," he says accusingly in a funny story where nothing is a joke—not life or death or the responsibilities of art—but everything may be joked about.

Paley's joking seems a way of searching within life's inevitabilities for a loophole—some surprise opening in the concatenation of events that seem to serious and acquiescent observers inexorably linked. Refusing to follow the absolute straight line of causality, which she sees as the tyranny of plot, Paley traces loops and twists and unexpected turnings that circumvent doom. These curlicues seem comic, jokes that Paley plays on life; and whenever her twistings of plot pivot around death, as in "Samuel," "A Little Girl," and "Friends," they allow the story a last laugh, for its final turn will openly defy death by invoking art. As long as the story lives, the person whose death it describes cannot be dissolved into nothingness. This notion that art confers immortality implies the timelessness of great literature; indeed, it traditionally defines greatness. Paley's stories show courage and aplomb by slipping themselves into this definition, for by their style, form, and tone—all Bronx derived—they relinquish every sign of portentousness, every means of literary inflation, that would seem to make them equal to the grand theme of the immortality of art. Still, the stories are clearly conscious of their purposes and processes as art; and like much contemporary fiction, they call attention to this art by self-reference: by stories within stories that are invented before our eyes, and by comments on stories that define the nature of fiction and its relationship to truth.

In the story "Friends," death cannot dissolve the "lifelong attachments" that make family and friendship inviolable to time. Pressed by time, dying Selena wants to think about her dead daughter Abby, who lives on in a mother's memory: "I want to lie down and think about Abby. Nothing special. Just think about her, you know." And all of the friends, Ann, Susan, and Faith, want to think about Selena. Faith has her own way of thinking, her way of inventing stories about what happened, of finding the truth in the facts. Her wise son Tonto protests against her versions of life, just as the father in conversation with his daughter had protested against her failure "to look tragedy in the face."

TONTO TO FAITH:
Here she goes with her goody-goodies—everything is so groovy wonderful far-out terrific. Next thing you'll say people are darling and the world is *so* nice and round that Union Carbide will never blow it up.

FAITH'S FINAL WORD:
Anthony's world—poor, dense, defenseless thing—rolls round and round. Living and dying are fastened to its surface and stuffed into its softer parts.

He was right to call my attention to its suffering and danger. He was right to harass my responsible nature. But I was right to invent for my friends and our children a report on these private deaths and the condition of our lifelong attachments.

("Friends")

Love between parent and child, one of the lifelong attachments in Paley's stories, permits disagreement without a rupture of relationship. Tonto lovingly serves his mother herb tea to soothe her sorrow over dying Selena, but also he mocks her way of seeing and telling the truth about the facts of life they both observe. Like the father in "A Conversation with My Father," he preempts the critic's role by challenging his mother as storyteller, accusing her of a whitewashing optimism that glosses over tragedy and, perhaps, the imminence of doom. Faith's defense is ignorance of various kinds: of who someone really is, of whom someone might become under pressure of the times. When Tonto will not allow this (nor will the critic), Faith resorts to simple assertion of what she knows, while at the same time she challenges what Tonto, or anyone, can know ultimately about someone else, even one's daughter or son.

A BRIEF DIALOGUE:
O.K., Faith. I know you feel terrible. But how come Selena never realized about Abby?

Anthony, what the hell do I realize about you?

Come on, you had to be blind. I was just a little kid, and *I* saw. Honest to God, Ma.

Listen, Tonto. Basically Abby was O.K. She was. You don't know yet what their times can do to a person.

("Friends")

Cynicism and hope, dissolution and attachments, endings and continuities—these oppositions create the vital thematic tension of Paley's stories. They do not avoid the losses in life they seem to cancel or absorb by their unique style, a style at once wise-cracking and poetic, tough and sentimental, sorrowing and comic. Though Faith wonders how anyone can really know her own times, she does try to discover their meaning, running a long distance to find out "what in the world is coming next" ("The Long-Distance Runner"); and the stories *do* know that children are killed by meaningless accidents or drugs or by the times; that women are deserted by their husbands and lovers; that little girls are beaten and raped and cannot go on living. Knowing all this, the stories distance us from loss by their wise smart-alecky tone, while they present a vision of life that would reconcile us to loss by valuing loyalty—that is, by making art an expression of faith in the meaningfulness of love for one's family and friends. After listening to Tonto, Faith accords herself the last word, insisting on her right to report in her own way on the death of lifelong friends. Despite criticism she cannot disregard, she remains loyal to her version of the ineffable facts of life and death, to her judgment that Abby and Selena are *basically O.K.,* worth thinking about and remembering and telling about even though they are, perhaps, unknowable. All one knows, all the story tells, elliptically and yet completely, is that friendships exist: they can be formed almost instantaneously between women; they last; and they survive death when friends remember each other and record their memories in stories.

Friendships in Paley's stories are inseparable from place, from the neighborhood streets, playgrounds, parks where urban congestion fosters intimacy and interest. Friendships, like geraniums, bloom in kitchens. Love runs up and down a flight of stairs and enters one flat and another in the housing projects. Paley's characters convene for coffee. They do not meet for cocktails or cookouts, for tennis games or ski parties; they do not cruise the Greek Isles (though in "Somewhere Else" they tour China "with politics in mind"). They would not run into each other in the fancy-food aisle of small-town New England co-ops. The streets of Brooklyn or the Bronx bring them together—streets where Paley formed the attachments that have been her lifelong concern as a writer.

A Writer's Writer:

Grace Paley's first collection of stories, *The Little Disturbances of Man*, appeared in 1959, when Paley was thirty-seven years old. In 1974, she published a second volume of stories entitled *Enormous Changes at the Last Minute*. These two collections have established her considerable reputation as a writer—an extraordinarily strong reputation considering that her early stories consistently met with rejection, her first book disappeared from print for several years, and her style, which does not appeal to everyone, stuns responsive readers in ways they find elusive. She achieves an almost inexplicable compression in her fiction. Even her short short stories, like "Love," produce the effect of totality: they tell of life, the whole of life, and not of incidents; and the art of their telling is so consummate and yet so neatly concealed—her stories are in their own way as seamless as Katherine Anne Porter's—that she has become, like Porter, a writer's writer. Her peers have praised her publicly. Philip Roth called her a "genuine writer of prose," and Herbert Gold, "an exciting writer." Susan Sontag, perhaps selling short Paley's deliberate artistry, called her "a rare kind of writer"—a "natural." Donald Barthelme said simply she was "wonderful." For many years during the sixties, Paley was an underground favorite, one whose book was passed from hand to hand, from one reader to the next, especially when *Little Disturbances* was out of print. Now she appears in such chic magazines as *Esquire* and the *New Yorker.* The Bronx is not out of her system, but like blue jean cloth and corduroy, used originally for workingmen's trousers, it has been accepted as fashionable material by the arbiters of style.

A Woman's Person:

I admire Paley as someone who eludes stereotypes, sexual or otherwise. Not prolific in her output over the years, she is not, on the other hand, *silenced.* I mean this in the way that Tillie Olsen has described silenced women: those who could and should but do not write. The spaces between publication are not blanks in Paley's life, but life itself—her life.

Paley was born in the Bronx in 1922. Her parents were Jews in flight from Czarist Russia, where their religion and their socialism placed their lives in jeopardy. In America, her father lived the Jewish immigrant success story: he studied and became a doctor (see Paley's introductory tribute in *Enormous Changes*); but he and her uncles, who gathered in the Bronx apartment kitchen to discuss life, retained their belief in socialism. She was *brought up,* to use her words, *with a lot of their particular kind of idealism: I just kind of inhaled their early lives.** In her own life she has persistently acted upon this idealism, a belief, essentially, in the possibilities for social justice—a faith that the will of *good people* like her parents might prevail. *You know the idea that you can't fight City Hall—well, you can.*

Readers who generally want more of her work may complain that Paley's political activism has usurped time from her writing, but Paley disagrees: *I don't think or talk in terms of a career as a writer, but I think about myself and most other people as leading whole lives. People really use the day the way they want to. They may not be doing the particular things I do, but they do things that are considered all right for others—like drinking for three hours in an afternoon. Tillie Olsen pointed this out to me. She said people were angry because I spent my time doing something else, but nobody criticizes the people who spend three hours simply drinking in the afternoon.*

Paley has always been a pacifist, and now the constant threat of nuclear arms proliferation keeps her busy. Her area for political activity has expanded from the neighborhood around Washington Square Park, to Washington, D.C., to the world. In 1961 she helped organize the Greenwich Village Peace Center, in which she served as secretary. In 1969, she traveled with her husband, the poet Bob Nichols, to Hanoi, trying, like her heroine Faith, to see "what in the world is coming next." Out of that visit eventually came the story "Somewhere Else," typically funny, oblique, complex, and comprehensive (see the *New Yorker,* October 23, 1978). She went to Moscow in 1973 to attend the World Peace Conference. A life now divided between New York and New England has not divided her political activities: *If you work where you are and you're serious, you have a chance for a good deal of change. For instance, out of over thirty-five towns in Vermont, over thirty voted— after a lot of hard work—to ban uranium mining in the state. Also the*

---

*Italicized passages are direct quotations from Paley in our August 1980 interview. See below, Questions and Answers.

passage of nuclear waste through many of these towns was banned.
Alert to dangers in New Hampshire as well as in Vermont, she
participated in the protest against the building of the Seabrook
nuclear plant. She has not avoided jail. Perhaps at least six days
in jail (served in 1966 for her sit-down protest against military
force) were inevitable for someone who had *inhaled* idealism
early and exhaled it everywhere—into the air of the neighborhood playground where mothers "became conscious of power
structure and power itself" as they gathered around the public
sandbox ("Northeast Playground"). In her fiction, as in her experience, women are political, aware of world events as well as of
sandbox group dynamics, a fact she sometimes presents comically. Here, for example, is the ending to the story "Northeast
Playground," one of my favorite passages.

PLAYGROUNDS AND POLITICS:
        The afternoon I visited [the playground], I asked one or two
simple questions and made a statement.
        I asked [two young unwed mothers], Wouldn't it be better if you
mixed in with the other mothers and babies who are really a friendly
bunch?
        They said, No.
        I asked, What do you think this ghettoization will do to your
children?
        They smiled proudly.
        Then I stated: In a way, it was like this when my children were
little babies. The ladies who once wore *I Like Ike* buttons sat on the south
side of the sandbox, and the rest of us who were revisionist Communist
and revisionist Zionist registered Democrats sat on the north side.
        In response to my statement, NO kidding! most of them said.
        Beat it, said Janice.

By the time she was seventeen, Paley had dropped out of
Hunter College—almost accidentally: *I would go to school, but I
could never get up to the classroom. I could sometimes get to the first floor,
but I couldn't get into the classroom. I would meet someone, and talk to
them, and that would be it. You know, a conversation anyplace stopped
me from doing anything. . . .* By the time she was twenty, she was
married to Jess Paley, her first husband, with whom she lived for
over twenty years and with whom she had a son and a daughter.
Her daughter, Paley said recently (while visiting a class at Dartmouth College), knows her better than anyone else—a tribute to

a mother-daughter relationship that visibly impressed the young women students listening to Paley talk about the influence of the city on her fiction. Her daughter was there too, listening. Her son has recently made her a grandmother, and like all grandmothers, she always happens to have in her purse a picture of the new baby.

She is much in demand for readings, lectures, and guest professorships. The summer of 1980 was interlaced with a flying trip to San Francisco, where she and her husband read from their works, and a two-week teaching assignment at Cazenovia College in upper New York state. She is admired and sought after by women, and she gives herself generously to their activities in the academy and in the community. The portrayal of women in her stories is original, warm, and intelligent. Women are as important to her as she is to them. Her enduring feeling for them grew naturally out of a shared daily experience of motherhood: *I still can't forget how much I learned about human life being not just with my own kids, but with other women and their children. I can never repay the debt that I have to the community of women with whom I raised my kids. I owe them a lot, and they owe me. I mean, we began in those days friendships that lasted for thirty years.* Her stories constantly repay such debts, lovingly and with interest.

During the year, she teaches at Sarah Lawrence College, dividing her time between her Manhattan apartment and her house in Thetford, Vermont. There, where children, stepchildren, and children's friends arrive and depart in unpredictable sequence, two dogs guard the grounds with deceptive ferocity. Recently, one of them was shot by an arrow. The quiet countryside allows no escape from man's disturbances, sometimes unmotivated except by archaic malice. Occasionally, Paley shops, as we know, in the Hanover Co-op, and she uses the Allen Street laundromat regularly. If you ran into her there, you would probably not suspect that she is a writer, a writer's writer, a teacher, public speaker, an active pacifist, and jailbird—though you would assume she is a housewife and mother. She would probably speak to you in the quick and interested way of her characters, and tell you right off that she is a grandmother. She says occasionally that she wants to lose a few pounds, but her life is too full, I think, and too absorbing to allow her to concentrate on a diet. Nevertheless, when she came for an interview, I prepared carrot sticks.

Questions and Answers—an Interview, Sort Of:*

The interview took place August 1980, not in an elegant Manhattan apartment overlooking the Hudson, and not between two sophisticates sipping drinks that clinked delicately as they spoke. We ate tuna fish sandwiches and carrot sticks and drank experimental coffee—I wasn't used to the stove—in the little dining room in the little college house into which I had recently moved. The boxes and disorder that I had warned Paley about, had tried to warn her away from, didn't bother her, she said. She liked to see how people lived. The short interview had taken a long time to arrange. I saw how busy and dispersed her life was as I tried, time after time, to catch her; and even now she was soon to elude me, running off to the White River Junction bus station to meet a stranger riding down from Montreal to interview her. Ah, well! Meanwhile, here we were, munching brain food and vitamins, and I was on the verge of exploring a mystery. How did she manage in her stories to make out of odd and minimal bits and pieces—little disturbances—a whole world? Even more mysterious than art was life. How did she manage to make for herself—as a woman and a writer—the whole life that she thought most people lived, though many people, especially women of her background and generation, would describe themselves as truncated, silenced, somehow incomplete? She knew how to place together incompatible fragments of experience to create unexpectedly a tense but harmonious whole. It was the secret of collage.

Question: I'd like to begin by remarking that you have taken many different roads in life, while most of us, like the speaker in Robert Frost's poem, take one and then regret the other roads not taken. You are a writer, teacher, lecturer, wife, mother, political activist, feminist—the list could go on. I don't

*I have edited the tapes that recorded our conversation, removing the hesitations of speech and its repetitions, cutting, condensing, occasionally transposing, and collating for the sake of clarity and smoothness.

want to present you as superwomen, and yet you've managed to follow many roads when most of us find it hard to follow one. I'd like ultimately to ask your secret about being able to make the combinations you do to achieve in your fiction and your life a sense of wholeness. Perhaps I could ask first which road, if any, has priority for you?

Answer: *I think at different times of your life, different roads, as you put it, are the road you're really on. It's not a question of preferring them; you happen to be walking on them, and there's just no way out. When your kids are small, or even when they're bigger, that's your main road. But, really, nobody travels only one road: it's not only hard to travel on one road; it's almost impossible. I think that's true for almost anybody in one way or another. Nobody lives without a personal life. What I do is not unusual.*

Question: I think many women find what you do exemplary and wonder how you do it.

Answer: *Well, you really do some things by neglecting other things, if you want to look at it in that negative way. Very often when I'm doing political stuff, I should be writing. This last couple of weeks I've been doing a lot of writing, but I did it by not going to a meeting in New York which I considered not only terribly important, but very meaningful to me. It was a convention in the southeast Bronx, which is my neighborhood, a place where I grew up and very important to me. I neglected that.*

Question: How do you decide what is politically important to you?

Answer: *I'm not really very cerebral about any of these things. I'm just pushed by the time and the weather as much as anything. A couple of years ago, not a lot of people were doing antinuclear plant work. It was something I thought about, the great terrors and dangers, and I was upset. I felt I had to go and do things. Today I feel other people are doing just as well and better than I.*

Question: You seem to have had a capacity to recognize very early what is crucial. How do you pick up early clues? Peace, of course, is a crucial issue.

Answer: *I think everybody thinks it is, and there's nobody who thinks war is good; but I happen to have always thought about these things. I believe in a kind of fidelity to your own early ideas; it's a kind of antagonism in me to prevailing fads.*

Question: How do you distinguish what is important from a fad?

Answer: *I'm trying to think about that. . . . One of the problems would be not knowing what happened last year or two years ago. Around Seabrook, for instance, one young man, whom I liked a great deal, had just gone into antinuclear plant work, and he was saying, "Never before has anything been done here." Well, you have to explain to people that there's a long, long history. The radical history of this country is now being brought back to the people who have forgotten it.*

Question: There is certainly a serious attempt now to recover what we have lost of our past—the radical past, women's history, the history of minority cultures. To pursue the subject of your political activities a little: what are some of the victories that you recall?

Answer: *I don't think in terms of victories. When you think how bad the world is right now, you don't think you've done anything. We're soon going to elect either Reagan or Carter, and I don't know how we're going to survive either. We're really small people fighting against fantastic powers. Still, there are local victories that make you feel you could go on from there, small victories that put you in a good mood for a year or so.*

Question: Why do you think we've come to the impasse you describe, to choices that many people consider nonchoices for the presidency?

Answer: *For one thing, the presidency has become less and less important than who owns the president—who has the money and the power to elect. Even in Vermont, millions of dollars are being raised to put in one candidate and beat another. Our country is so rich: I think terrible things come from extreme wealth and greed. And terrible things come from poverty.*

Question: To switch, rather abruptly, from one road to another—from politics to writing—let me ask you what fosters or hinders your work as a writer. Children, for instance: you have said that when your children were small, then it was clear that the road you have to take was that of a mother.

Answer: *Well, you don't have to. What I say is not how I think other people should live. I think that if people have great difficulty in*

*being with their children, they shouldn't be with them. I'm powerfully
pro-choice—not just on whether or not you should have a baby, but on
how you should raise it. Some people couldn't do a worse thing than stay
with their kids. It's hard for them; it's hard for the kids. For me, it was just
a continuation of street life. I was fascinated by them. I mean, here it is
twenty-five, thirty years later, and I still can't forget how interesting the
whole thing was.*

Question: Then you didn't feel the conflict between wanting to write and wanting to care for your children that's described with such agony by poets like Sylvia Plath and Adrienne Rich?

Answer: *If Sylvia Plath could have gotten through the next year
or two . . . Her period with those kids was probably the hardest, when
they're very little, very demanding. Then, if you're trying to do something
. . . but I can't speak exactly about that because one of the things I lacked
at the time was ambition. It's not that I didn't want to be a writer; it's not
that I didn't want to struggle. It's just that I was writing. I was writing at
about the same rate that I was writing at other times. I was writing mostly
poetry, and it wasn't that good. It really wasn't. And nothing I could do
improved it. I mean, I worked on it and I worked on it and I worked on
it. It stayed kind of—I won't say third rate, but second rate. And I knew
it. I would every now and then write a really good poem, but I mean
every now and then. I guess if you really want to write, anything else can
stand in your way: going to school, having to clean the house, whatever
you do. For me, having small kids didn't stand in my way any more than
having to have a job. Before I had kids, I worked full-time.*

Question: Did you feel the lack of a mentor? Many young women today feel handicapped by not having women mentors, or any mentors, in the way a young man has.

Answer: *What do you mean by a man having a mentor?*

Question: He has someone, a teacher, who's interested in his career and takes it seriously.

Answer: *Well, there were great English teachers when I was a
kid, wonderful women, and they encouraged me. I think they existed in
high schools everywhere, women who should have been teaching in colleges but couldn't, you know, would never have been hired in those days.
Now that I think of Hunter, and of N.Y.U., I remember there were mostly
men. Of course now at Sarah Lawrence there are plenty of women, a
whole bunch of us.*

Question: How did you find your medium, your unique story form?

Answer: *People ask, "What is your influence?" I think you come to think through subject material you're interested in. In my early thirties, I really become involved in the lives of the women around me. I had this subject matter really pummeling me, but I thought, "Aah, who'd be interested?" Most of the literature of the time came out of the Second World War, and it seemed to me that what I had to say was not really interesting; and so it sat in my head for a long, long time. I was reading Joyce, Proust, Virginia Woolf, Gertrude Stein.*

Question: What particular Gertrude Stein? Do you remember?

Answer: *Oh, I loved* Three Lives. *Those three things had a very strong sound for my ear. . . . When I wrote my first couple of stories, because of the poetry, I worked aloud from the very beginning. I would read a paragraph to myself and then type it, and then I'd reread it and I'd take it apart. And every day I'd reread what I wrote the day before aloud. That became my method.*

Question: You said you feared being cut off from ordinary life, the parks, the streets, the women and children—the source of what you write.

Answer: *Yes, I just loved the streets, and I love them to this day. We played in the streets all the time, and the grown-ups were in the streets all the time, and we had sandwiches in the streets, and someone would throw an apple down from the fourth floor so that you didn't have to come up. I remember all that with a great deal of affection. The streets are something I care about. I'm never averse to sitting down outside . . . with friends.*

Question: Well, it used to be a spectacle. People would take their folding chairs or boxes and sit all day on the street, just watching. It was more exciting than watching a movie. You knew all the characters and something interesting was always happening. A surprise!

Answer: *That's right. . . . Yeh. . . . Yeh.*

We sat and chewed carrot sticks, and then she ran off to meet the bus at White River Junction—in Vermont.

Ann Beattie's Magic Slate

or The End of the Sixties

Ann Beattie

ON ANN BEATTIE

Ann Beattie has said that she has a clear memory of me sitting up on the bed of a Hilton Hotel room, my legs outstretched, asking her questions. She was being interviewed for a teaching position and I was on the interviewing committee. I had my legs outstretched because I was exhausted, not for any more interesting reasons that she, with her inventive mind, might have imagined. I remember her too—her long dangling hair, hippie look, and her dazzling achievement as a young writer. Her stories had already appeared in prestigious magazines, and done so with impressive regularity. I supported her as persuasively as I could for the position of teacher of creative writing—but to no avail. A young man was hired. Beattie continued to publish regularly, and in time, she produced two volumes of stories and a novel. Writing about her work was enjoyable, somehow immediately personal. The journal that had asked for a review-essay did not want a ponderous scholarly piece, and I could do as I pleased, enter into the essay as I entered into Beattie's fictional world. By now, this review describes the early stages of a career that has continued to develop. Beattie's latest collection of stories, The Burning House, *seems to me her most perfected, the work of a glittering writer. The style is typically snappy and modern, syncopated. Beattie's mood, however, is sometimes nostalgic and often bleak. The combination of verve and depletion makes all her stories memorable. Grace Paley, an older writer, also has verve, but she writes of things yet to come and changing, while Beattie, a young writer from whom hope might be expected, tells of the end of things—love affairs, marriages, dreams. Both writers represent, I think, moods of different periods: Paley of the thirties, which for all its human miseries inspired a hope for change; and Beattie, of the sixties, when hope was also high, only to be followed by a disillusionment from which some never recovered. Both Beattie and Paley have a comic strain, but the smile or laughter they induce is different. The variety of American women's writing is rich; and the new voices that emerge, even when they tell a bittersweet story, are good to hear. Meanwhile, Beattie's own story continues, with a little ironic twist. This year she is to be a celebrated guest, reading her latest stories, at the college that had once refused her a job.*

The weather forecast is for snow.

"Victor Blue" *in* Distortions

Entering Ann Beattie's fictional world through her collection
of stories, *Secrets and Surprises,* I drift through desolate
landscapes with numb aimless characters who are nowhere
wherever they are, and wherever they are is where I do not want
to be. For them, the climate of all seasons is adversary and the
same. "We are thinking about spring," she says in "Octascope,"
but it is "the dead of winter"—"It will rain, or snow." Rain
shrouds the New England countryside and the tomblike house
where "they are trapped together by rain" in "Weekend." Traps
can cripple before they kill. The trap of "Tuesday Night" gets a
mouse by its paw; then it must be beaten to death with a screw-
driver. I do not want to be trapped—not again. I still feel the
exquisite pain of being trapped by Hemingway, Salinger, and
Didion, writers whose nihilism gives Beattie inspiration. I do not
want to wander—as I have with Kerouac—in a pointless world,
or to come to rest in the *dead* of winter. I want to get out of
fantasized landscapes of nothingness.

At the moment, reality offers no escape. Outside the snow
falls as thickly, as pallingly, as in the stories. Soon I shall see
nothing. The streets and mountains of New Hampshire are disappearing under lowering skies. It is two o'clock of a December
afternoon. The storm has begun. Soon the driving will turn
hazardous. Cars will swerve and skid, and death will strike of a
sudden as it does in "Starley," killing a young man who crosses
the snowy street for a bag of ice cubes.

Sudden pointless death stalks Beattie's world, a world of the
young in perpetual mourning. The walking dead—the numbed,
or stunned, or stoned, or mad—mourn the buried and check
their calendars by the dates of their dying. "In 1969 Joseph died
in Vietnam," his sister recounts in "A Clever-Kids Story," and at
the end of every summery day in 1969 she sits on the dock and
smokes grass, and never recovers from her loss. Beattie's stories
are elegiac, but no ceremony, not even that of writing a formal
lament for the dead, can lay to rest persons and purposes gone
with the end of the sixties. *Chilly Scenes of Winter,* the novel that
precedes *Secrets and Surprises,* is a slow dirge to this end—to the
termination of a decade and to the purposes that died with

33

public figures marked for violence. Jack Kennedy. Bobby Kennedy. Martin Luther King. The mystery of their assassination remains inviolable, something pure in our midst. In *Chilly Scenes of Winter,* Charles counts the dead for whom the decade must make an accounting, those the young adulated and lost to an overdose taken accidentally or on purpose. "The song is over," Charles says. "Janis Joplin is dead. Jim Morrison's *widow* is dead." So is Brian Jones. Rod Stewart is rumored dead. Elvis is as good as dead, having turned forty. The massive deaths for which there can be no accounting are barely mentioned.

In *Secrets and Surprises,* references to Vietnam are infrequent but overt and predictable. Jane warned Joseph in "A Clever-Kids Story" not to go—to run away to Canada. Now his life is ended. In "Shifting," Natalie told Andy "not to go to Vietnam." Now he tells her, "You were right"—and he has lost a leg and the use of his arms to prove it. Now he is listening, but "she had nothing to say." The achievement of Beattie's stories is the way they fill the silence that remains when the song is over, the way they say *nothing* when there is nothing to say.

But these are the facts, and the trivia is more interesting.
"Wally Whistles Dixie" in Distortions

Some people find trivia interesting; they can make up stories through an accumulation of the insignificant. When meaning or purpose has been erased, trivia can fill the leftover blanks—those visible on a page of writing, those suspended elusively in time. In daily life, trivia often fill the voids in time, and for a while keep us from confronting their meaninglessness and menace. The events that fill the time of Beattie's fictions are random, disjointed, brief, often idiosyncratic, and marked by an inconsequentiality that displaces attention from silence, death, and nothingness to daily attempts to stay confusion. "I'm mad because you just add to the confusion," Estelle tells her little boy in "It's Just Another Day in Big Bear City, California"—the day that spacemen Donald and Fred (retarded) appear to take pictures of Estelle and her husband, Big Bear (no relation to the city or the story's title). "This is a random landing. . . . We found you by accident," the spacemen explain to the drunk and disconcerted couple. As disconcerting as spacemen to Estelle is a Coke machine that won't work, part of the general disorder of everyday details—of hors d'oeuvres in which liver is "hidden," of broken plastic milk glasses, blue velvet birds on a birthday card, a valentine's quilted taffeta heart, a La-Z-Boy recliner, human intestines used as a jumping rope at mortuary school, and a 1965 Peugeot. The Peugeot is the last thing Estelle's brother thinks of, wondering why he is not thinking of his mother or father or sister rather than his car, as he lies dying in Vietnam. The background for the day's confusion—"just another day"—is the sixties, thrust visibly before us as the pictures of Estelle's album. Estelle's snapshots of the sixties "really kill" Bobby, who begins to laugh "uncontrollably." Loss of control comes easily to Beattie's characters, always on the edge of hysteria, panic, or madness. Clutching at trivia is their way of steadying themselves. You try not to go crazy by making glazed pots in "A Reasonable Man," or by listening ritualistically, obsessively, for a phone call; or by writing down an account of the routine moments of your day in "Victor Blue," a story in *Distortions.*

Mr. Edway's "secret book" in "Victor Blue" gives us a code for reading Beattie. Like her story, the book keeps a meticulous record of inconsequential progress, that of a violet, a kitten, a library book (when borrowed, read or not read, and returned). It lists recipes, TV programs, meals (eaten or not eaten), weather forecasts and actual weather, all of which Mr. Edway epitomizes in one word—"Trivia." So thoroughly do trivia displace attention, his and our own, that we hardly realize that Mrs. Edway is in agony with terminal cancer and deliberately oversedating herself until she dies.

Such displacement suggests that the true subject of Beattie's stories may be too painful to confront directly. The pain of living for a useless death must be camouflaged. This is the function of massing trivial details, comic or grotesque in *Distortion,* and in *Secrets and Surprises* so utterly mundane that they begin to seem in Beattie as they are in Barthelme, self-parodic. The short story will be sustained by trivia; a sudden revelation of the significance they have hidden, as a hostess hides liver in a hors d'oeuvre, will surprise and satisfy. But the novel becomes monotonous when insignificant details multiply and recur. In *Chilly Scenes of Winter,* trivia are as abundant and unsustaining as Charles's Hydrox cookies, available always in the novel as they are in the supermarket. Cookies may show Charles's childishness, but in a way that hardly makes us care. Writers who display life's smallness, sameness, boredom, and futility run the risk of a mimetic novel. Beattie is more exciting, more creative with *nothing,* as a short story writer than as a novelist—at this stage in her career. By its scope and duration, the novel means to enlarge. Under a magnifying glass we see trivia enlarged, but we know their real effect is diminution.

In "Dwarf House," the first story of *Distortions,* Beattie shows men and women literally diminished. James is only "four feet, six and three-quarters inches tall"; but a little man, especially when he reaches the age of thirty-eight, can want what any man wants, though his dimension seems to distort normal values and make them questionable. At the end of the story, against his mother's wishes, James marries the little woman he loves—and the wedding sets the world against a perspective described by his mother's bitter aphorism: "Real love comes to naught. I loved your father and we had a dwarf." MacDonald echoes his mother as he listens to Tammy Wynette sing "D-I-V-O-R-C-E": "Everything is for nothing." At the wedding, MacDonald sees the dwarfs "swarm" around the happy couple, and he is reminded of ants he saw converge upon a piece of Hershey bar. Everything sweet in life is devoured; we are left with nothing. Still, the bride is radiant at the wedding, and MacDonald kneels to her and to all beautiful brides and happy marriages. The story ends with his ambiguous gesture, and with the tension between marriage as a strangely diminished ritual and yet one beautifully if precariously sustained.

Secrets and Surprises contain fewer surprises than *Distortions*—no spacemen or dwarfs appear, no child prodigies like Wally living in a tree in "Wally Whistles Dixie." The muting of surprise entails a loss of humor, idiosyncracy, and tension, and of the quirky charm that I admired for just missing cuteness. Clarity and craft compensate for these losses. The new stories evoke a less ambiguous view of aimlessness than "Dwarf House" and other earlier stories, like a favorite of mine called "Wanda's"; and none matches the story I consider Beattie's consummate achievement, one which merges the typical elements of her art into an original, striking, and haunting work—"The Lifeguard."

In *Secrets and Surprises,* the trivia are more minute and unattractive than in *Distortions,* the characters in greater bondage to them—like the nameless obsessed *She* of "A Reasonable Man," for whom going to the cleaners is an event, and the typically "depressed" *I* of "Tuesday Night," for whom "some time to do just what I want to do" is excruciatingly eventless. Beattie seems merciless to women trying to "liberate" themselves, like this *I* of "Tuesday Night" (or that screwy lesbian of *Chilly Scenes of Winter*). Such women become aimless once they aim to discover, assert, or free themselves, because they have a self only in relationship to a man. Divorced from Henry and about to be dumped by Dan, the Tuesday Night woman exists in limbo, like the mouse in her apartment, caught in a trap by one paw. To the partially trapped, freedom seems possible, but Beattie is as brutal to the Tuesday Night woman as Dan to the mouse he bludgeons to death. Time is the woman's trap. Released into time—one night a week, like the maid's night off—the woman chooses trivia, lacking energy, imagination, or experience for significant action (she does not know, as we already do, that significant actions—like those of the sixties—also end in nothing). Here are some of the things the woman does on her Tuesday nights: she reads "a dirty magazine," calls long-distance and discusses varicose veins, bakes four loaves of bread, burns a pie crust, gets "depressed" and drinks Drambuie, browses through *Vogue,* tries yoga, sees a movie, sips a milk shake, and reminisces about necking with a high-school date. Surface and depths in the story exist on the same plane, which is to say the story is all surface with nothing more implied, nothing more at stake, than what appears as trivia. In Hemingway's understated stories, surface and depths were as distinct and inseparable as in the two-hearted river where Nick went fishing. In Flannery O'Connor's stories, women acted vacuously, but their actions were implicated in the eternal drama of good and evil, significant to the damning or salvation of the soul. I am not suggesting conversion to Catholicism for Beattie. I am indicating the aesthetic problem—Hemingway's problem in his finest and most understated stories—of creating interesting and significant stories out of the trivia that surface in our time—that become merely surface without depths, except for the empty abyss of nothingness.

He really thought that he would always be in control, that he
would always be the storyteller.

"A Clever-Kids Story" in Secrets and Surprises

Always the weather is beyond control. Already it has forced
day into night, though it is only four o'clock in Hanover, New
Hampshire, where the snow still falls. Outside it is so dark that
when I look through the window I see my reflection framed in
black. I know conditions are temporary. I know skiers are
happy: for them something good will come of this falling blackness. Still it is eerie to watch a world disappear, leaving only a
room where every window mirrors my self against a void. There
is the telephone. I could call out to check if everything is still
there; or the phone might ring here. It might be Jay asking how
I am doing, if I am finishing; and I might tell him it is all under
control. I might make up a little story about the snow and the
void and the stories that fill my mind while the storm takes
possession.

In "A Clever-Kids Story," Joseph the storyteller who thought
himself "indestructible" is killed in Vietnam. Because he could
order his stories, he could not imagine chaos beyond his control,
though his sister tries to warn him, to prevent him from going:
"He didn't understand how bad, and how pointless, things were
in Vietnam. No matter what I said, his attention didn't focus on
it, and I couldn't make him understand." Though Joseph is "a
clever kid," clever enough to make the impossible sound "reasonable," he does not understand that life is different from art
and eludes the artist's shaping. He can imagine kindness and
miraculous rescue in his stories, but he cannot imagine the disorder and the destruction of the world whose violence awaits him.
Disorder envelops Joseph and Jane as children—their mother
has an abortion, their father bums around, their houseguest
cries and is not entirely recovered from his breakdown. As Janet
remembers the summers in New Hampshire and tries to understand what happened and why she could not save Joseph from
Vietnam, she sees that the divorce between storytelling and life
was already there in childhood, just as the beginnings of her
parents' divorce were there, but neither she nor Joseph understood: "As Joseph was fabricating stories that spring, strange
things were happening that we didn't know about." Years later

her lover sleeps in Joseph's bed; he offers her sex, but she wants a story, such as a child tells, such as she tells when she speaks of her brother: "As I got older, if I told people about my brother, the stories would always be about my brother as a child—I got older, but Joseph was still frozen in childhood."

"A Clever-Kids Story" shows J. D. Salinger's abiding influence upon Beattie and upon the art and function of her storytelling. Like Salinger, she values childlike innocence, precociousness, and whimsy. At her best, she tells stories that embody these qualities while she shows them imperiled. Whatever anxieties of her own her stories master, they show no way for the reader to control the world or his or her self. Characters break down or die as they do in Salinger; when they live, they often seem "frozen in childhood" like Holden Caulfield and Phoebe. Beattie's extended tribute to Salinger is her novel *Chilly Scenes of Winter,* which posits a life for Holden if he can survive to the age of twenty-eight, Charles's age in the novel. The allusions to *The Catcher in the Rye* and *Nine Stories* are specific in Beattie's novel, while the general tone of her book—its charm, colloquialism, malaise—evokes Salinger's world and supports the oblique references to him: a character named J.D.; a hero who is "obsessed with going to Bermuda" and who "felt like a great savior"; a brother-sister relationship of two against the world; and a sense of the world's betrayal of the innocent. Sentimentality also prevails. Charles loves a young woman so sentimental that cut flowers sadden her. When characters are not sad or wistful, they are "numb" and "depressed." " 'Everybody's so pathetic,' Sam says. 'What is it? Is it just the end of the sixties?' " Writing in the seventies about the sixties, Beattie seems frozen in the fifties. Her sense of the world is apocalyptic: things have fallen apart, and no one is in control. "J.D. says it's the end of the world"— Charles reports the verdict of a dropout hippie who has had too many beers. The imputation to Salinger is *cute,* a quality often attributed to him, and not entirely accurate, though it conveys an indelible influence upon Beattie's fiction. To be whimsical, sentimental, and *cute* about the end of the world, to search among its debris for true love as Charles still does, to feel "sorry for everybody" you want to save but are too "depressed," to verge on the maudlin and at the same time suggest a pristine innocence—these are qualities the characters of *Chilly Scenes of*

Winter share with Salinger's characters who are from another time, not waste products of the sixties, and not perhaps the most suitable emblems of the seventies—though of all Beattie's qualities the most distinctive is contemporaneousness. This comes as much from a naming of brand names, rock and country music stars, faddish foods and manners, like smoking pot, places where people from New York go, like Vermont and New Hampshire (where Salinger went), as from a literary style already called, like Salinger's, *"New Yorkerish."* The combination of sentimentality and slickness which Salinger maintained in a precarious and striking balance characterizes Beattie's fiction and points to an accomplishment she must transcend as she grows as a storyteller.

Storytellers often retell stories, their own and others'. It is a way of demonstrating the "indestructibility" that Joseph unwisely took for granted—showing that a good story and a good storyteller never die. It may be a sign of depletion, or of impatience—the rush to write another story before you have another story to tell; or an urge to perfectibility, the desire to say what you said, but perfectly this time. One story might be called "on the road," and of course has been called that by Jack Kerouac in the famous novel of the fifties which looms over Beattie's aimless wanderers. They are not wild, like Kerouac's Dean Moriarty, not inspired like him with a mad sense of America, of the West, not driven toward "It," the center of Time that only a Holy Goof, a modern Saint, can penetrate. But they are as circular and futile in their movements, and as obsessive. In "Hale Hardy and the Amazing Animal Woman," Hale Hardy, a college dropout (naturally), becomes obsessed with seeing the Grand Canyon because he has read a book, *Lolita.* "That book put women in his mind. He thought it might be a good idea to pick up some woman and drive across the country with her. . . . Eat ice cream with some woman, peering into the Grand Canyon." How listless and unprovoked this desire is compared to Humbert Humbert's obsessive passion for Lolita. The attenuation and diminution of desire show again that everything comes to nothing, even stories of inordinate passion. "What state is this," Robert asks, confused by pot and life, when he arrives finally in Colorado, driven both by aimlessness and obsession, but without the frantic joy that was the companion to Kerouac's Dean Moriarty and Sal Paradise—at least at times, at the beginning of the road. When Hale Hardy gets to the Grand Canyon, he gazes into a "vast pit," the familiar abyss of nothingness; when Robert gets to Colorado in the story- "Colorado," he is where he has always been, in the state of confusion.

These are typical men, dropouts of the fifties who have let twenty years slip by without affecting their consciousness. The women also are reenacting a story already told, most effectively and economically in Joan Didion's novel *Play It As It Lays*, to which there is an indirect but unmistakable allusion in Beattie's current story "A Reasonable Man." Like Salinger's characters and Kerouac's, Didion's woman is trying to maintain her tenuous control, though she has slipped into certifiable madness. So has Beattie's nameless *She* in a story that recapitulates the state of obsession and paralysis of women in earlier Beattie stories, "The Parking Lot," "Four Stories About Lovers," and most notably, "Downhill." *She* is obsessed with a telephone that remains "inexplicably silent," becoming the symbol (as it was for Maria in *Play It As It Lays*) for breakdown in communication, solipsism, and nothingness—a world annihilated by disorder cannot generate meaningful messages. Nihilism lapses into silence. Women can achieve a delicate equilibrium in Beattie's world if they are "simple," like Lenore in "Weekend." That means they love to cook, care for children, and nurture Peruvian ivy and shattered but arrogant men. Laura of *Chilly Scenes of Winter* is the loveliest of such women, and Charles pursues her obsessively because she is as sweet and airy as the orange soufflé he craves—and which at the end she is making for his delectation. In "Starley," life picks up for Donald in the summer of 1976: "He had a girl friend, Marilyn, who was excessively kind. She made a lobster stew that made his eyes water with pleasure." That was 1976 when, the story implies, you had better be "simple," an object of comfort and desire; or else you might go mad. In your madness, you might dream as *She* does (as does Didion's Maria) of domestic bliss, the only thing that can save you—your child, your husband, your home—all that you would preserve from the devastations of time (as Maria would preserve "Damson plums, apricot preserves, Sweet India relish and pickled peaches"). In "Shifting," Natalie makes what Marge Piercy has called "small changes." She learns how to drive a shift car, though her husband does not teach her, and she learns that "isolation" can be beautiful if it is captured as a gesture in art. "This was in 1972, in Philadelphia," the last line of the story informs us—still a long way to go. Like Natalie, Diana in "La Petite Danseuse de Quatorze Ans" admires a statue, this time of a young dancer "poised for a moment before she moves." The most modern of Beattie's women are arrested in such a moment, not yet moving, but poised—uncertainly poised—before they might make a gesture which could advance them into the world that came into being when the sixties ended. Maybe that world gives women only the illusion that they might assume control and become the tellers of their own story. In "Distant Music," Sharon hears the incidents of her life retold in a hit song that her former lover Jack has written. That is his version, lacking the ironic twist she knows but is not telling.

He took, instead, a Captain Magic slate. He liked to write on it and draw pictures, then zip up the top part and watch it all disappear.

"The Lifeguard" in Distortions

The snow has stopped. Soon the snowplows will come. The roads will clear, and I shall get out. This essay will come to an end and leave me thinking about the sense of ending in Ann Beattie's stories—stories that end in irresolution, suspension, irony, or erasure. As though scenes were etched upon a magic slate, they disappear quickly after they make themselves visible because they lack consequence. They describe the trivia left around after the end of the sixties; they deny importance to the trivia; they leave us with *nothing*. They leave us in the *dead* of winter, though we know the snow has stopped; and even if it comes again, we know that winter must yield to another season. Is it entirely delusory to think summer will be different?

Beattie's vision of the sixties is by no means unique. That the decade left us with a daily expectation of loss—the TV becoming our magic slate where people and promises were shown and erased—becomes an explicit statement in a novel as radically different from Beattie's fiction as Walker Percy's *Lancelot,* published in 1977: "We were wondering who was going to get assassinated next. Sure enough, the next one did get killed. There it was, the sweet horrid dread we had been waiting for. It was the late sixties and by then you had got used to a certain rhythm of violence." The effect of this violence is inertia, symptomatic of a sense of helplessness and futility. This sense is by no means unique to Beattie's fiction. I find it permeating a fine Canadian novel that has an almost uncanny resemblance to *Chilly Scenes of Winter*—Richard B. Wright's *The Weekend Man*, published in 1970. The weekend man and Beattie's Charles would understand each other.

So much for the erasure. Now for the magic—all the wonderful, indelible aspects of Ann Beatie's secrets and surprises. She has the secret of exact infallible perfectly timed dialogue and of smooth transitions at difficult junctures. Her stories turn into surprises because their aimlessness is leading nowhere and any twist or turning is unexpected and turns adventitiousness into inevitability. I like the moments of violence that intrude suddenly upon apathetic characters. Nick's two muggings in "A Vintage Thunderbird" are the best things that happen to him— sudden, simple, weird, frightening, evoked as if by magic through Beattie's language. The sudden manic madness with which *She* runs on the beach at the end of "A Reasonable Man" breaks though the story's inertia and creates excitement and tension and fear. The authority of Beattie's detail is indisputable and shocks us into a gasp of pleasure at recognizing the familiar as inevitable. Most of all the magic is in sentences.   *If she were the piece of sculpture and if she could feel, she would like her sense of isolation.   She could remember how light, how buoyant, she had felt being tossed high in the air, and thought that perhaps being powerless was nice, in a way.   Behind the house is a ruined birdhouse, and some strings hang from a branch, with bits of suet tied on. The strings stir in the wind.   I stare at her and imagine her dress disappearing, her shoes kicked off, beautiful Danielle dancing naked in the dusk.   She stood amid the scattered clothes, wondering if it could be true. "Wait a minute," he said. "Wait." "Wait for what?" she whispered.*

Revolutionary Turnings:

The Mountain Lion Reread

Jean Stafford

ON JEAN STAFFORD

The summer of 1974 I was searching for a copy of The Mountain Lion—*nowhere to be found. I had been asked by the book editor of a journal if there was a neglected novel I wished to reconsider, and with sudden certainty I named* The Mountain Lion. *I remembered reading it years before, though why it should now come immediately to mind I could not have said. Indeed, I had forgotten more than I remembered about the novel, and I had no idea what I would discover upon reconsideration. Yet the book was my unequivocal choice. The problem was that I could not find it anywhere. It had gone out of print, and I was at the time in Cape Cod, searching in an unscholarly haphazard way. I looked at people's summer bookshelves and, as chance would have it, at last found a copy, its pages loose and yellowing. I had to make a hard bargain for the book because as soon as I wanted it the owner began to reconsider its value. I still have this little loose-leafed paperback, which initiated a study of all of Jean Stafford's work. Today this work is being reviewed by various critics interested in American women writers; and Stafford is assuming a place that, ironically, she might not wish to occupy. Soon after my reconsideration of* The Mountain Lion *was published, I was asked to write an introduction to a reissue of the novel. I was pleased to see it coming back into print, but I could not foresee Stafford's displeasure nor her rejection of my piece. Apparently, she disliked the frames into which I was placing her novel. She considered the book purely comic, I was told, but though I saw it as satiric and witty, I could find little comedy in a girl's suffering because she was different—not pretty, but alarmingly perceptive. I did not find the novel's ending evocative of laughter. The last words, pronounced over the dead girl's body, reverberated harshly: "Lord Jesus. The pore little old piece of white trash." In 1974 I may not have remembered those words precisely. Nevertheless, I had remained haunted by the memory of a young girl's fate in* The Mountain Lion—*the memory of waste.*

Like the whirling circle of fireworks that Jean Stafford describes in *The Catherine Wheel*, her novel *The Mountain Lion* is brilliant in its revolutions. Its action turns upon an overturning of expectations: a subversion of forms, myths, and manners which it draws on only to demolish. It is social satire, comedy of manners, Western romance, hunting adventure, fairy tale, and *Bildungsroman*—all of these, and none. For it refuses the demands of each of these forms as though in deliberate revolt against them. It subverts the traditional theme of initiation by arresting the growth of the children, Ralph and Molly Fawcett, with terrible finality. It subverts the myth of the American West—of open space as freedom—by denying the future promised by a once-boundless land. It subverts the myth of the East—of inviolable ideas as freedom—by creating the past and preserving it as ashes. For all its abundance—an extraordinary richness of detail as well as motif—it leaves us with a wasted sense of emptiness. This is the residue of its brilliant and destructive tour de force, an appropriate and typically clever turn, since the novel is about residue. We are reminded of this by the literal presence of ashes in a conspicuous place in the novel, in Mrs. Fawcett's parlor. This macabre and comic touch, the preservation of Grandfather Bonney's remains, shows Mrs. Fawcett's infatuation with the past, an infatuation shared by Miss Pride in *Boston Adventure* and by Katherine in *The Catherine Wheel*. All three characters wish that time could be stopped so that the present would exist as a perpetual past. A vain wish, since time as we trace it around the clock moves intransigently through its revolutions; and Stafford's concern as novelist is with resistant characters caught in this movement and destroyed.

In *The Catherine Wheel*, the destruction is stunningly graphic: Stafford's heroine is consumed in flames, turned to ash, on a whirling wheel of fireworks. This flaming circle, a spectacle intended for pleasure, resembles a medieval instrument of pain, a "spinning rack" that tortured victims by its turnings. I suggest the analogue—that we as readers are pained as we are pleasured by the brilliant spectacle of Stafford's art. *The Mountain Lion* hurts us not only because of the fate of the children, but more pervasively because of the devastating picture of America it presents. Judging with a moral absoluteness that reminds us of the Puritan heritage it both satirizes and sustains, the novel denies

greatness to America in any form. It shows everything diminished, like Miss Runyon's miniature houses in Covina; or everything come to an end, like the species of wonderful wild animals
in Colorado.

Showing man diminished is the satirist's stock-in-trade, as we
know from Swift's Lilliputians; and showing the end of his
world, as Stafford does in her novels, is the work of the apocalyptic writer. *The Mountain Lion* belongs to the wasteland tradition of apocalyptic writing, but we have failed to recognize this
because it dazzles us with liveliness, only to shock us with loss. We
are left with the sense of things ended: the West depleted and
left to childish men like Uncle Claude; Covina, California, overrun by pests, a disaster area like Los Angeles in Nathanael West's
apocalyptic novel *The Day of the Locust;* and the East evaporated
to a gaseous gentility belched up by Reverend Follansbee at tea.

Everything ends—the novel ends—with Molly's death. This
death effects the most complete revolution, turning the book we
have been enjoying as comedy to pathos and melodrama. If we
have not anticipated the death, then we must admit we are incor-
rigible American optimists, believers in fairy tales. For we expect
ugly ducklings to turn into swans; and lost children, like Hansel
and Gretel, to find safety at home; and wise children, who see
the emperor naked, to achieve acclaim. But Molly dies, ig-
nominiously, her epitaph an insult. *The Mountain Lion* brings its
revolutions to an end with violence; while like fireworks, for a
brief and brilliant duration, it sparkles—with the wit, satire, and
startling rectitude, both moral and verbal, that enliven all of
Stafford's fiction.

As a social satirist, Jean Stafford is a stern uprighteous judge
whose standards for human being and human conduct no
character meets. In *The Mountain Lion*—of greater scope than
either *Boston Adventure* or *The Catherine Wheel,* her other novels—
she surveys the American scene, East and West, to find everyone
everywhere reduced to caricature. She presents us with our
familiar stereotypes, which is a way of preserving our prejudices,
and her own. In Mrs. Fawcett she produces a typified suburban
mother: fussy, supercilious; addicted to cleanliness, ritual, and
gentility; and always apprehensive, possessing her children
through her fear and her guilt. We might laugh her off, except
for her implication in her father's death, an example to Ralph

and Molly of how members of a family can destroy each other. The tea-drinking, discreetly belching, chinless, platitudinous Reverend Follansbee is also familiar; but he cannot be wished away, as Molly tries to do, nor can his small revengeful cruelties be circumvented. He hounds Molly and makes Ralph vomit. Miss Runyon the postmistress, suspected of having "set her cap for Mr. Kenyon," is everyone's spinster: a respository of silly fears, silly interests (like the Sunday "funnies"), and sexual repressions. To escape her fate, young girls like Leah and Rachel must keep their hair curled, their complexions pink, and their clothes frilly so that young men will want to marry them. Winifred Brotherman, for a while a stereotyped "tom-girl," turns at marriageable age into another coquette, exchanging her blue jeans for party dresses, and her horse for her boyfriend's car. She taunts Molly by a transformation that the lank, dark, slouching girl cannot effect. Molly is susceptible, however, to the prejudices that run rampant through *The Mountain Lion*, to our monumental shame. Here is the area where generosity abounds—in distrust of "others," of Japanese, Germans, blacks, Catholics (Jews are put in their place in *Boston Adventure*). Poor people show up at the ranch as migrant scarecrows, arriving, multiplying, and then disappearing into the night. Had they stayed and shed their visibility, Molly might have found a friend such as Emily Vanderpool finds in Stafford's story "Bad Characters," a girl's account of her Colorado childhood: the friend gets Emily arrested for "lifting," but meanwhile saves her from herself. The stereotyped "bad characters" around Ralph and Molly offer no outside chance of rescue: neither the menacing Mexican gardener, a "bad man" who sings "bad songs" in Spanish; nor the wised-up little Japanese children who tell of impossibly bad things men and women do; nor the wizardly old wizened black cook Magdalene at the ranch who "botches" goats without mercy, and eats beaver tails and calf testicles with relish.

In their comic-strip outlines, and in their mindlessness, Stafford's characters are cartoon figures: flattened, glossy, gross. But they represent the adult world where eventually the children must find their grown-up roles. Insofar as Ralph and Molly understand this, we can understand their reluctance to assume these roles, and their desperate eagerness to find others. Ralph wants "to go out West," to run away from civilization, like Huck-

leberry Finn; and Molly starts "to go crazy," like Holden
Caulfield in *The Catcher in the Rye,* a novel that *The Mountain Lion*
in various ways anticipates. Like Holden and his sister Phoebe,
Ralph and Molly band together against the adult world; but
unlike them, they lose their coherence, a devastating, irrevers-
ible loss, as they approach this world through an inevitable journey from childhood to adolescence.

Stafford portrays this journey in images derived from Freudian dream psychology and from Puritan brimstone sermons, sex
and sin being synonymous in Ralph's mind and, perhaps, in
hers. Her novel rings with Calvinistic overtones, sounded by the
motif of poisoned blood. Is it coincidence that Grandfather Bonney died of blood poisoning, and that Ralph and Molly, "half
poisoned," suffer profuse nosebleeds? The novel implies that
evil is an inherited contamination that streams through human
history and catches the young in its dirty course. "Molly, tell me
all the dirty words you know," Ralph cries in the dark tunnel of
adolescence where he feels sexual desire as his soul's damnation.
Stafford supports this moral judgment by corroborative language—"corruption," "vileness," "black, sinful mind"; and by
evocations of hell. Throughout the journey scene she conjures
up vile fogs and crepuscular darkness; bats and snakes and
corpselike humans; sulphur and suffering and the devil himself.
This melodramatic vision of hell merges with sexual nightmare
as Ralph dreams of a precipitous fall amid swarming snakes, and
as Stafford exploits conventional Freudian symbols of train and
tunnel, one entering the other in darkness. All this is clever and
contrived, and dates the novel, but also makes it the permanent
impression of a sensibility of the times. It reminds us of a naive
era when some people grew up thinking that corruption was
simply sex, while some people never grew up because they died
of such naiveté. Ralph seeks innocence and manhood, perhaps
an impossible coalescence. Molly is implicated in his quest because she is the only one he finds untainted by sex (he does not
understand repression): "Molly, alone . . . did not urge him to
corruption."[1] His older sisters threaten his innocence by arousing incestuous fantasies—from which Molly alone can save him
by a fanatical purity. In desiring both innocence and manhood,
Ralph faces a dilemma that seems indigenous to American

fiction and, perhaps, to American life. How he tries to deal with this dilemma is his story in *The Mountain Lion*.

When early in the novel Ralph cries, "Golly *Moses,* I'd like to go out west", he expresses the pristine wish of the mythic figure of American culture—the roving young hero who leaves civilization for the still uncontaminated places in the continent—wilderness, prairie, or mountain—where he can enact the timeless ritual of initiation to manhood. As in myth, Ralph is summoned to his journey by a mysterious messenger: Grandfather Kenyon, a "half legendary" visitor, a "sort of god of September". Kenyon resembles at times an Indian, at times a "massive, slow-footed bear", both fabulous creatures of the West. When Ralph enters Colorado he comes upon the landscape of fable: of immeasurable mountains, forests, glaciers, glades, streams, valleys, and pastures; and of animals—coyotes, elk, deer, bighorn, beavers, cattle, and horses; and of rangy strong men and hunting rituals; and of golden light that transfigures everything, including a mountain lion, into dream. Here he too is transfigured from a puny frightened inept child to hunter. Equipped with his gun he prepares to join the male tribe by fulfilling its ritual. Alone and unafraid he will find a sacred spot in the wilderness where he will confront a legendary animal, one personified by a name. In the mystically charged encounter that brings together hunter and prey, the boy will acquire courage and skill and pride—and become a man. The greatest account of this myth in American fiction—one that embodies the tension of merging innocence with manhood—is William Faulkner's "The Bear." Ike McCaslin, the boy who hunts Old Ben in a southern wilderness, casts his indelible shadow over Ralph hunting Goldilocks on a Colorado mountain (and more recently, over Norman Mailer's character D.J. hunting Grizzer, old "Mr. Bear," in an Alaska frontier in *Why Are We in Vietnam?*). Like Ike, womanless and childless, and like Uncle Claude, the same, when Ralph enters the hunt he commits himself to a ritual that excludes women. For the West is the symbolic country where boys become men; and where girls, even the closest of sisters, become not only extraneous or intrusive, but also threatening. As a female, Molly encumbers Ralph in his obsessive stalking of the mountain lion and the masculinity that is its trophy. Her con-

stant presence reminds him of a part of himself he can no longer
endure, and indeed, must annihilate, if he is to grow up—the
feminine part of his nature.

Thus *The Mountain Lion* presents us with a study of childhood
ambivalence and social intolerance. For the society Ralph will
enter does not tolerate shared or ambivalent sex roles: it demands clear-cut identity. This demand destroys both Ralph and
Molly as it divides them from each other and involutes their love
with hate. It destroys them because they have been too integrally
a part of each other—almost as one in thought and feeling, and
even with simultaneous nosebleeds—to be separated by the unequivocal sex roles society prescribes. Ralph is too sensitive to
become like Claude—the strong solitary male defined in the
great masculine myth of the West; and Molly is too "ugly"—and
too smart, quirky, cantankerous, and critical—to become a coquette, like Rachel and Leah. Molly dies—in what I take to be a
sacrificial ceremony disguised in the novel as accident. She is
sacrificed so that Ralph can live, and live up to the myth of the
West, to an image of manhood that makes violence and destruction its consummation. "Learning the ways of a man," "proving
his worth or manliness," Ralph inherits the confused values
transmitted through the hunt. Killing, he learns, is an art.
Through killing, as through art, one enters the world of ritual
where time is stopped and the past kept intact. Thus, killing may
turn into an act of love; for as one stops time, one stops change
and keeps the object of one's love forever fixed in its perfection,
like the figures on Keats's Grecian urn. If Ralph's is the logic of
madness, it nevertheless informs romantic literature. Ralph becomes a romantic hero when he determines to kill the mountain
lion, an animal whose beauty arouses his erotic fantasy, because
he loves her: "Goldilocks . . . would be killed . . . out of his own
love for her golden hide". Once he has her dead, he can possess
her forever: "have her stuffed and keep her . . . all his life".
Ralph also wants Molly immutable; and his love and his desire
for possession are implicated in the accident that assures him
that Molly will never change. Perhaps mistakenly, Ralph loves
Molly for the "innocence" in which he seeks his own salvation.
But he sees innocence despoiled by time and change which have
already tainted him. If Molly grows up she too may fall into the
pit of snakes, which already she fears with phobic terror; if she

grows up she may lose her virginal purity—she may become a woman. Ralph's dilemma dooms his sister. Wedged between a cult of violence and a cult of virginity, she is crushed to death. And she collaborates in this fate. She too does not want to grow up and have to cope "with all the tommyrot with which people were constantly trying to ruin her life". To deny this "tommyrot," she willfully deludes herself that a girl can marry her brother, or barring that, her horse. She refuses the knowledge into which we all must fall; her innocence is indistinguishable from ignorance and fear. Rather than face life, Molly wishes to die, and she reveals this wish by her negation of her body. She tries consciously never to be conscious of her body, and she speaks of it ominously as "a long wooden box with a mind inside." We can guess that Ralph in his oneness with his sister intuits her death wish; and we know he shares it. When his initiation rite demands violence, he finds a way to fulfill this wish with apparent impunity, because the hunt sanctifies killing. Through a ritual that sublimates murderous instincts, Ralph tries to save his sister—from life, from violation, from herself. At the same time, by making her the scapegoat in his rite, he tries to save himself. So both children are sacrificed, and the myth of the West, which separates boys from men, and men from women, prevails. Seeing Ralph step into this myth and rigidly enact its ritual, we cannot believe he kills Molly without unconscious design or without cultural sanction. We have become too highly sophisticated in our reading of the intentions of a person or a society to think that accident, even one so obviously contingent as Ralph's, strikes gratuitously, without motive or purpose, as a purely freak occurrence. Within the novel, Molly is seen as a freak, and chosen for her destiny.

Why does Molly *want* to die? She knows and tells: "I know I'm ugly. I know everybody hates me. I wish I were dead". I need not elaborate here on the involuted meanings that revolve about a woman's physical appearance, nor figure the price any American woman must pay for being ugly—for being defined as ugly, that is, by her culture. At the end of Katherine Anne Porter's famous novella "Old Mortality," an elderly maiden aunt reveals to the young heroine the persecution she has suffered because of her protruding teeth and receding chin: "All my life the whole family bedeviled me about my chin. My entire girlhood

was spoiled by it. Can you imagine . . . people who call themselves civilized spoiling life for a young girl because she had one
unlucky feature?"[2] All of Molly's features are unlucky: height,
"heavy eyebrows," dark skin, "prominent nose," lank black hair,
weak eyes. In Ralph, her double, these features turn to advantage as he grows tall, dark, and handsome, and, by a miracle
reserved only for him, no longer needs eyeglasses. Molly's pretty
older sisters, smugly on their way to marriage, serve as foil and
reprimand to the quirky, awkward, critical, contentious little girl
who strikes everyone as a "discord," being opposed to all "in
temperament, in capacity, in propensities." These last are not
Jean Stafford's words but Charlotte Brontë's describing Jane
Eyre, another child misfit. Jane Eyre develops inner strength by
becoming contemptuous of all those she could "never please"
because she was not by nature a "sanguine, brilliant, careless,
exacting, handsome, romping child."[3] She grows up to take a
respected place alongside a grateful Rochester, now blind,
crippled, and dependent upon her love. Like Jane, little Maggie
Tulliver in *The Mill on the Floss* is also quick-witted and satiric;
like Molly, dark in complexion and moods; and like both, a
"discord" because she is smart and does not hide her brains or
her pride in having them. Maggie grows up to be beautiful and
desired, triply desired by two lovers and her brother. Her fate—
to die locked in her brother's arms—would have been a consummation for Molly, separated abruptly and irrevocably from
Ralph as he conforms to a myth of masculinity. An American
girl, caught between the culture of a superannuated East, as
depicted in the novel, and a boisterous, male West, Molly can
find no place for herself, no vindication. Unlike Jane, she never
learns to assert an identity by making moral choices that would
allow her to live and eventually prevail. Unlike Maggie she never
turns from ugly duckling into swan. Perhaps beauty, or mere
prettiness, might have saved her from death, though not from
the inanity that seems in the novel inseparable from female survival. Molly's sisters can grow up because they remain fairy-tale
creatures, two pretty Goldilockses who will trip through life
without ever getting lost or encountering menace, or ever
threatening the suburban Disneyland world in which they live.
They pay for their immunity to danger and disapproval with
insipidity; they grow up by never really growing up, and their

rites of passage are spurious, though presented in the novel as common to girls. They do not suffer as Molly does, but in their own way they are as blighted by prettiness as Molly is by her intelligence—her "handicap," her mother calls it—and her appearance.

That women are judged by appearance, whether beautiful or ugly, Stafford sees as their misfortune. In her Jamesian story "The End of a Career," Stafford's heroine discovers that being blessed with rare and exquisite beauty is a form of curse. All her life she has cared for her beauty as though it were a sacred jewel whose brilliance must not be allowed to dim; that has been her career and the waste of her life. For at the end she learns what we should have known all along, that appearance is superficial, though it may be all in a woman that society values. The young woman in another story, "The Echo and the Nemesis," finds beauty and intellectual brilliance burdens too heavy for her to carry. So she splits her personality in two, bestowing beauty on one self and brains on the other: a solution of insanity, painful and full of diabolical self-punishment. She eats herself into obesity—a fate worse than death for the American woman. In *The Mountain Lion,* Molly's brains cannot save her from the blight of her looks; and her character is demoralized by her acceptance of society's judgment that her looks are ugly. The ugly looks she gives to others—making gross faces at them—reflect what she has seen mirrored to her as an identity and a judgment. Molly collaborates in her own destruction when she accepts this image as her own. She is Stafford's brilliant study in introjection. Finally hating herself for the same reasons others hate her, because she assaults their sense of female beauty, she wants to erase herself from view, to disappear, to die. Though she is precocious, ambitious, critical, and discerning, her talents go to waste; her epitaph is "trash." Conventional beauty and simpering ways would save her, she thinks: "If only she had yellow hair, she thought, she would be an entirely different kind of person". But the image in the mirror does not reflect Shirley Temple. She comes to hate the image so much that shortly before she dies she adds her own name to her "list of unforgivables". Then she breaks down and cries, "and all the time she cried she watched herself in the mirror, getting uglier and uglier until she looked like an Airedale". In death she resembles "a monkey." Her limp body evokes the judgment with which the book ends: "The pore little old piece of white trash".

Although *The Mountain Lion* is Ralph's story, it tests us by our judgment of Molly. We sympathize with Ralph's desire for autonomy, and we see he has been betrayed by the male tribe that he thinks will grant it. In time the stereotyped "gosh darn" weekend-whooping cowhands at the ranch deprive him of his dream of the West. In time Uncle Claude, his only possible model for manhood, reveals "a ponderous stupidity, a sort of virile opacity" that masks indifference to suffering, and malice to those who suffer or allow themselves, like Molly, to be "unhealthy"—that is, introspective, thoughtful, "bookish," critical, and smart (like Jean Stafford).[4] But though he is alone, Ralph can enter and be entertained in the world closed to Molly—because he is male, and handsome, and willing to accommodate to the "fat merchants" against whom he and Molly were once allied. But Molly remains intransigent; perhaps that is what we mean when we call her neurotic. And even if she would accommodate to the world as shown in the novel, she would not be accepted because her looks are hopeless. She tries. Even at the last, grown tall, her latest misfortune as a girl, she is still trying to cope, by stooping and sidling through the school hall like a crab. But such maneuvers make her more of a freak: more eccentric, more isolated, more unhappy, and finally, hopeless.

Can we imagine for Molly a life that does not end in futility, madness, or death? In 1947, reviewers of *The Mountain Lion* did not trouble themselves over this question, though they admitted being shocked by the "unexpected horror" with which the book ended. They were troubled, however, by the possibility that readers might miss the "terrible" "underlying truth" concealed almost entirely, they feared, beneath a brilliant surface—that of Stafford's witty, subtle, and highly sophisticated style. In his *New York Times* review, Howard Mumford Jones expressed the worry that "naive readers may miss the deeper psychological developments of the tale." This was a shared apprehension. As another reviewer wrote: " 'The Mountain Lion' is likely to beguile many a reader into thinking that he has hold of merely a shrewdly perspective and amusing novel of children, when what he really has in his hand is a charge of psychological dynamite." Such doubts about the common reader's ability to understand

The Mountain Lion show the critics responding to an uncertain tension within the novel between form and theme, or between expectation and fulfillment. This is the tension I ascribe to *The Mountain Lion*'s revolutionary turnings, its radical movements away from the expectations that its traditional forms arouse. That this tension produces in the reader both pleasure and pain—pleasure at the expectation of the familiar, and shock at "unexpected horror"—still another reviewer clearly discerned: "though you read it [*The Mountain Lion*] with amusement, you will feel it aching in you like a tooth for days." All these responses suggest that *The Mountain Lion* creates confusion in the reader: she thinks she is reading one kind of book, a traditionally amusing one, but she feels and reacts to another. No doubt Jean Stafford imagined herself writing one kind of book, a humorous satire well within the tradition of the American Western; but she could not imagine within that tradition a life for an odd young adolescent girl since, traditionally, none existed. Thus, *The Mountain Lion* describes a critical impasse in consciousness—of a character who cannot grow up in the West, and of a writer who cannot imagine for this character any destiny other than early death. That we do not entirely accept Molly's death as an inexplicable and intrusive accident, and that, unlike early reviewers, we wonder about ways to circumvent this accident, seem to me cause for celebration. For beyond the revolutions in its chosen literary traditions that *The Mountain Lion* shows us when we approach it formalistically, it reveals as a social document a revolution—or the possibility of a revolution—in consciousness. Today we can imagine what thirty-five years ago Jean Stafford could not—a future for Molly. That future requires another literary form, one in process of being shaped. I mean the novel that will present a portrait of the artist as a young woman; a novel of initiation that will describe female rites of passage. Molly Fawcett had dreamt of becoming a poet, but she lacked not only a typewriter (for which she wrote letters of solicitation comic to us and futile to her); she lacked a sense of the reality of this possibility, examples for a way of life she could barely imagine, let alone live. She belonged like the mountain lion to an endangered species, for which at the time there were no plans for preservation. In hunting Goldilocks, Ralph imagined that death would preserve this graceful, rare golden creature. Art, Jean Stafford's art as novelist, has preserved Molly, an awkward adolescent misfit. But life itself—and the revolutions it brings in understanding, manners, taste, social vision, and sympathy—makes it possible for us to preserve the life we see wasted by death in art. The possibility of a life for Molly that we can now imagine into the novel gives it its most radical and hopeful turning upon itself, and revitalizes as it revolutionizes us as readers.

After Long Silence:

Tillie Olsen's "Requa"

Tillie Olsen

ON TILLIE OLSEN

In 1982 when I was asked to speak on Tillie Olsen at the New England meeting of the College English Association, I was perplexed on two accounts. How could one maintain a critical demeanor, not become deferential or diffident, when the writer was sitting there on the stage waiting to be honored? And what could one say to an audience that one assumed knew Olsen's work, had taught her stories, and probably written about them in critical journals? I spoke about "Requa," her least known work, in the spirit of celebration that I think this essay conveys. For in creating "Requa," Olsen had prevailed as a woman and a writer—and against obstacles which she, more than anyone else, has brought to public attention. The occasion was made memorable by Olsen's spontaneous reading from "Requa": quiet, deeply felt, powerful. Her voice brought back memories of earlier readings I had heard, the first, in 1973 when I was teaching Tell Me a Riddle *in a short story course. I had invited Olsen to our campus as a guest speaker. The audience that came to hear her was small, but responsive; some cried as her voice lapsed into silence at the end of the story. I date an important insight back to Olsen's visit of 1973, a significant year to me, since it was Willa Cather's centennial. The occasion was marked on my campus by a display of photographs from a new book that traced Cather's life pictorially. Tillie Olsen was deeply moved to see in the photographs of Nebraska the landscape of her own childhood. I began to sense then, dimly perhaps, what has now become clear: that women writers have common roots, not necessarily geographic, as in this instance; that they inspire and give strength to each other; that when one finds or recovers her voice, she enables many others to speak.*

No one has written so eloquently about silences as Tillie Olsen, or shown as poignantly that a writer can recover her voice.[1] In her most recent fiction, a long story called "Requa," Tillie Olsen reclaims once more a power of speech that has proved at times extremely difficult to exercise. Silence followed the publication, almost fifty years ago, of sections from her early and still unfinished novel *Yonnondio*.[2] Then came *Tell Me a Riddle*,[3] bringing Olsen fame but not the sustained power to write she needed, and for another long period her voice was stilled. In 1970 "Requa" appeared, an impressive work which received immediate recognition and was reprinted as one of the year's best stories.[4] For apparently fortuitous reasons, it is now little known, though as Olsen's most innovative and complex work of fiction, it deserves critical attention. Complete but unfinished, "Requa I" is a still-to-be-continued story that develops the theme of human continuity in ways which seem almost subversive. Its form is discontinuous, as though to challenge its theme; the text broken visibly into fragments separated from each other by conspicuous blank spaces—gaps the eye must jump over and the mind fill with meaning. However, the story repudiates the meanings that might be inferred from its disintegrated form, and from its imagery and setting, both influenced by literary traditions of the past that Olsen continues only to subvert. "Requa I" evokes the poetry of the twenties in its wasteland motifs, and novels of the thirties in its realistic portrayal of America's Great Depression. Waste and depression are Olsen's subjects in "Requa," but Olsen's voice, resonant after long silence, is attuned to her vision of recovery—a vision central to this essay, which hopes to show how the process of recovery, described and enacted in "Requa," produces a work of art.

In his poem "After Long Silence," Yeats had defined the "supreme theme" of recovered speech as "Art and Song." Patently, these are not the themes of Olsen's story. "Requa" is about uneducated, unsung working people struggling against depression, both the economic collapse of the thirties, the time of the story, and the emotional depression of its protagonist, fourteen-year-old Stevie. The story begins with Stevie traumatized by his mother's death and the loss of everything familiar. Alone and estranged from the world, he is being taken by his Uncle Wes from his home in San Francisco to a small California town set by the Klamath River. Here men fish for salmon, hunt deer, and lead a life alien to a city boy. Stevie arrives at this town—named by the Yorok tribe Rek-woi or Requa—broken in body and spirit. A wreck of a child, still dizzy from the long bumpy truck ride, heaving until he "can't have 'ary a shred left to bring up,'" he seems utterly defeated: unable "to hold up." "All he wanted was to lie down" (54); and from the beginning, this wish leads to Stevie's withdrawal. He refuses to speak; he sees human faces dimly or not at all; he huddles in bed, hiding under his quilt and rocking. A "ghostboy" with dazed eyes and clammy green skin, he seems ready to lie down forever. But the story turns aside from death to describe a miraculous recovery, nothing less than Stevie's resurrection. For at the end of "Requa" the silent numb boy springs spectacularly to life. In the "newly tall, awkward body" he has grown into, he runs, rassles, "frisks" about like a puppy; and when at last Stevie does lie down, he falls into a sweet sleep from which, it seems, he will awaken rested and restored.

Given the story's time and place, that recovery should become its pervasive action seems as miraculous as a boy's resurrection. For the time is 1932, and the setting a junkyard, the natural stopping place for dispossessed people on the move during America's Great Depression. "Half the grown men in the county's not working," Wes tells the boy—no jobs anywhere. Wes himself works in the junkyard, a realistic place described in encyclopedic detail and a symbolic setting suitable to the theme of loss and recovery.[5] At the junkyard, mounds of discarded and disjunct things represent tangibly a vision of disorder, disintegration, and waste. "U NAME IT—WE GOT IT," the yard sign boasts: tools, tees, machine parts, mugs, quilts, wing nuts, ropes, reamers, sewing machines, basket hats, "Indian things," baby buggies, beds, pipe fittings, five-and-dime souvenirs, stoves, Victrolas. These wildly proliferating abandoned things form "heaps piles glut accumulation" (64); but the growing lists of material objects Olsen interjects into the story—or rather, makes its substance—undermine a common assumption that accumulation means wealth. On the contrary, things can reveal the poverty of a person's life. All the souvenirs that Stevie's mother had accumulated, now passed on to her son, are "junk"—"Jesus, what junk" (60). The more souvenirs the story mentions, the more it shows how little the mother had, though obviously she wished to possess something pretty even if it was only "a kewpie doll [or a] green glass vase, cracked" or a

> coiled brass snake   Plush candy box: sewing stuff: patches, buttons in jars,   stork scissors,   pincushion doll   taffeta bell skirt glistening with glass pinheads

(60)

But things that at first seem worthless take on a strange incandescence in the story, initially perhaps because of the narrator's tone—a musing, mysterious, reverent tone that imbues isolated objects with emotional meaning. And the lives that seem wasted in the story also begin to glow. The dead mother's felt presence becomes stronger and brighter, and shines through characters who help her son and through Stevie himself as he begins to recover. Even the junkyard changes. Piled with seemingly useless things, it gives promise of renewal, for the "human mastery, [the] human skill" which went into making machines, now broken and disassembled, can be applied again, and the strewn parts made to function. Olsen's wasteland inspires "wonder" at the technological genius which can rehabilitate as well as invent, though it has rampantly destroyed. Olsen expresses no nostalgia for a bygone pastoral era which many American writers wish recovered. She visualizes instead a reclamation in the modern world of the waste its technology has produced. In her story everything can be recycled, and anything broken and discarded put to new use. Nothing is beyond the human imagination which can create even out of waste, the "found" objects in a junkyard, a poetic text. Placed side by side, the names of these objects begin to form a concrete poem which the story will interrupt, continue, and complete as it moves along. The first stanza, a listing of ingenious devices, implicitly extols human inventiveness and skill:

> Hasps switches screws plugs faucets drills
> Valves pistons shears planes punchers sheaves
> Clamps sprockets coils bits braces dies.

(65)

If these disconnected nouns form also a litany of waste, it is one that introduces the hope of redemption, for Olsen describes "disorder twining with order," a combination that qualifies chaos and may signify its arrest. Moreover, Olsen's final inchoate sentence traces a search through the "discarded, the broken, the torn from the whole; [the] weathereaten weatherbeaten: mouldering" for whatever can still be used or needed, for anything that can be redeemed (65).

At the junkyard, Stevie sees people as depleted as himself still hoping for redemption. The faceless, nameless migrant workers who stop to pick up a used transmission or discarded tire reflect widespread social disintegration; but like the migrant workers in John Steinbeck's *The Grapes of Wrath,* they persist in trying, struggling, moving. Battered as they are, they refuse the temptation to lie down, and they trade their last possession, a mattress or gun, for whatever will keep them going. "We got a used everything," Evans the yard owner says (67), seeing to it that trashed and broken things are fixed and made usable again for people on the move. Evans is tough and wants the "do-re-mi," but whatever his motives, he is crucially involved in the process of recovery. His yard attracts people whose lives have been shattered, the dispossessed migratory workers and, in time, Stevie. The junkyard also sustains Wes, who keeps his own self intact as he makes broken parts useful, working capably and even happily, "Singing . . . to match the motor hum as he machines a new edge, rethreads a pipe" (65). Meanwhile Wes is trying to make a new life for his nephew: "I'll help you to catch hold, Stevie," he says, "I promise I'll help" (61). Other characters, barely identified, also help, and the story sketches in the outlines of people variously involved in the boy's recovery. Besides Evans, who gives Stevie a chance to work, the Chinese cook at the boardinghouse keeps him company, and the sympathetic landlady takes him on an outing that will complete his recovery.

As "Requa" describes the "concern" which underprivileged or struggling characters show for each other, it raises Olsen's thematic questions about human responsibility, and about the relationship between love and survival. Implicitly it asks why Wes, a lone workingman, should give his skill and energy to make trash useful to others and an alienated boy valuable to himself, and why anyone should care, as everyone does, whether a "ghostboy" recovers. The story thus restates Olsen's recurrent riddle, which is, essentially, the mystery of human survival as evidenced by people who continue to live and to care even though their lives seem broken and futile, and life itself full of pain. If human existence has meaning, as Olsen's fiction asserts, then suffering, bereavement, poverty, despair, all inseparable from day-to-day survival in a wasteland, must be explained. So must the secret of recovery, which prevails against depression.

This is a complicated achievement already described in Tillie Olsen's earlier stories. In "I Stand Here Ironing," a pockmarked girl becomes beautiful, her talent realized, her unhappy deprived childhood, never forgotten, transcended; and a mother, recalling this childhood, straightens out confused emotions as she irons, and gains a sense of her own identity.[6] Before the grandmother dies in "Tell Me a Riddle," she too searches through the past to see what of value she can retrieve; and as she becomes reconciled to her own painful life, now coming to an end, she finds meaning and continuity in all human existence. Olsen can describe such recoveries because she has a strong sense of history as both a personal past which gives one a continuous identity and a social legacy which links generations. This legacy, however, is neither whole nor yet complete, for history is a dump heap strewn with broken promises and wrecked hopes, among which lie examples of human achievement. Someone must sort through the junk of history, redeem its waste, and salvage whatever can be useful for the next generation. This is the task of reclamation which Tillie Olsen has assumed as a writer and assigns to her characters, often unnoted, unlikely, inarticulate people for whom she speaks. Indeed, this is why she must recover her own speech, no matter how long her silence, so that Wes, and Stevie, and the dying grandmother can have a voice.[7]

In "Requa" Stevie continues the quest of the grandmother in "Tell Me a Riddle." Different as they are, the resurrected boy and the dying woman are both searching for a transmittable human past that will give significance to their present struggle. Both need a history as reusable as Wes's rethreaded pipes. The grandmother finds hers in the record of humanity's continuous progress toward self-realization. She appropriates this history as a shared "Heritage": "How have we come from the savages, how no longer to be savages—this to teach. To look back and learn what humanizes man—this to teach" (81).* Young as he is, Stevie also looks back to learn from his past the secret of recovery, of how he might claim his rightful place as a human being. As the story begins he seems dehumanized, so broken and apathetic that he is unable to relate to anyone else or to himself, unable to see the people in the boardinghouse or the beauty of the country-side that will in time shake him with "ecstasy." Described as a "ghost-boy," he appears doomed to inanition, but the story struggles against this fate and insists in hushed portentous tones that something will save him: "the known is reaching to him, stealthily, secretly, reclaiming" (65). Both mysterious and obvious, the *known* is Stevie's personal past, experiences from which he will in time draw the strength to live. This strength comes mainly from the remembered love of his mother, the person in his past who has provided him with a "recognizable human bond" which must sustain him and matter more than the losses that life makes inevitable. Even in his withdrawal, a quest for "safety" from the shocks he has suffered, Stevie recognizes that the bond is holding, that Wes is taking the place of his mother by showing "concern." Wes is in Stevie's "corner," willing to share whatever he knows. "I got so much to learn you" (64), he says, looking to the future; and looking back at the past, he vows not to let Stevie "[go] through what me and Sis did" (56). Though he is an orphan, Stevie belongs to a family bound together by ties which Olsen insists can remain irrefrangible, even in a landscape of waste. When Wes becomes helpless, falling on his bed in a drunken stupor, Stevie tends to his uncle as once he himself had been cared for by his mother. He takes off Wes's muddy shoes and covers his body with blankets: *There now you'll be warm,* he said aloud, *sleep sweet, sweet dreams* (though he did not know he had said it, nor in whose inflections)" (70). Then he stares at the sleeping face in a crucial moment of recognition: "Face of his mother. *His* face. Family face" (71).

Once Stevie can see clearly the *"human bond"* created by the human family, he begins to see objects and people that had been vague: the windows in the dining room which had been "black mirrors where apparitions swam"; the Indian decorations on the wall; the bizarre family resemblance between a bearded face and

---

*Olsen omitted the word "man" in the Delta twelfth edition of the story.

the face of his landlady. The forces of reclamation are finally reaching Stevie, forces shaped by the care and concern which have linked generations together in an endless chain of human relationships. Thus, though "Requa" describes the fragmentation of a life disrupted by death, it creates in the end a vision of relatedness that gives the displaced person somewhere to belong. Wes's loyalty to his sister's child makes possible Stevie's recovery of the life he lost when his mother died; and Stevie's consciousness of recovery begins when he recognizes the face of his mother in any human being who cares for another—his uncle, his landlady, himself. In an unexpected way, Olsen speaks of the power of mother love as a basis for the continuity of one's self and of one's relationships with others. History keeps a record of these relationships, preserving and fostering the ties of one generation to another; and literature extends these ties as it creates a bond of sympathy between the reader and such unlikely characters as Stevie, whose experience of depression and death is universal.

As the story continues, work reinforces a recovery made possible by extended acts of love, and Stevie's apprenticeship period at the junkyard proves therapeutic. Understanding perhaps that he can learn from things as broken as he is, Stevie has begged to work with Wes rather than attend school. As he undertakes the task of sorting out the accumulated junk in the yard, the story begins to sort out its contents, separating order from disorder; and Stevie sorts out his life. He bungles and fails at his job in the junkyard, but he keeps trying because "*the tasks*" are there, "*coaxing.*" Describing these tasks, ordinary daily labor, Olsen dignifies the manual worker and his work. Stevie sees Wes showing "concern" for a trashed car as "he machines a new edge, rethreads a pipe." A man's labor expresses his love; and a boy's tasks pull him "to attention, consciousness"; they teach him "trustworthiness, pliancy"; they force him "to hold up" (65). The salvaging effect of work, even the work of salvaging, dramatizes the theme of "Requa" and shows Olsen's experience of the thirties still shaping her social vision. During the Great Depression she had seen jobless men lose their self-respect, and she learned a simple tautological truth: economic recovery, as well as the recovery of a broken individual, comes with work. Even a seemingly menial task, as she would show in "Requa," can be redemptive. Instinctively, Stevie knows this and wants a job, "A learn job, Wes. By you" (63). Work will bond him to another and teach him the secret of survival. At the junkyard Stevie slowly acquires skill and patience whch give him a sense of self-respect. He can put things together, including himself. As he sorts through heaps of waste, he finds a rhythm to his life: the incremental repetition of tasks produces a sense of pattern and continuity, of meaning. He is becoming someone who keeps working, making order, and making himself into an integrated person, like Wes. Slowly, "coaxed" by his tasks, he too is showing "concern."

The climactic moment of Stevie's return to life occurs, oddly enough, as he commemorates the dead. On Memorial Day, Mrs. Edler, the landlady, takes Stevie to church for a requiem celebration and then to several cemeteries. At church, encountering other "families, other young" who remember their dead, he realizes that loss, like love, constitutes a human bond. Moreover, as long as the dead are remembered they are never entirely lost, for the human community includes both mourners and the mourned. At the cemetery, Stevie embraces a stone lamb that may represent the ultimate inexplicability of death, the mystery of its arbitrariness as it claims an infant's life. The quaint consoling verse on the lamb tells that the baby is safely sleeping, and it seems to lull Stevie to rest: "The lamb was sun warm. . . . He put his arm around its stone neck and rested" (74). Calmly embracing a figure of death, Stevie at last finds peace at the *Requiescat in Pace* Cemetery. His story, however, is not over, for the act of recovery is never entirely consummated. "Requa" concludes with the word "reclaiming," after which there is neither the end parenthesis the text requires nor a final period—as though the process of reclamation still goes on and will continue with no sign of ending.[8]

In the last scene, Stevie's "newly tall" body suggests that time has effected recovery simply by letting the boy grow; but that natural gathering of strength which comes with the body's maturation needs the reinforcement of human relationship and love. A faceless woman, merely a name in the story, Mrs. Edler or Mrs. Ed, has taken Stevie in hand and acted as catalyst for his recovery.[9] She does this, apparently, because she feels sorry for an orphan boy, though Olsen's characterization of Stevie raises questions of why she should care and so mother him. For Stevie is a silent, withdrawn, and ghostlike boy, if not sleeping then vomiting, and awake or asleep, dripping with snot. However, the characters in "Requa" have a clairvoyance that comes from caring, and they see beyond appearances, just as they communicate without words, or with curses and insults that express love. Throughout the story, Wes calls Stevie "dummy" and "loony" and swears the boy will end in the crazy house; but Wes's insults in no way affect his action nor show disaffection. Rather they express frustration as he waits for Stevie's recovery. Wes's happiest moment comes at the end of the story when he looks at the blissfully sleeping boy and says, "Blowing out the biggest bubble of snot you ever saw. Just try and figger that loony kid" (74).

Olsen's style in "Requa" is conspicuously varied. Lyrical passages are juxtaposed to crude dialectic speech, and stream-of-consciousness passages to objectively seen realistic details. Numerous lists of things represent a world of objects proliferating outside the self; but a mind encompasses these objects and tries to find in their disorder a way of ordering an inner tumult expressed by the story's roiling fragments. Like the junkyard, the story is the repository of bits and pieces: sentences broken into phrases, phrases separated into words, words isolated by blank spaces. Single words on a line or simply sounds—"aaagh/aaagh"—mark the end of narrative sections, some introduced by titles such as *"Rifts"* and *"Terrible Pumps."* Even the typography is discontinuous, so that the text seems a mosaic of oddly assorted fragments. In creating a visibly discontinuous text, in effect, turning "Requa" into a design upon the page, Olsen attracts attention to her form which, however, always refers the reader to a social world that "Requa" presents as real, recognizable, and outside the fiction. Still, "Requa" exists as an object: its varied typography creates truncated patterns of print that catch the eye; words placed together as lists or as fragmentary refrains form distinct visual units; blocks of nouns separated from the text produce concrete poems; intervening spaces turn into aesthetic entities. Mimetic of her theme, Olsen's form is enacting the story's crucial phrase: *"Broken existences that yet continue"* (65). As a text, "Requa" is broken and yet continuous, its action extending beyond its open-ended ending. The story transforms a paradox into a promise as it turns the polarities of fragmentation and continuity into obverse aspects of each other. Merged together, the broken pieces of "Requa" create an integrated self as well as an aesthetic entity. The story enacts a process of composition to show broken existences continuing, order emerging from disorder, art from images of waste, and speech from the void of silence.

Among the many reasons for silence that Tillie Olsen has enumerated, another may be added. Perhaps what the writer has to say is too painful to express: that mothers die, children sorrow, working families are evicted from homes and left with nothing to trade for a gallon of gasoline. Olsen speaks of knowledge ordinarily repressed, and while she dignifies her characters and their work, her story denies the cherished illusion that childhood in America is a happy time of life. But "Requa" preaches no social doctrine; unlike the novel *Yonnondio*, which also describes a child caught in a period of depression, it preaches nothing at all, although a preacher's fragmentary phrases of consolation help restore the boy.[10] Rather, the story contains a secret which must be pieced together from disconnected fragments, inferred from blank spaces on the page, melded out of poetic prose and vomit, snot, and violence. This secret, that broken existences can continue, is stated explicitly. Left unsaid is another truth which both affirms and subverts the view of the poet. Yeats had described speech after long silence as an extended discourse upon Art and Song—"we descant and yet again descant." In "Requa," Olsen has said nothing about art. Her speech, resumed after ten years of silence, simply *is* art. This is the secret inherent in Tillie Olsen's story of recovery in which a child's renewed will to live becomes inseparable from an artist's recovered power to write.

Meridel Le Sueur's "Indian" Poetry

and The Quest/ion of Feminine Form

Meridel Le Sueur

ON MERIDEL LE SUEUR

This essay grew out of a talk given at a conference held at Stanford University, the subject, women writing poetry in America. The conference commemorated what would have been Sylvia Plath's fiftieth birthday. At the time, I was studying Meridel Le Sueur's prose—elegant, strong, "singing" it was always called, highly figurative, rhythmic, lyrical. Reading this prose, I could imagine the poetry Le Sueur might have written. Indeed, I reset certain passages into lines, demonstrating to myself, illegitimately of course, that except for lineation, her prose was lyrical poetry. If so, it was not the poetry she chose to write. Instead, she produced—or rather, as the essay indicates, re-produced—assertive, drumming chants, "renderings" of Native American oral poetry.

To the ear of the modern reader used to fragmented confessional lyrics, Le Sueur's renderings were strange—alienating and even ugly. They were, a word I use in the essay, vertiginous. The poems seemed to be circling, the landscape circling, the world in a dizzy whirl catching time in its movement, so that the past and present were not only continuous but also simultaneous. Women were dying, their bodies dismembered and frozen, and at the same time a perennial child was always being born. Many poems ended with the act of arrival or of coming home, or with a traditional "Thanks!" for the life given and the hope renewed. As I read and reread the poems of Rites of Ancient Ripening, *chanting them, singing them, I found myself unexpectedly hurling the lines into the air, this when I was alone and at some routine task, like driving. I realized that they were becoming less estranged, part of my consciousness; they were making me repeat: I am, I am, I am a woman. I am a woman speaking. I am a woman singing to you. Come—that emphatic command of the poems—Come, let us sing together. Then, for all the reservations I had about the poetry, which I registered in the essay, I understood why I had chosen to speak about Meridel Le Sueur on the occasion of the fiftieth birthday that Sylvia Plath never reached. Le Sueur was in her eighties. Her voice had never been silenced, though a multitude of forces might have silenced her as they had other women. She had never stopped singing, and she chose the form of her song from native traditions which celebrated an eternal returning. Her noetic image, an Indian image,*

was the circle, which included all and never ended. Her belief in
renewal may help sustain those who, like Sylvia Plath, despaired. Her
example is important to remember, for she is, as she has said, a survivor.

Meridel Le Sueur's "Indian" poems in *Rites of Ancient Ripening*[1] represent her quest for a "feminine" form of expression radically opposed to a modern "male" poetry she sees filiating from T. S. Eliot—poetry fragmented in style and vision, death-obsessed, and sterile. Native American song offered Le Sueur images of wholeness and fertility that she was seeking, images of corn, earth, and woman as one. Though Le Sueur's mythic woman anguishes over a history of blood and dismemberment, her chant calls for remembering, rebirth, and wholeness; in vatic tones, she announces her recuperative power. However, Le Sueur's appropriation of native materials raises questions about the act of appropriation, condemned in the poems as rape—of the land and of woman; about "Indian" poetry that homogenizes sacred rituals and separates them from their cultural contexts; about "feminist" poetry that alienates white readers by its unfamiliar forms, and natives by its "white shamanism"; and about the strategy of combining the voices of groups historically deprived of power in order to achieve poetic and political force.

One must note the irony of discussing these issues in a critical essay, a form which by its conventions seems to repudiate the poems' theme of communality. For by making the poems an object of study, the essay establishes a distance between subject and object—between the reader's self and the poems' persona— that Le Sueur wants eliminated; and by subordinating some ideas to others, it creates a hierarchical order that she is trying to subvert by giving major importance to minority motifs. Moreover, the essay's linear form violates the principle of circularity essential to Le Sueur's vision of life as well as to the poems' pattern of continuous return.

One moves to the central quest/ion of the poems, however, by

73

seeing the irony of placing *Rites of Ancient Ripening* within a discourse whose conventions Le Sueur opposes in order to discover a place for her poetry within a literary canon she wishes to subvert. For like all of Le Sueur's writing—like her extraordinary life[2]—the poems are radical and subversive, alienated from a mainstream, their thematic tensions produced by the insistent presence of an Other—Woman, Indian, Earth. Speaking as one, these three personae represent a body separate from and subject to the white American male. This polarization of politicized sexual bodies raises the critical question of Le Sueur's "Indian" poems: how can a radical minority voice, one associated with an Other, change a majority's consciousness? Inseparable from this question is another: how can radical politics combine with a radical poetics to create a form Le Sueur would consider feminine?[3] Controversial as it may be, Le Sueur's pursuit of this form explains her aesthetic decisions in *Rites of Ancient Ripening*. The first, of course, was her rejection of the modern lyric as unsuited to her sensibility as a woman. The second was her recovery of indigenous poetic traditions that, ironically, had become alien. Through them she hoped to realize a goal she had set before all women writers—that they create their own literary language.[4] Le Sueur believed that in everyday speech, women used a language of their own. "Listen to women talk," she has said. "Women have a different rhythm and tempo. . . . good woman gossip . . . taught me . . . about women's words and language."[5] Le Sueur has described herself as a lifelong listener who from childhood on has sought to hear and record the speech of women. In talk, gossip, letters, journals, diaries—in women's personal expressions—she found, she believed, a genderized language, one that she had tried from her earliest writings to shape into a literary medium.[6]

A brief backward glance at Le Sueur's stories and reportage shows her experimenting with a lyrical and lush prose that captured, she thought, a woman's emotional responses to the rhythms of wind, rain, growing grass—the rhythms of the earth. In "Wind," a story written in the thirties, a sudden rain excites the young wife to a sexual consummation that comes not from her husband but from the lightning that "pierced her body" and the "freshening wind" that blew over and through her.[7] The story reimagines a union between woman and the metamor-

phized gods who appeared in classical myths as natural forces—
gods who reappear in modern guise in Le Sueur's early stories
"Psyche" and "Persephone."[8] The Demeter-Persephone relationship, as her readers know, has deeply inspired Le Sueur because
it linked daughter to mother and both to the earth, a relationship crucial to her poems. Seeking essential, enduring, and pro-
creative relationships, Le Sueur turned indiscriminately to pagan myths, Native American traditions, and Christian belief.
The story "Annunciation," as the title indicates, resonates to
Christian themes, describing birth as a composite miracle: a
woman bears a child, a tree bears fruit, the story creates a social
consciousness, and the narrator, a work of art.[9] Though the
autobiographical "I" of "Annunciation" is personalized (unlike
the vatic "I" of the poems), the place localized, and the fruit
specifically named, the particular becomes universal and the secular sacred though an allusive association of the girl's pregnancy
with that of the Virgin Mother. The imagery of spiraling that
will become central to the poems is already explicit: the woman
sees the tree's trunk "spiraling upwards from below, its stem
straight, and from it, spiraling the branches . . . and from the
spiraling branches . . . the forked stems and from the stems,
twirling fragilely the tinier stems holding outward . . . the half-
curled pear leaves."[10] Like Le Sueur's current experimental
novels, "Annunciation" seems a web of intricately returning images: scraps of paper, the magnolia tree, pear tree, the landlady,
Karl's anger. These and other elements appear, disappear, and
reappear, circling back to themselves and around each other like
the "circling within me" of the girl.[11]

Like her stories, Le Sueur's reportage was rich in imagery,
lyrical, and impassioned. A well-known piece, "Eroded Woman"
identified a widow's "deep exhaustion" with the depletion of the
earth by describing woman and lead mine as exploited and sorrowing.[12] Le Sueur's interviewing technique in the report is one
she would recommend to her own interviewer thirty years later:
"you should write entirely differently. . . . Perhaps circular, going
inward and opening up an illumination about a woman. That
might be a good way to interview and write about another
woman—by loving her."[13] The interviewer in "Eroded Woman"
(Le Sueur) is neither objective nor distanced; she enters into the
being of another woman by intuiting a "virginal delicate life"

within her used and uncared-for body. In the unlit room, the two strangers sit "close together"; they will sleep together in the only bed of the sparse isolated house. Thus the interview becomes an act of communion between Le Sueur and the widow, a woman who represents the "underground" people that Le Sueur was joining by her descent to a "lower continent." Another well-known report, "I Was Marching," describes Le Sueur's first experience of communal action as a physical union so intimate that her very breath merges with the "gigantic breath" of the striking workers.[14] Woman and the social world, woman and woman, woman and earth—these relationships, thematic to Le Sueur's prose, assume cosmic significance in the poems of *Rites of Ancient Ripening*.

The poems, made equivocal here by quotation marks, are obviously "Indian" in style—a borrowed style that has appropriated from Native American songs their vocables, images, and symbolic codings of colors, numbers, and natural phenomena. Corn is blue or red; thunder, blue; the female shell, white. Four is a sacred number, the winds coming from four directions, the water coming "on the four paths of the eagles." Rain is advisedly He or She. Formally, the poems imitate ceremonial chants with their repetitions and refrains, their emphatic rhythms and drumlike commands, their parallel lines ("I am the daily bread / I am the daily breast"), and traditional vocables ("A hey a hey a hey"). Allusions to rituals, some as familiar as the smoking of peace pipes, enhance the "Indian-ness" of the poems, as do references to myths and to mythological figures—Changing Woman, Katchina girls, White Buffalo Woman, Corn Maid. The poems are "Indian" also in their (simulated) oral delivery; all are spoken or chanted in vatic tones, the "I" impersonalized as a timeless woman, a progenitor of life in the past and now a recuperative spirit. Recuperation, imagined as an act of remembering or of resurrecting, emerges as a dominant theme because the sacred circle of life that the poems would celebrate has been shattered; Le Sueur is invoking ancient rites in order to reunite alienated forms of being—human being and nature.[15] She remembers also truncated parts of the past so that the battles of Wounded Knee and Vietnam are (for her) the same—both instances of oppression. The poems constitute a symbolic victory over this oppression as they rejoin—if only in song—the dismembered parts of wars' victims.

Though *Rites of Ancient Ripening* has been published as her own poetry, Le Sueur describes herself as "rendering" Native American songs, translating and interpreting them and, as the word implies, giving them back or restoring. I have traced several poems back to particular sources. One, for example, is a Papago song freely translated into two lines:

> Where am I running from, that I come here?
> Am I a crazy woman with a painted face?[16]

As if in antiphonal response to these questions, Le Sueur's longer poem begins with a prostitute's assertion, "I am a crazy woman with a painted face," and continues with her wanderings in the streets of Gallup, "beneath the guns" of white men and "among the thrushes." A more complicated example of rendering involves the Sioux myth of White Buffalo Woman bringing her people the sacred pipe.[17] "Behold this and always love it!" she cries, as does the speaker of the poem entitled "Behold This and Always Love It." The poem renews the promise of the original Buffalo Woman by describing her second coming, a coming made perpetual by drumming repetitions of the present participle:

> Coming   coming   coming.
>   . . .
> From far away she is coming   coming
> From all the roads she is coming   coming.

"Make the Earth Bright   And Thanks" restores a restoration as it offers Le Sueur's version of a translation of Black Elk's account of the Sun Dance and the "Crying for a Vision" ritual.[18] "We are crying for a vision," the poem says, weaving together words, phrases, lines, and vocables from ceremonies described in *The Sacred Pipe*, an intricate and ingenious interweaving which eliminates the young man and the grandfather of Black Elk's story and replaces them, significantly, with a grandmother. Clearly, Le Sueur was subverting (and so collaborating in the destruction of) the original ceremony when she omitted from her poem such lines as "Our Grandfather's voice is calling to me" and "Grandfather, behold me!" Instead, she gives "Thanks" to a primordial woman, the "grandmother / of the center of the world."

If the render means to give back or restore, it implies also to give up—to cede, yield, lose. *Ancient Rites* evokes a sense of loss by recalling tribal cultures that have yielded to the destructive pressures of history and by showing traditional rites separated from their contexts. Recognizing this loss, Le Sueur tries to reinstate the sacred meanings of words like "smoke," "sage," "pollen" with her glossary of "Indian Symbols," a preface that effects an uneasy compromise with the text by offering to make alien (Native American) linguistic codes accessible as "Indian" speech. However, the glossary's homogenizing definitions emphasize the artifactuality of the poems—that they present a white person's image of the "Indian."[19] Le Sueur tries to avoid stereotyping by recalling the real victims of history, particularly in poems grouped together as "Winters of the Slain." Among these, "Dead in the Bloody Snow" is striking as a woman's account of the slaughter at Wounded Knee. Graphically, in gruesome detail, a woman tells how a dream—"a beautiful dream," Black Elk had called it—was buried beside the dismembered and frozen bodies of a people. Black Elk's own farewell to this dream was poignant: "you see me now a pitiful old man who has done nothing, for the nation's hoop is broken and scattered. There is no center any longer, and the sacred tree is dead."[20]

Fragmentation and death are, of course, motifs of the modernist poetry that Le Sueur was consciously, even angrily, rejecting. She said recently, "I consider the darkest time of my life in '23 when T. S. Eliot published The Wasteland"; "The Wasteland is about death . . . straw men, going out with a whimper . . . a terrible influence."[21] Elsewhere she has quipped, "Fortunately, Eliot didn't speak of hollow women,"[22] a remark that must be taken as a misprision, for wasteland women are as emptied of life as the poem's Lil after her abortion. When Eliot's leisured lady cries, "What shall I do now? What shall I do?" she expresses a neurasthenic despair that Le Sueur was finding pervasive in modern poetry. Criticizing its pessimism—"We must write optimistically," she says[23]—Le Sueur implicitly repudiated the modern lyric as the expression of an individual concerned only with a dissociated self. Though line after line in *Rites of Ancient Ripen-*

ing begins with "I," the poems are not about private emotions; rather, the "I," decentered from the self, speaks for all people as witness to what has been (history) and what is to come (prophecy). Through her "Indian" poems, Le Sueur was trying to revive the communal purposes of Native American songs, which were inseparable from ceremonies that created and preserved social cohesiveness.[24] Unlike Eliot's hollow women, the generative female of "Dead in Bloody Snow" knows what she can do, for she can make a poem emanate from her words, "I sing."

In Native American traditions, singing represented an exercise of power. Originally the gift of the gods, song was inseparable from sacred ceremony and dance. Singing not only described events, both personal and communal; singing shaped events by influencing the supernatural forces that controlled the world. Such effectiveness of the word within a cultural context appealed to Le Sueur, who had always believed that language should be a means of persuasion, of social action, and of change. In Native American sacred songs, she was finding another mode for the expression of this view of art—a political view formulated in the thirties as the aesthetic of proletarian literature. Alien as her poems may seem to this literature, they continue her long quest for an art dedicated to action. In 1981 she was still declaring that the "time of the private artist is over," an assertion that led her again to disavow Eliot as a purveyor of pessimism.[25] On the "arid plains" of his wasteland, one could hope to find only fragments; but Le Sueur wanted wholeness, symbolized for her by the circle, an entire, continuous, embracing figure, central but by no means exclusive to Native American cultures.

These were cultures she had encountered early in her life and to which she always returned. When she came to write her poems she had only to remember the Indian girls she danced and played with as a child in Oklahoma, and the Mandan Indian woman Zona, who had taught her that "the circle never ends."[26] In an autobiographical essay, Le Sueur interweaves Zona's wisdom with stories her mother and grandmother told as the three women sat in a circle sharing their experiences. Intimacy between "the ancient people and the newly come" (native and whites) constituted a personal experience for Le Sueur as

she remembered how "In the beginning of the century the Indian smoke still mingled with ours."[27] Moreover, Le Sueur's life
on the Midwest prairies reinforced Indian stories of the earth's
fecundity and the life-giving power of grass, "one of the richest
foods on earth." Inevitably, Earth, Woman, and Indian merged
in her memories (as they would in her poems), all interrelated in
the turning and returning movement of the circle of life, its
forms springing forth from the earth and growing, ripening,
and dying; then springing forth again. Corn, the source of life in
Native American creation myths, has always obsessed Le Sueur
as a poetic symbol (indeed, she is now writing a complex
scientific and visionary history of corn).[28] Speaking through the
personae of such mythic Indian women as Corn Maiden (who
had plucked the corn from her breast to give to humans) and of
Changing Woman (who had enacted the process of eternal rejuvenation), Le Sueur could assert at once her belief in the female's progenitive power, in her own alien-ness or political difference, in the communal function of art, and in the integrity or
oneness of human life and nature. Moreover, she could reinforce her own identity as a prairie woman by using a symbolic
language that sprang from the landscape.

At the same time Le Sueur's "Indian" poems allowed her to
pursue her quest for "feminine" forms of expression. Since the
twenties and thirties, when male editors criticized her for writing
about "funny" things like birth, Le Sueur knew that her subject
matter, like her experience, must be different from Faulkner's
and Hemingway's, that she could not write about "killing an old
bear" or about "fighting, fishing, and fucking."[29] Nor could she
use the male writers' language or narrative form, both of which
she thought reflected destructive impulses: "The more you nar-
rate," she said, "the more you externalize. Most writing is to
externalize and objectify and actually kill what you're looking
at."[30] She resented the styles of discourse she had inherited because they violated her sensibility, just as, she believed, they violated the landscape they described as there to be possessed and
conquered—like the poem's Corn Maid, raped: "Almost all my
language comes from the English poets, the nature poets, all
those bastards. When they look at a sunset, they look at nature
like they do a woman—they want her, to possess her. Now I don't
look at a landscape that way."[31]

Rites of Ancient Ripening represents Le Sueur's experimenta-
tion with a literary language belonging to an Other, a language
that she believes is "freer than ours, not based on intellectual
logic," linear progression, or a preponderance of nouns.[32] Writing in 1970 of the "spirally return" of the past that makes for a
continuous present, Le Sueur supported her views on circularity
by citing Native American speech: "Indians have no word for
progression of time or sequence, for past, present and future.
Their word for time means . . . unfolding . . . the immediate
germinal presence of the entire spiral of growth, instantaneous,
reappearing."[33] This vision of life as a process of continuously
spiraling emergence underlies Le Sueur's opposition to linear
narrative forms. Developed by male writers, these forms reflect,
she believes, their desire to bring stories—and life—to an end.
Endings, points, targets—such analogical terms reveal men's destructive tendencies, while the nouns of traditional literary style,
famous in Hemingway's texts, mask their ineffectuality: "we
name hunger and make studies of global hunger, but in the
meantime the hungry people just keep on getting hungrier."[34]
Thus, Le Sueur has condemned naming as "a conquering and
objectifying action."[35] Inspired by the Hopi language (as she
understands it), Le Sueur is now writing a "nameless novel,"
seeking through this experimental form to express the sense of
relatedness intrinsic to her poems. In Hopi, she points out,
"there is only the relationship, not the naming."[36] Women also
value relationship, she believes, and to express their sense of
communality they require literary forms other than those transmitted by male-created traditions. This other-ness Le Sueur
thought she could find in the chants and sacred songs of the
Native Americans, since they defy linear narrative forms by
their repetitions, parallel lines, and images of rebirth and circularity. "Everything an Indian does is in a circle," Black Elk has
said; "the Power of the World always works in circles, and everything tries to be round. . . . The sky is round . . . the earth is
round like a ball. . . . The sun comes forth and goes down in a
circle . . . the moon . . . the seasons. . . . The life of a man is a
circle."[37]

In *Rites of Ancient Ripening,* the life of woman becomes an
eternal circle through an identification of her body with the
earth. Highly condensed figures of speech assume this

identification. Such figures recur as the poems describe a "meadowed breast" and "horizon belly" ("All Around Me, Come!"); or direct a bird to "fly over the low horizon / of my breast" ("Strike Us to Bud"); or depict trees "tilt[ing] upon me like young men" ("Rites of Ancient Ripening"); or cry out, "Do not plow my flesh" ("Lost Mother Lode"). Sometimes the woman encircles the earth, which she can move, hold, and hand to her children ("I Hear You Singing in the Barley Ripe"). Sometimes she contains it in her body: "In my lap I hold the valley"; "In my breast I hold the middle valley" ("Rites of Ancient Ripening"). Because the rootedness Le Sueur ascribes to Native Americans has become precarious, her women must plead for renewal. In poem after poem, the female "I" implores a male "You" to quicken her seed:

> I lie prone   father husband
> Open me kernel, green unfurl me
> . . .
> Reach green to my hungry breast
>   into my dust of fire and thorn
> And face me to your knife of love.
>
> ("Green Unfurl Me")

Like sexual desire, this language eludes logic. Particular images are enigmatic because they are allusive, referring to the biological processes of corn fertilization and to the mythic origins of corn in a woman's breast. However puzzling poems like "Green Unfurl Me" are, they convey a woman's passion for the man with whom she maintains an intense but ambiguous relationship as she prays for his sperm in return for her "power." "As I lie on the earth," she says, "Be upon me / Take me / I am powerful!" ("All Around Me, Come!").[38] Excerpted, the lines suggest a mutual relationship, woman and man giving and taking from each other life-infusing force. But the poems as a whole, any individual poem and all together, do not imply full reciprocity. Only a woman speaks in Le Sueur's poems, and as she announces immediately, she speaks for her sex: "I am a woman speaking for us all" ("Hush, My Little Grandmother"). "Us all" includes mother, grandmother, child; mythic females identified with earth and its fruit; and historic figures who tell a tale of tribal annihilation.

In "Dead in Bloody Snow," the first lines establish the authority of the "I" to describe the Battle of Wounded Knee: "I am an
Indian woman / Witness to my earth / Witness for my people."
Validating this witness is Black Elk, whose words are echoed in
Le Sueur's final line denoting "a people's dream that died in
bloody snow."[39] If Le Sueur was seeking in Native American
tradition a spiritual vision of cosmic harmony, she could not
separate her ideal from the brutal history Black Elk remembered. "Dead in Bloody Snow" requires the Indian woman to
rise from the dead because she has been killed, her tribe annihilated, and her "people's vision" destroyed. "I came toward
you shouting," the woman cries in "Behold Me! Touch Me!",
shouting not in exultation but in fear: "Do not let them kill me
before you speak to me." If heard, her words would eradicate
the past and its "trail of tears"—or more precisely, they would
restore the (romanticized) age that had preceded dislocation and
death:

> I come toward you shouting
> To call you to the land of meeting, brothers.
> Fat buffalo   stalwart people   and a holy tree
>   of liberty flourishing for all birds
>   for all children.
>   ("Behold Me! Touch Me!")

Needless to say, the buffalo are gone, and the shouting seems a
rhetorical strategy to deny the fact of genocide. Though the
poem insists upon "return" or resurrection in lines proclaiming
the woman's power to nurture life—"I am the daily bread / I am
the daily breast"—it also recognizes her powerlessness: "Do not
let them kill me."

Le Sueur's polarization of genocide and resurrection as a
thematic conflict suggests an acculturation more profound than
the acquisition of particular native symbols and myths, for central to the poetry of contemporary Native American women, an
important spokesperson for them has shown, is the memory of
racial extermination intertwined with the hope for racial renewal.[40] Le Sueur discovered this dichotomy for herself as she
tried through the syncretic form of *Rites of Ancient Ripening* to
merge two sensibilities into one, that of the traditional Indian (as
she best understood it) and that of a generic woman (as

epitomized by her own desire to create and care for life). Intended to reinforce the strength Le Sueur finds in both groups,
this merging cannot help calling attention to their shared victimization. Summer may appear in "Strike Us to Bud," and the
speaker may promise fertility and harvest, but such assurances
are necessitated by the presence of "napalmed children," "rockets," and "the holocaust of burning cities." In defiance, the
poem's "I" will "shake my rattles," but with the knowledge,
shared by the reader, that rattles have been proved ineffectual
against guns and that neither Native Americans nor women
have prevailed against the powers that make war. In view of
these failures, woman's assertiveness may seem compensatory,
and woman herself a static figure who speaks but does not act.
Traditionally, mythic heroines engage in action and become
known, become themselves, through what they do. Le Sueur's
"I" invokes other to act, while, characteristically, she speaks or
sings: "I am a woman come to speak"; "I sing holding my
severed head"; "I want to talk to the people"; "I send my voice of
sorrow / calling calling."

This voice is commanding, even when the woman lies
"prone." It never falters in its song, however devastating the
subject. Recalling a past at once historical and mythic, the voice
announces the theme of recuperation. In the long poem, "Rites
of Ancient Ripening," a vertiginous cosmic circling effected by
repetitions, parallels, and transformative images—"My body a
canoe turning to stone / Moves . . ."—makes this theme a felt
experience of return. As in the story "Annunciation," everything
that appears in the poem reappears: the woman, the horizon,
stones, dust, feathers, seeds, birds, hunters ("great hunters returning"), summers, flowers, memories, songs, ceremonies.
Grinding the corn, an ancient action, the old woman produces
new life in her "bowl," a synonym the glossary says, for "earth,
womb, Mother Clay":[41]

> All was ground in the bodies bowl
>   corn died to bread
>   woman to child
>   deer to the hunters.

The poem celebrates a transcendence over death achieved as life
revolves through eternal cycles of change. "Release my seed and

let me fall," the luminous woman cries, accepting age as a phase
in the process of ripening, and death as a prelude to requickening. Le Sueur embodies this requickening in the child who carries the seeds of the future. Indeed, this "perpetual child" is
already an "ancestor" like the grandmother she will become:[42]

> Beautiful child, appearing in constellations
> In all differences and repetitions
> Future ancestors in a rain of seed.
> Child   mother   grandmother   child again
> I am singing it   I am singing it
>   ("I Hear You Singing in the Barley Ripe")

Le Sueur's bequest in this song is the earth revolving in life-
producing processes, passing from mother to daughter and supporting an eternal series of transformation: of seed to corn to
bread; of child to mother to grandmother to child again; of life
to death to rebirth into new life.

If this vision is universal, central to world religions and made
peculiarly American in Walt Whitman's *Leaves of Grass,* in Le
Sueur's poems it is native (and so alien) and offered by a woman
who affiliates herself with Native American mothers by reiterating a traditional creed: "Women never birth enemy faces" ("No
Enemy Faces"). While "Winters of the Slain" describes men
slaughtering their enemies, the grouped poems of "Changing
Woman" and "Surround of Rainbows" show women bringing
the pipe of peace and calling all to "be together / as bread."
Bread made from corn ground by women, milk flowing from
their "globular" breasts, children "budded" from their bodies—
images of woman's "begetting" multiply to contrast with men's
violence. Le Sueur's most lyrical lines describe a woman's rebirth
through her child. "Before you, child," the woman says in
"Budded with Child," "I never knew the breast of milk / the arm
of love"; and in "Sprang Seed to Wind," she speaks again of a
child's coming:

> Before you came
> I never slept with hope
>   or hoped for flesh.
> Sprang seed to wind
>   spiraled petal to light

Or leapt from root to calyx
   or sprang through time and space
      Alive!
Child, you always bring the summer
   of earth and flesh.

Monosyllabic, rhythmic and emphatic, alliterative, simple but abstract and compressed, the lines attempt to transcend time and space, their rhythms suggesting a leaping movement as though the woman were springing to life and spiraling with the seed sprung newly into the wind. Here Le Sueur is at her best—concentrated, intense, celebratory, her voice released and free—above all, freed from conventions suited to poetry of personal confession, despair, or weakness, of lamentation over a broken fragmented world. Le Sueur wanted to see a restored whole world. She did not deny the violence of the past; rather, she inscribed the history of genocide within poems that celebrate an eternal process of return: the closing and enclosing of a sacred circle in which forms of being could coexist, each sustaining the other, each in its time dying so that the perpetual child could be reborn. Her poems conclude with salutations and images of arrival. "Let the Bird of Earth, Fly!" and "Make the Earth Bright" end with a traditional "Thanks." "Strike Us to Bud" ends with a promise to "reach harvest . . . make cob"; "Corridors of Love" with "the resurrected heart"; "Come to My Singing" with arrival "home." The volume ends with "Our sisters / Singing. / choruses of millions / singing ("Dòan Kêt").

If Le Sueur's poems permit woman to sing triumphantly of her difference and her power, they also raise aesthetic, political, and perhaps even moral problems. They may strike white readers as stylized and stilted, their form producing not community but alienation: "When I first began reading Meridel's poetry," Le Sueur's most intimate critic confessed, "I found her land imagery alien to my urban experience. Her incorporation of Indian symbols was foreign to my Christian eyes and ears, and the voluptuous metaphors which sing of the land as a woman left me blushing with embarrassment."[43] *Rites of Ancient Ripening* intensifies the eroticism characteristic of Le Sueur's prose by constant allusions to Changing Woman or Corn Maiden. "Come, come," they command the male: "Touch me!"; "Take Me"; "face me to your knife of love." Accustomed to the personal "I" of contemporary poems, readers might respond to Le Sueur's frenetic personae as women in love rather than mythic principles of fertility, the embodied spirits of procreation. Objecting less to the sexuality than the misappropriation of native material, a reviewer who admired Le Sueur's prose wished that she had never written the poems, that she had left traditional forms to Native Americans who might have observed the tribal distinctions Le Sueur ignored.[44] For in her desire to create an ideal figure, she presented a homogenized universal "Indian"; and in her desire to imagine an ideal society— a "global village," a "cosmic circle"—she conflated native cultures and so violated tribal history. Indeed, history becomes unrecognizable in Le Sueur's introductory remarks, highly conditional statements that imply a past of unrelated and unrealizable possibilities.[45] One was that frontier, village, and church might have come together to create communality—a view that overlooks the inherent tensions between the frontier and the villages it had left behind. Another possibility Le Sueur suggests is that whites and natives might have united—or may yet unite (Le Sueur's verbs are ambiguous). At the same time, she proclaims a precedence of natives over whites by pointing to their historical priority; Indian cultures, she noted, existed long before those of ancient Greece and Rome. As enigmatic (and historically or philosophically indefensible) as Le Sueur's introductory remarks are in *Ancient Rites,* their intention is clear. They propose the appropriation of an Indian vision of life by modern white society. By detaching native traditions from their historical contexts, Le Sueur was making native vision and secret sacred song seem transferable from one culture to the next, from one aesthetic form or language to another, from an individual to others.

Modern Native Americans have objected to this apparently easy assimilation of their culture and to poetry that professes to recreate their sacred beliefs.[46] To them "white shamanism" reflects a disarray within the white's society and psyche. A recent poem by a Native American (Hopi) woman inveighs against white poets who think that through imitative gestures, words, and dress—a "temporary tourism"—they can achieve "instant and primal knowledge":

> You think of us only
> when your voice
> wants for roots,
> when you have sat back
> on your heels and
> become
> primitive.
>
> You finish your poem
> and go back.

("For the White Poets Who Would Be Indians")[47]

The poem allows for no exception, and from a Native American perspective none seems permissible; but Le Sueur's political and personal commitment to Native American integrity has been lifelong, made many years before the sixties popularized Indian clothes and bathos, and it persists in her current support of Native American land rights. I do not wish to claim native authenticity for Le Sueur (a claim she might, in fact, make through her great-grandmother, a full-blooded Iroquois). On the contrary, I wish to elaborate upon the problems that her Indian style raises for her poetry and politics and her quest for a "feminine" form. Having condemned historical acts of appropriation as illegal violent seizures—the seizure of twenty-four million acres of Sioux territory she described as so bloody that the prairies and rivers ran "red"[48]—Le Sueur herself may be accused of making literary appropriations by using the traditions of others for her own purposes. However admirable and renewing these purposes may be, they cannot be separated from personal motives, for as the poem quoted above would suggest, Le Sueur's affinity as a white poet for Native Americans (like her attraction to working-class people) reflects her own dislocation and search for roots. Years ago Le Sueur described rootlessness as a Midwest blight: "The Prairie of the Middle West is very large. Nothing has ever been rooted there," she said, "Now it is blowing away because nothing has been rooted. . . . The rooted things have been torn up by the greed for lumber, coal, iron, railroads, and wheat. Man has not been rooted in it either."[49]

The hope of Le Sueur's poems is that woman may be rooted in this prairie, a synecdoche for the earth which all poetic traditions identify with a primal mother. "The body repeats the landscape," Le Sueur has written, describing how her "embryonic eye . . . went from mother enclosure to prairie spheres curving into each other."[50] In her poems the roundness of the mothering woman's breast repeats the prairie's horizon curve, which in Native American myths extended endlessly to inscribe a cosmic circle. Le Sueur believed that woman—all women, including her Vietnamese sisters[51]—could form such a cosmic circle, inclusive, embracing, appropriate to both an ancient and a modern vision of life.[52] She was speaking symbolically, prophetically, imagining an act of sexual difference which would, paradoxically, create oneness of spirit and vision. *Rites of Ancient Ripening* ends militantly with a prophecy of peace as women of the entire world join to "light the bowl of life." Their power lies in the song that Native Americans believed could move the earth. Le Sueur has always described power as rising from below. She believed that what has been submerged would in time emerge—a seed planted in the earth, an oppressed class, race, or sex "trapped far below ground in American life," a buried vision. Many creation myths describe female figures (Persephone or White Shell Woman) rising from below, and Native American traditions in particular emphasize the chthonic origins which Le Sueur preferred to generative decrees handed down from above. Based upon such decrees, she believed, Christianity had instituted a hierarchical order she found invidious, one which placed men above women, capitalist class above workers, whites above natives:

Drawn up [she said]. Leaf from root. Everything is drawn UP. If you had this sense instead of that devilish Christian sense that all is from above, given to you by some patriarchal god. Even Michelangelo's God holding out his finger to Adam is puerile. How much of those Christian images in the poetry of Eliot and Pound is so infantile![53]

No one would stand above or fall below another in the circle that embraced all forms of life in Le Sueur's "Indian" poetry. No one would be outside or apart, even though the poems seek to concentrate revolutionary power by uniting two outsiders: Native and Woman, perennial Others. Described as victims of history, together they were to achieve power not by victimizing others, but by inspiring them to join in communal rites. To be revitalized these rites required, she believed, a language that was non-hierarchical, non-possessive, non-aggressive. As women had created life, so also, Le Sueur thought, they could create or recover literary forms consonant with the rites of ripening. The returning lines, repetitions, parallelisms, reiterated vocables, transformative metaphors of Native American song—all suggesting patterns of circularity—seemed to Le Sueur an-Other possibility, an escape from the fragmented anguished lines of modern poets whose lyrics confessed confusion and defeat. In *Rites of Ancient Ripening* the "resonance" of woman's song shows her undefeatable, even though she bears witness to massive and continuous violence—genocide, murder, dismemberment, rape. The poems are not easy, not in their memories, their indictments, or their images, but to avoid them for the difficulties of their alien forms would be to deny a hope of recuperation. As poems created by the combined voices of minority figures, *Rites of Ancient Ripening* will neither change the consciousness of the American majority nor "feminize" its literary forms, but the promise of its chant reverberates to perennial rhythms of renewal as women sing:

> Child   mother   grandmother   child again
> I am singing it   I am singing it.
> Look my children the earth is about to move.
> I am humming to you   I am singing to you
> I circle round and round the earth.
>   . . .
> My children   My children   Here it is   I hand it to
>   you
>   the earth!
>   the earth!
>   ("I Hear You Singing in the Barley Ripe")[54]

In *Rites of Ancient Ripening,* Meridel Le Sueur sings the green earth back into existence, and if the magical power of words in which Native American chanters believed could be recovered, her song might be widely heard, perhaps even heeded. Meanwhile, her "Indian" poems express a woman's desire for the return to a vision of the past that promises a future. Circling through time, the poems themselves enact a process of recovery, renewing ancient songs as a modern woman's language, as her hope. The hope is perennial—for rain, harvest, home, for birds, not rockets, to fly over us, and for the earth to be bright.

The Forgotten Reaping-Hook:

Sex in *My Ántonia*

Willa Cather

ON WILLA CATHER: I

*I remember that the title of this essay seemed insistent, though I wished
it would change. I knew that an article with the word* sex *in it would
never be accepted by an academic journal. Indeed, "Sex in* My Ántonia*" seemed a contradiction in terms. For as an idealistic writer who
celebrated pioneer virtues, Willa Cather seemed above or beyond sex.
Why* My Ántonia *perplexed me, when others felt certain of its themes, I
cannot say precisely; but as the essay indicates, I was troubled by
criticism that called the novel a masterpiece and yet pronounced many
parts of it extraneous. Extraneous to what, I wondered, except critical
preconceptions of what a Cather novel should be and how it should
celebrate an American past which the critics seemed to agree was glorious. This judgment was not unequivocally supported by history. The
history of the railroads, depicted in Cather's fiction as the realization of
a great pioneering dream, was riddled with greed, corruption, and
exploitation. Jim Burden, a railway lawyer, begins his reminiscences in*
My Ántonia *while on a train; he recalls a glorious past which
somehow has led to his vacuous present. To ask if he is a narrator whose
memory can be completely trusted is to wonder whether Cather is
a simple writer whose characters say what she as well as they mean
without equivocation or omission. By its internal contradictions,
the text itself seemed to question Jim Burden's credibility; and once that
foundered so did accepted interpretations of the novel which, I believe,
had been subtly influenced by the novelist's sex. Women writers would
naturally be expected to celebrate the virtues of home, earth mother,
children—the nurturing of a new-born nation. They would not penetrate the dark depths of life. Men like Cather's contemporary Theodore
Dreiser penetrated, while women created a soothing seamless surface. If
implicitly Cather was being stereotyped, the revealing and nefarious
stereotypes perpetuated in her novel were ignored, along with the violence that marred an idyllic vision of the pioneer past. Today, Cather's
simplicity is no longer taken for granted and her romantic vision of the
past no longer passively accepted. The violence of days past needs
to be remembered, and as a writer who celebrated the power of memory,
Willa Cather does not let us forget.*

Our persistent misreading of Willa Cather's *My Ántonia* rises from a belief that Jim Burden is a reliable narrator. Because we trust his unequivocal narrative manner, we see the novel as a splendid celebration of American frontier life. This is the view reiterated in a current critique of *My Ántonia*[1] and in a recent comprehensive study of Cather's work: "*My Ántonia* shows fertility of both the soil and human beings. Thus, in a profound sense *My Ántonia* is the most affirmative book Willa Cather ever wrote. Perhaps that is why it was her favorite."[2] Critics also elect it *their* favorite Cather novel: however, they regret its inconclusive structure, as did Cather when she declared it fragmented and unsatisfactory in form.[3] David Daiches's complaint of thirty years ago prevails: that the work is "flawed" by "irrelevant" episodes and material of "uncertain" meaning.[4] Both critical positions—that *My Ántonia* is a glorious celebration of American life and a defective work of art—must be reversed once we challenge Jim Burden's vision of the past. I believe we have reason to do so, particularly now, when we are making many reversals in our thinking. As soon as we question Jim's seemingly explicit statements, we see beyond them myriad confusions which can be resolved only by a totally new reading. This would impel us to reexamine Jim's testimony, to discover him a more disingenuous and self-deluded narrator than we supposed. Once we redefine his role, *My Ántonia* begins to resonate to new and rather shocking meanings which implicate us all. We may lose our chief affirmative novel, only to find one far more exciting—complex, subtle, aberrant.

Jim Burden belongs to a remarkable gallery of characters for whom Cather consistently invalidates sex. Her priests, pioneers, and artists invest all energy elsewhere. Her idealistic young men die prematurely; her bachelors, children, and old folk remain "neutral" observers. Since she wrote within a prohibitive genteel tradition, this reluctance to portray sexuality is hardly surprising. What should intrigue us is the strange involuted nature of her avoidance. She masks sexual ambivalence by certainty of manner, and displays sexual disturbance, even the macabre, with peculiar insouciance. Though the tenor of her writing is normality, normal sex stands barred from her fictional world. Her characters avoid sexual union with significant and sometimes bizarre ingenuity, or achieve it only in dreams. Alexandra Bergson, the heroine of *O Pioneers!*, finds in recurrent reveries the strong transporting arms of a lover; and Jim Burden in *My Ántonia* allows a half-nude woman to smother him with kisses only in unguarded moments of fantasy. Their dreams suggest the typical solipisism of Cather's heroes, who yield to a lover when they are most solitary, most inverted, encaptured by their own imaginations. As Alexandra dispels such reveries by a brisk cold shower, their inferential meaning becomes almost comically clear. Whenever sex enters the real world (as for Emil and Marie in *O Pioneers!*),[5] it becomes destructive, leading almost axiomatically to death. No wonder, then, that Cather's heroes have a strong intuitive aversion to sex that they reveal furtively through enigmatic gestures. In *A Lost Lady*, when young Niel Herbert, who idealizes the Forrester's sexless marriage, discovers Mrs. Forrester's love affair, he vents his infantile jealousy and rage the only way he can—symbolically. While the lovers are on the phone, he takes his "big shears" and cuts the wires, ostensibly to prevent gossip, but also to sever a relationship he cannot abide. Ingenious in rationalizing their actions, Cather's heroes do not entirely conceal an underlying fear of physical love; and the connection between love and death, long undiscerned in Cather's work, can be seen as its inextricable motif. Even in her first novel, *Alexander's Bridge*, the hero's gratuitous death— generally thought to flaw the work—fulfills the inherent thematic demand to show physical passion as disastrous. Here, as in *O Pioneers!*, illicitness is merely a distracting irrelevance which helps conceal the fear of sexuality in all relationships. *O Pioneers!* reduces the interval between love and death until they almost coincide. At three o'clock, Emil races "like an arrow shot from the bow" to Marie; for the first time they make love; by evening they are dead, murdered by the half-demented husband.

In *My Ántonia*, Jim Burden grows up with an intuitive fear of sex, never acknowledged, and in fact, denied; yet it is a determining force in his story. By deflecting attention from himself to Ántonia, of whom he can speak with utter assurance, he manages to conceal his muddied sexual attitudes. His narrative voice, reinforced by Cather's, emerges firm and certain; and it convinces. We tend to believe with Jim that his authoritative recitation of childhood memories validates the past and gives meaning to the present, even though his mature years stream before him emptied of life, intimacy, and purpose. Memory transports him to richer and happier days spent with Ántonia, the young Bohemian girl who signifies "*the country, the conditions, the whole adventure of . . . childhood.*"[6] Because a changing landscape brilliantly illumines his childhood—with copper-red prairies transformed to rich wheatfields and corn—his personal story seems to epitomize this larger historical drama. Jim uses the coincidence of his lifespan with a historical era to imply that as the country changed and grew, so did he, and moreover, as his memoirs contained historical facts, so did they hold the truth about himself. Critics support Jim's bid for validity, pointing out that "*My Ántonia* exemplifies superbly [Frederick Jackson] Turner's concept of the recurring cultural evolution on the frontier."[7]

Jim's account of both history and himself seems to me disingenuous, indeed, suspect; yet it is for this very reason highly pertinent to an understanding of our own uses of the past. In the introduction, Jim presents his memoirs as a spontaneous expression—unselected, unarranged, and uncontrolled by ulterior purpose: "*From time to time I've been writing down what I remember . . . about Ántonia. . . . I didn't take time to arrange it; I simply wrote down pretty much all that her name recalls to me. I suppose it hasn't any form, . . . any title, either*" (2). Obviously, Jim's memory cannot be as autonomous or disinterested as he implies. His plastic powers reshape his experience, selecting and omitting in response to unconscious desires and the will. Ultimately, Jim forgets as much as he remembers, as his mind sifts through the years to retrieve what he most needs—a purified past in which he can find safety from sex and disorder. Of "a romantic disposition," Jim substitutes wish for reality in celebrating the past. His flight from sexuality parallels a flight from historical truth, and in this respect he becomes an emblematic American figure, like Jay Gatsby and Clyde Griffiths. Jim romanticizes the American past as Gatsby romanticizes love, and Clyde money. Affirming the common, the prototypic, American dream of fruition, all three, ironically, are devastated—Gatsby and Clyde die violently, while Jim succumbs to immobilizing regressive needs. Their relationship to the dream they could not survive must strike us oddly, for we have reversed their situation by surviving to see the dream shattered and the Golden Age of American history im-

pugned. Out of the past that Jim idealized comes our present
stunning disorder, though Jim would deny such continuity, as
Cather did. Her much-quoted statement that the world *broke* in
1922 reveals historical blindness mistaken for acuity.[8] She denied
that "the beautiful past" transmitted the crassness, disorder, and
violence that "ruined" the present for her and drove her to
hermitic withdrawal. She blamed villainous men, such as Ivy
Peters in *A Lost Lady*, for the decline of a heroic age. Like her,
Jim Burden warded off broad historical insight. His mythopoeic
memory patterned the past into an affecting creation story, with
Ántonia a central fertility figure, "a rich mine of life, like the
founders of early races." Jim, however, stalks through his myth
as a wasteland figure who finds in the present nothing to compensate him for the loss of the past, and in the outer world
nothing to violate the inner sanctum of memory. "Some
memories are realities, are better than anything that can ever
happen to one again"—Jim's nostalgic conclusion rationalizes his
inanition. He remains finally fixated on the past, returning to
the vast and ineffaceable image that dominates his memoirs—
the Nebrasks prairie yielding to railroad and plough. Since this
is an impersonal image of the growth of a nation, and yet it
seems so personally crucial to Jim, we must be alerted to the
special significance it holds for him. At the very beginning of the
novel, we are told that Jim "*loves with a personal passion the great
country through which his railway runs*" (2.) The symbolism of the
railroad penetrating virgin fields is such an embarrassingly obvious example of emotional displacement, it seems extraordinary
that it has been so long unnoted. Like Captain Forrester, the
unsexed husband of *A Lost Lady,* Jim sublimates by traversing the
country, laying it open by rail; and because he sees the land grow
fertile and the people prosper, he believes his story to be a celebration.

But neither history's purely material achievement, nor
Cather's aesthetic conquest of childhood material, can rightfully
give Jim Burden personal cause to celebrate. Retrospection, a
superbly creative act for Cather, becomes for Jim a negative
gesture. His recapitulation of the past seems to me a final surrender to sexual fears. He was afraid of growing up, afraid of
women, afraid of the nexus of love and death. He could love

only that which time had made safe and irrefragable—his memories. They revolve not, as he says, about the image of Ántonia, but about himself as a child. When he finds love, it seems to him the safest kind—the narcissistic love of the man for himself as a boy. Such love is not unique to Jim Burden. It obsesses many Cather protagonists from early novels to late: from Bartley Alexander in *Alexander's Bridge* to Godfrey St. Peter in *The Professor's House.* Narcissism focuses Cather's vision of life. She valued above all the inviolability of the self. Romantically, she saw in the child the original and real self; and in her novels she created adult characters who sought a seemingly impossible reunion with this authentic being—who were willing to die if only they could reach somehow back to childhood. Regression becomes thus an equivocal moral victory in which the self defies change and establishes its immutability. But regression is also a sign of defeat. *My Ántonia,* superficially so simple and clear a novel, resonates to themes of ultimate importance—the theme of identity, of its relationship to time, and of its contest with death. All these are subsumed in the more immediate issue of physical love. Reinterpreted along these lines, *My Ántonia* emerges as a brilliantly tortuous novel, its statements working contrapuntally against its meanings, its apparently random vignettes falling together to form a pattern of sexual aversion into which each detail fits—even the reaping-hook of Jim's dream:

One dream I dreamed a great many times, and it was always the same. I was in a harvest-field full of shocks, and I was lying against one of them. Lena Lingard came across the stubble barefoot, in a short skirt, with a curved reaping-hook in her hand, and she was flushed like the dawn, with a kind of luminous rosiness all about her. She sat down beside me, turned to me with a soft sigh and said, "Now they are all gone, and I can kiss you as much as I like." (147)

In Jim's dream of Lena, desire and fear clearly contend with one another. With the dreamer's infallibility, Jim contains his ambivalence in a surreal image of Aurora and the Grim Reaper as one. This collaged figure of Lena advances against an ordinary but ominous landscape. Background and forefigure first contrast and then coalesce in meaning. Lena's voluptuous aspects—her luminous glow of sexual arousal, her flesh bared by a short skirt, her soft sighs and kisses—are displayed against shocks and stubble, a barren field where the reaping-hook has done its work. This landscape of harvest and desolation is not unfamiliar; nor is the apparitional woman who moves across it, sighing and making soft moan; nor the supine young man whom she kisses and transports. It is the archetypal landscape of ballad, myth, and drama, setting for *la belle dame sans merci* who enchants and satisfies, but then lulls and destroys. She comes, as Lena does, when the male is alone and unguarded. "Now they are all gone," Lena whispers, meaning Ántonia, his threshold guardian. Keeping parental watch, Ántonia limits Jim's boundaries ("You know you ain't right to kiss me like that") and attempts to bar him from the dark unexplored country beyond boyhood with threats ("If I see you hanging around with Lena much, I'll go tell your grandmother"). Jim has the insight to reply, "You'll always treat me like a kid"; but his dream of past childhood games with Ántonia suggests that the prospect of perpetual play attracts him, offering release from anxiety. Already in search of safety, he looks to childhood, for adolescence confronts him with the possibility of danger in women. Characteristically, his statement that he will prove himself unafraid belies the drift of his unconscious feelings. His dream of Lena and the reaping-hook depicts his ambivalence toward the cycle of growth, maturation, and death. The wheat ripens to be cut; maturity invites death.

Though Jim has declared his dream "always the same," it changes significantly. When it recurs in Lincoln, where he goes as a university student, it has been censored and condensed, and transmuted from reverie to remembrance:

As I sat down to my book at last, my old dream about Lena coming across the harvest-field in her short skirt seemed to me like the memory of an actual experience. It floated before me on the page like a picture, and underneath it stood the mournful line: *"Optima dies . . . prima fugit."* (175)

Now his memory can deal with fantasy as with experience: convert it to an image, frame it, and restore it to him retouched and redeemed. Revised, the dream loses its frightening details. Memory retains the harvest-field but represses the shocks and stubble; keeps Lena in her short skirt, but replaces the sexual ambience of the vision. Originally inspired by the insinuative "hired girls," the dream recurs under the tranquilizing spell of Gaston Cleric, Jim's poetry teacher. As his name implies, Cleric's function is to guide Jim to renunciation of Lena, to offer instead the example of desire sublimated to art. Voluptuous excitement yields to a pensive mood, and poetry rather than passion engages Jim: "It came over me, as it had never done before, the relation between girls like those [Lena and "the hired girls"] and the poetry of Virgil. If there were no girls like them in the world, there would be no poetry" (175). In his study, among his books, Lena's image floats before him on a page of the *Georgics,* transferred from a landscape of death to Virgil's bucolic country-side; and it arouses not sensual desire, but a safer and more characteristic mood: nostalgia—"melancholy reflection" upon the past. The reaping-hook is forgotten. Lena changes from the rosy goddess of dawn to an apparition of evening, of the dimly lit study and the darkened theater, where she glows with "lamp-light" rather than sexual luminosity.

This preliminary sublimation makes it possible for Jim to have an affair with Lena. It is brief and peculiar, somehow appropriating from the theaters they frequent an unreal quality, the aspect of play. In contrast to the tragic stage lovers who feel exquisitely, intone passionately, and love enduringly, they seem mere unengaged children, thrilled by make-believe people more than each other. "It all wrung my heart"; "there wasn't a nerve left in my body that hadn't been twisted"—Jim says, his histrionic (and rather "feminine") outbursts pertain not to Lena but to Marguerite Gauthier as impersonated by "an infirm old actress." Camille's "dazzling loveliness," her gaiety and glitter—though illusory—impassion him far more than the real woman's sensuality. With Lena, he creates a mock drama, casting himself in the stock role of callow lover pitted against Lena's older suitors. In this innocuous triangle, he "drifts" and "plays"—and play, like struggle, emerges as his memoirs' motif. Far from being random, his play is directed toward the avoidance of future responsibilities. He tests the role of lover in the security of a make-believe world where his mistress is gentle and undemanding, his adversaries ineffectual, and his guardian spirit Cleric, supportive. Cleric wants him to stop "playing with his handsome Norwegian," and so he does, leaving Lena forever and without regret. Though the separation of the stage lovers, Armand and Camille, wracks them—"Lena wept unceasingly"— their own parting is vapid. Jim leaves to follow Cleric to Boston, there to study and pursue a career. His period of enchantment has not proved one of permanent thrall and does not leave him, like Keats's knight, haggard and woebegone.

Nevertheless, the interim in Lincoln has serious consequences, for Jim's trial run into manhood remains abortive. He has not been able to bypass his circular "road to Destiny," that "predetermined" route which carries him back finally to Ántonia and childhood. With Lena, Jim seems divertible, at a crossroads. His alternatives are defined in two symbolic titles symbolically apposed: "Lena Lingard" and "Cuzak's Boys." Lena, the archetypal Woman, beckons him to full sexuality. Ántonia, the eternal Mother, lures him back through her children, Cuzak's boys, to perennial childhood.

If Jim cannot avoid his destiny, neither can he escape the "tyrannical" social code of his small town, Black Hawk, which permits its young men to play with "hired girls" but not to marry them. The pusillanimous "clerks and bookkeepers" of Black Hawk dance with the country girls, follow them forlornly, kiss them behind bushes—and run. "Respect for respectability" shunts them into loveless marriages with women of money or "refinement" who are sexless and safe. "Physically a race apart," the country girls are charged with sensuality, some of them considered as "dangerous as high explosives." Through an empty conformist marriage, Jim avoids danger. He takes a woman who is independent and masculine, like Ántonia, who cannot threaten him as Lena does by her sheer femininity. Though Lena may be "the most beautiful, the most *innocently* sensuous of all the women in Willa Cather's works,"[9] Jim is locked into his fantasy of the reaping-hook.

Jim's glorification of Lena as the timeless muse of poetry and the unattainable heroine of romance requires a closer look. For while he seems to exalt her, typically he works at cross-purposes to demean her—in his own involuted way. He sets her etherealized image afloat on pages of poetry that deal with the breeding of cattle (his memoirs quote only the last line here):

So, while the herd rejoices in its youth
Release the males and breed the cattle early,
Supply one generation from another.
For mortal kind, the best day passes first.

(*Georgics*, Book III)

As usual, Jim remembers selectively—only the last phrase, the novel's epigraph—while he deletes what must have seemed devastating counsel: "Release the males." Moreover, the *Georgics* has only factitious relevance to Lena (though I might point out that it undoubtedly inspired Cather by suggesting the use of regional material and the seasonal patterning of Book I of *My Ántonia*). If anything, the allusion is downright inappropriate, for Virgil's poem extols pastoral life, but Lena, tired of drudgery, wants to get away from the farm. Interested in fashion and sensuous pleasure, settling finally in San Francisco, she is not really the muse for Virgil.

Jim's allusion does have a subtle strategic value: by relegating Lena to the ideal but unreachable world of art, it assures their separation. Mismatched lovers because of social class, they remain irreconcilable as dream and reality. A real person, Jim must stop drifting and study; he can leave the woman while possessing Lena the dream in remembered reverie. Though motivated by fear and expediency (as much as Sylvester Lovett, Lena's fearful suitor in Black Hawk), he romanticizes his actions, eluding the possibility of painful self-confrontation. He veils his escape by identifying secretly with the hero Armand Duval, also a mismatched lover, blameless, whose fervid affair was doomed from the first. But as a lover, Jim belongs as much to comedy as to melodrama. His affair fits perfectly within the conventions of the comedy of manners: the sitting room, Lena's "stiff little parlour"; the serving of tea; the idle talk of clothes and fashion; the nuisance pet dog Prince; the minor crises when the fatuous elder lovers intrude—the triviality. Engaged with Lena in this playacting, Jim has much at stake—nothing less than his sexuality. Through the more serious drama of a first affair, he creates his existential self: an adult male who fears a sexual woman. Through his trivial small-town comedy of manners, he keeps from introspection. He is drifting but busy, too much preoccupied with dinner parties and theater dates to catch the meaning of his drift. His mock romance recalls the words he had used years earlier to describe a childhood "mock adventure": "the game was fixed." The odds are against his growing up, and the two mock episodes fall together as pseudo-initiations which fail to make him a man.

Jim's mock adventure occurs years back as he and Ántonia explore a series of interconnected burrows in prairie-dog-town. Crouched with his back to Ántonia, he hears her unintelligible screams in a foreign tongue. He whirls to discover a huge rattler coiling and erecting to spring. "Of disgusting vitality," the snake induces fear and nausea: "His abominable muscularity, his loathsome, fluid motion, somehow made me sick" (32). Jim strikes violently and with revulsion, recognizing even then an irrational hatred stronger than the impulse for protection. The episode—typically ignored or misunderstood by critics—combines elements of myth and dream. As a dragon-slaying, it conforms to the monomyth of initiation. It has a characteristic "call to adventure" (Ántonia's impulsive suggestion); a magic weapon (Peter's spade); a descent into a land of unearthly creatures (prairie-dog-town); the perilous battle (killing the snake); the protective tutelary spirit (Ántonia); and the passage through the rites to manhood ("You now a big mans"). As a test of courage, Jim's ordeal seems authentic, and critical opinion declares it so: "Jim Burden discovers his own hidden courage and becomes a man in the snake-killing incident."[10] But even Jim realizes that his initiation, like his romance later, is specious, and his accolade unearned: "it was a mock adventure; the game . . . fixed . . . by chance, as . . . for many a dragon-slayer."

As Jim accepts Ántonia's praise, his tone becomes wry and ironic, communicating a unique awareness of the duplicity in which he is involved. Ántonia's effect upon Jim seems to me here invidious because her admiration of his manhood helps undermine it. Pronouncing him a man, she keeps him a boy. False to her role as tutelary spirit, she betrays him from first to last. She leads him into danger, fails to warn him properly, and finally, by validating the contest, closes off the road to authentic initiation and maturity.

Jim's exploration "below the surface" of prairie-dog-town strikes me as a significant mimetic act, a burrowing into his unconscious. Who is he "below the surface"? In which direction do his buried impulses lead? He acts out his quest for self-knowledge symbolically: if he could dig deep enough he would find a way through this labyrinth and learn the course of its hidden channels—whether "they ran straight down, or were horizontal, . . . whether they had underground connections." Projecting upon the physical scene his adolescent concern with self, he speaks an analytic and rational language—but the experience turns into nightmare. Archetypal symbol of "the ancient, eldest Evil," the snake forces him to confront deeply repressed images, to acknowledge for the only time the effect of "horrible unconscious memories."

The sexual connotations of the snake incident are implicit. Later in Black Hawk they become overt through another misadventure—Wick Cutter's attempted rape of Jim, whom he mistakes for Ántonia. This time the sexual attack is literal. Wick Cutter, an old lecher, returns in the middle of the night to assault Ántonia, but meanwhile, persuaded by Ántonia's suspicions, Jim has taken her place in bed. He becomes an innocent victim of Cutter's lust and fury at deception. Threatened by unleashed male sex—the ultimate threat—he fights with primordial violence, though again sickened with disgust. Vile as the Cutter incident is—and it is also highly farcical—Jim's nausea seems an overreaction, intensified by his shrill rhetoric and unmodulated tone. Unlike the snake episode, this encounter offers no rewards. It simply reduces him to "a battered object," his body pommeled, his face swollen. His only recognition will be the laughter of the lubricious "old men at the drugstore." Again Ántonia has lured him into danger and exposed him to assault. Again he is furious: "I felt that I never wanted to see her again. I hated her almost as much as I hated Cutter. She had let me in for all this disgustingness" (162). Through Wick Cutter, the sexual urge seems depraved, and more damning, ludicrous. No male in the novel rescues sex from indignity or gives it even the interest of sheer malevolence (as, for example, Ivy Peters does in *A Lost Lady*).

Also unexempt from the dangers of sex, Ántonia is seduced, exploited, and left with an illegitimate child. When finally she marries, she takes not a lover but a friend. To his relief, Jim finds husband and wife "on terms of easy friendliness, touched with humour" (231). Marriage as an extension of friendship is

Cather's recurrent formula, defined clearly, if idiosyncratically, by Alexandra in *O Pioneers!*: "I think when friends marry, they are safe." Turning words to action, Alexandra marries her childhood friend, as does Cécile in *Shadows on the Rock*—an older man whose passion has been expended on another woman. At best, marriage has dubious value in Cather's fiction. It succeeds when it seems least like marriage, when it remains sexless, or when sex is only instrumental to procreation. Jim accepts Ántonia's marriage for its "special mission" to bring forth children.

Why doesn't he take on this mission? He celebrates the myth of creation but fails to participate. The question has been raised bluntly by critics (though left unanswered): "Why had not Jim and Ántonia loved and married?"[11] When Ántonia, abandoned by Donovan, needs Jim most, he passionately avers, "You really are a part of me . . . I'd have like to have you for a sweetheart, or a wife, or my mother or my sister—anything that a woman can be to a man" (208). Thereupon he leaves—not to return for twenty years. His failure to seize the palpable moment seems to one critic responsible for the emotional vacuum of Jim's life: "At the very center of his relation with Ántonia there is an emptiness where the strongest emotion might have been expected to gather."[12] But love for a woman is not Jim's "strongest emotion" and cannot mitigate fear, nostalgia, or even simple snobbery. Nothing in Jim's past prepares him for love or marriage, and he remains in effect a pseudo-bachelor (just as he is a pseudo-lover), free to design a future with Ántonia's family that excludes his wife. In his childhood, his models for manhood are simple regressive characters, all bachelors, or patently unhappy married men struggling, like Mr. Shimerda, Chris Lingard, and Ole the Swede, for and against their families. Later in Black Hawk, the family men seem merely vapid, and prophetically suburban, pushing baby carriages, sprinkling lawns, paying bills, and driving about on Sundays (105). Mr. Harling, Ántonia's employer in Black Hawk, seems different; yet he only further confuses Jim's already confused sense of sexual roles, for he indulges his son while he treats his daughter as a man, his business partner. With Ántonia, his "hired girl," Mr. Harling is repressive, a kind of superego, objecting to her adolescent contacts with men—the dances at Vannis's tent, the evening walks, the kisses and scuffles on the back porch. "I want to have my fling, like the other girls," Ántonia argues, but Harling insists she quit the dances or his house. Ántonia leaves, goes to the notorious Cutter, and then to the seductive arms of Larry Donovan—with consequences that are highly instructive to Jim, that can only reinforce his inchoate fears. Either repression of sex or disaster: Jim sees these alternatives polarized in Black Hawk, and between them he cannot resolve his ambivalence. Though he would like Ántonia to become a woman, he wants her also to remain asexual.

By switching her sexual roles, Ántonia only adds to his confusion. As "hired girl" in Black Hawk and later as Cuzak's wife, she cooks, bakes, sews, and rears children. Intermittently, she shows off her strength and endurance in the fields, competing with men. Even her name changes gender—no adventitious matter, I believe; it has its masculine variant, Tony, as Willa Cather had hers, Willie. Cather's prototype for Ántonia, Annie Pavelka, was a simple Bohemian girl; though their experiences are similar, Ántonia Shimerda is Cather's creation—an ultimately strange bisexual. She shares Cather's pride in masculinity and projects both her and Jim's ambivalent sexual attitudes. Cather recalled that "much of what I knew about Annie came from the talks I had with young men. She had a fascination for them."[13] In the novel, however, Lena facinates men while Ántonia toils alongside them. "I can work like mans now," she announces when she is only fifteen. In the fields, says Jim, "she kept her sleeves rolled up all day, and her arms and throat were burned as brown as a sailor's. Her neck came up strongly out of her shoulders, like the bole of a tree out of the turf. One sees that draught-horse neck among the peasant women in all old countries" (80). Sailor, tree, draught horse, peasant—hardly seductive comparisons, hardly conducive to fascination. Ántonia's illegitimate pregnancy brutalizes her even more than heavy farmwork. Her punishment for sexual involvement—and for the breezy pleasures of courtship—is thoroughgoing masculinization. Wearing "a man's long overcoat and boots, and a man's felt hat," she does "the work of a man on the farm," plows, herds cattle. Years later, as Cuzak's wife, her "inner glow" must compensate for the loss of her youthful beauty, the loss, even, of her teeth. Jim describes her finally as "a stalwart, brown woman, flat-chested, her curly brown hair a little grizzled"—his every word denuding her of sensual appeal.

This is not to deny that at one time Jim found Ántonia physically desirable. He hints that in Black Hawk he had kissed her in a more than friendly way—and had been rebuffed. But he is hardly heartbroken at their impasse, for his real and enduring love for her is based not on desire but on nostalgia. Childhood memories bind him more profoundly than passion, especially memories of Mr. Shimerda. In their picnic reunion before Jim departs for Lincoln, Ántonia recounts her father's story of transgression, exile, and death. Her miniature tale devolves upon the essential theme of destructive sex. As a young man, her father succumbs to desire for the family's servant girl, makes her pregnant, marries her against his parents' wishes, and becomes thereby an outcast. His death on the distant prairie traces back to an initial sexual act which triggers inexorable consequences. It strips him of all he values: his happy irresponsible bachelor life with the trombone player he "loves"; his family home in beautiful Bohemia; his vocation as violinist when he takes to homesteading in Nebraska; and his joy in life itself. For a while, a few desultory pleasures could rouse him from apathy and despair. But in the end, he finds the pattern of his adult life, as many Cather characters do, unbearable, and he longs for escape. Though Ántonia implies that her poppa's mistake was to marry, especially outside his social class (as Jim is too prudent to do), the marriage comes about through his initial sexual involvement. Once Mr. Shimerda acts upon sexual impulse, he is committed to a woman who alienates him from himself; and it is loss of self, rather than the surmountable hardships of pioneer life, that induces his despair. Suicide is his final capitulation to destructive forces he could have escaped only by first abnegating sex.

Though this interpretation may sound extreme—that the real danger to man is woman, that his protection lies in avoiding or eliminating her—it seems to me the essence of the most macabre and otherwise unaccountable episode in *My Ántonia*. I refer to that grisly acting out of male aversion, the flashback of Russian Pavel feeding the bride to the wolves. I cannot imagine a more graphic representation of underlying sentiments than we find here. Like most of the episodes in Jim's memoirs, this begins innocently, with the young bride drawing Peter, Pavel, and other guests to a nearby village for her wedding. But the happy evening culminates in horror; for the wolves are bad that year, starving, and when the guests head for home they find themselves rapidly pursued through a landscape of terror. Events take on the surreality of nightmare as black droves run like streaks of shadows after the panicking horses, as sledges overturn in the snow, and mauled and dying wedding guests shriek. Fast as Pavel drives his team, it cannot outrun the relentless "back ground shadows," images of death. Pavel's murderous strategy to save himself and Peter is almost too inhuman to imagine: to allay the wolves and lighten his load, he wrests the bride from the struggling groom, and throws her, living bait, to the wolves. Only then does his sledge arrive in safety at his village. The tale holds the paradigm for Mr. Shimerda's fate—driven from home because of a woman, struggling for survival against a brutal winter landscape, pursued by regret and despair to death. The great narrative distance at which this episode is kept from Jim seems to me to signify its explosiveness, the need to handle with care. It is told to Jim by Ántonia, who overhears Peter telling it to Mr. Shimerda. Though the vignette emerges from this distance—and through Jim's obscuring nostalgia—its gruesome meaning focuses the apparently disjunct parts of the novel, and I find it inconceivable that critics consider it "irrelevant."[14] The art of *My Ántonia* lies in the subtle and inevitable relevance of its details, even the most trivial, like the picture Jim chooses to decorate a Christmas book for Ántonia's little sister: "I took 'Napoleon Announcing the Divorce to Josephine' for my frontispiece" (55). In one way or another, the woman must go.

To say that Jim Burden expresses castration fears would provide a facile conclusion; and indeed his memoirs multiply images of sharp instruments and painful cutting. The curved reaping hook in Lena Lingard's hand centralizes an overall pattern that includes Peter's clasp knife with which he cuts all his melons; Crazy Mary's corn knife (she "made us feel how sharp her blade was, showing us very graphically just what she meant to do to Lena"); the suicidal tramp "cut to pieces" in the threshing machine; and wicked Wick *Cut*ter's sexual assault. When Lena, the essence of sex, appears suddenly in Black Hawk, she seems to precipitate a series of violent recollections. First Jim remembers Crazy Mary's pursuit of Lena with her sharpened corn knife. Then Ántonia recalls the story of the crazy tramp in details which seem to me unconsciously reverberating Jim's dream. Like Jim, Ántonia is relaxed and leaning against a strawstack; similarly, she sees a figure approach "across the stubble"— significantly, his first words portend death. Offering to "cut bands," within minutes he throws himself into the threshing machine and is "cut to pieces." In his pockets the threshers find only "an old penknife" and the "wish-bone of a chicken." Jim follows this anecdote with a vignette of Blind d'Arnault, a black musician who, as we shall see, represents emasculation; Jim tells how children used to tease the little blind boy and try "to get his chicken-bone away." Such details, I think, should not be considered fortuitous or irrelevant; and critics who have persisted in overlooking them should note that they are stubbornly there, and in patterned sequence.

I do not wish to make a case history of Jim Burden or a psychological document of *My Ántonia*, but to uncover an elusive underlying theme—one that informs the fragmentary parts of the novel and illuminates the obsession controlling Cather's art. For like most novelists, Cather writes out of an obsessive concern to which her art gives various and varied expression. In *My Ántonia*, her consummate work, that obsession has its most private as well as its most widely shared meanings. At the same time that the novel is highly autobiographical, it is representatively American in its material, mood, and unconscious uses of the past. In it, as in other novels, we can discover that Cather's obsession had to do with the assertion of self. This is the preoccupation of her protagonists, who, in their various ways, seek to assert their identity, in defiance, if necessary, of others, of convention, of nature, of life itself. Biographers imply that Cather's life represented a consistent pursuit of autonomy, essential, she believed, to her survival as an artist. Undoubtedly, she was right; had she given herself to marriage and children, assuming she could, she might have sacrificed her chance to write. Clearly, she identified writing with masculinity, though which of the two constituted her fundamental drive is a matter of psychological dynamics we can never really decide. Like Ántonia, she displayed strong masculine traits, though she loved also feminine frilleries and the art of cuisine. All accounts of her refer to her "masculine personality"—her mannish dress, her deep voice, her energetic stride; and even as a child she affected boyish clothes and cropped hair. Too numerous to document, such references are a running motif throughout the accounts of Mildred Bennett, Elizabeth Sergeant, and E. K. Brown. Their signifiance is complex and perhaps inescapable, but whatever else they mean, they surely demonstrate Cather's self-assertion: she would create her own role in life, and if being a woman meant sacrificing her art, then she would lead a private and inviolate life in defiance of convention.

Her image of inviolability was the *child.* She sought quaintly, perhaps foolishly, to refract this image through her person when she wore a schoolgirl costume. The Steichen photograph of her in middy blouse is a familiar frontispiece to volumes of her work; and she has been described as characteristically "at the typewriter, dressed in a childlike costume, a middy blouse with navy bands and tie and a duck skirt."[15] In life, she tried to hold on to childhood through dress; in art, through a recurrent cycle of childhood, maturity, and childhood again—the return effected usually through memory. Sometimes the regressive pattern signalized a longing for death, as in *The Professor's House* and *Death Comes for the Archbishop;* always it revealed a quest for reunion with an original authentic self. In *My Ántonia,* the prologue introduces Ántonia and the motif of childhood simultaneously, for her name is linked with *"the country, the conditions, the whole adventure of . . . childhood."* The memoirs proper open with the children's journey into pristine country where men are childlike or project into life characters of the child's imagination (like Jake who "might have stepped out of the pages of 'Jesse James' "). The years of maturity comprise merely an interim period—and in fact are hardly dealt with. For Jim, as for Cather, the real meaning of time is cyclical, its purpose to effect a return to the beginning. Once Jim finds again "the first road" he traveled as a wondering child, his story ends. Hardly discernible, this road returns him to Ántonia, and through her, to his real goal, the enduring though elusive image of his original self which Cather represents by his childhood shadow. Walking to Ántonia's house with her boys—feeling himself almost a boy again—Jim merges with his shadow, the visible elongation of self. At last, his narcissistic dream comes to fulfillment: "It seemed, after all, so natural to be walking along a barbed-wire fence beside the sunset, toward a red pond, and to see my shadow moving along at my right, over the close-cropped grass" (224). Just as the magnified shadow of plow against sky—a blazing key image—projects his romantic notion of the West, so "two long shadows [that] flitted before or followed after" symbolize his ideal of perennial children running through, imaged against, and made one with the prairie grass.

Jim's return "home" has him planning a future with Cuzak's boys that will recapitulate the past; once more he will sleep in haylofts, hunt "up the Niobrara," and travel the "Bad Lands." Play reenters as his serious concern, not the sexual play of imminent manhood, but regressive child's play. In a remarkable statement, Jim says, "There were enough Cuzaks to play with for a long while yet. Even after the boys grew up, there would always be Cuzak himself!" (239). A current article on *My Ántonia* misreads this conclusion: "[though] Jim feels like a boy again . . . he does not *wish* that he were a boy again. . . . He has no more need to cling to the past, for the past has been transfigured like the autumn prairie of old."[16] Such reasoning falls in naively with Jim's self-deception, that the transformation of the land to country somehow validates his personal life. Jim's need to reenter childhood never relents and becomes even more urgent as he feels adult life vacuous. The years have not enriched him, except with a wealth of memories—"images in the mind that did not fade—that grew stronger with time." Most precious in his treasury of remembered images is that of a boy of ten crossing the prairie under "the complete dome of heaven" and finding sublimity in the union of self with earth and sky. An unforgettable consummation, never matched by physical union, he seeks to recreate it through memory. Jim's ineffable desire for a child more alive to him than his immediate being vibrates to a pathetic sense of loss. I believe that we may find this irretrievable boy in a photograph of young *Willie Cather,* another child who took life from imagination and desire.[17]

In a later novel, *The Professor's House,*[18] Cather rationalizes her cathexis on childhood through the protagonist's musings. Toward the end of his life, Professor Godfrey St. Peter discovers he has two identities: that of his "original" self, the child; and of his "secondary" self, the man in love. To fulfill himself, "the lover" creates a meretricious "design" of marriage, children, and career, now, after thirty years, suddenly meaningless. The professor's cyclic return to his real and original self begins with solitary retrospection. All he wants is to "be alone"—to repossess himself. For, having yielded through love to another, he has lost "the person he was in the beginning." Now before he dies, he longs for his original image as a child, an image that returns to him in moments of "vivid consciousness" or of remembrance. Looking back, the professor sees the only escape from a false secondary life to be through premature death: death of the sexual man before he realizes his sexuality and becomes involved in the relationships it demands. This is the happy fate of his student Tom Outland, who dies young, remaining inviolate, pure, and most important, self-possessed: "He seemed to know . . . he was solitary and must always be so; he had never married, never been a father. He was earth, and would return to earth" (263).

This romantic mystique of childhood illuminates the fear of sex in Cather's world. Sex unites one with another. Its ultimate threat is loss of self. In Cather's construct, naively and of course falsely, children are asexual, their love inverted, their identity thus intact. Only Ántonia manages to grow older and retain her original integrity. Like Tom Outland, her affinity is for the earth. She "belongs" to the farm, is one with the trees, the flowers, the rye and wheat she plants. Though she marries, Cuzak is only "the instrument of Ántonia's special mission." Through him she finds a self-fulfillment that excludes him. Through her, Jim hopes to be restored to himself.

The supreme value Jim and other Cather characters attribute to "old friendships" reflects a concern with self. Old friends know the child immanent in the man. Only they can have communion without causing self-estrangement, can marry "safely." They share "the precious, the incommunicable past"—as Jim says in his famous final words. But to keep the past so precious, they must romanticize it; and to validate childhood, they must let memory filter its experiences through the screen of nostalgia. Critics have wondered whether Jim Burden is the most suitable narrator for *My Ántonia*. I submit that Cather's choice is utterly strategic. For Jim, better than any other character, can control his memories, since only he knows of but does not experience the suffering and violence inherent in his story. And ultimately, he is not dealing with a story as such, but with residual "images in the mind." *My Ántonia* is a magnificent and warped testimony to the mind's image-making power, an implicit commentary on how that creative power serves the mind's need to ignore and deny whatever is reprehensible in whatever one loves. Cather's friend and biographer said of her, "There was so much she did not want to see and saw not."[20] We must say the same of Jim Burden, who held painful and violent aspects of early American life at safe distance, where finally he could not see them.

Jim's vignette of Blind d'Arnault, the black piano player who entertains at Black Hawk, is paradigmatic of his way of viewing the past. Its factual scaffolding (whether Cather's prototype was Blind Boone, Blind Tom, or a "composite of Negro musicians") seems to me less important than its tone. I find the vignette a work of unconscious irony as Jim paints d'Arnault's portrait but meanwhile delineates himself. The motif of blindness compounds the irony. D'Arnault's is physical, as though it were merely futile for him to see a world he cannot enter. Jim's is moral: an unawareness of his stereotyped, condescending, and ultimately invidious vision. Here, in his description of the black man, son of a slave, Jim's emblematic significance emerges as shamefully he speaks for himself, for Cather, and for most of us:

[His voice] was the soft, amiable Negro voice, like those I remembered from early childhood, with the note of docile subservience in it. He had the Negro head, too; almost no head at all, nothing behind the ears but the folds of neck under close-cropped wool. He would have been repulsive if his face had not been so kindly and happy. It was the happiest face I had seen since I left Virginia. (122)

Soft, amiable, docile, subservient, kindly, happy—Jim's image, as usual, projects his wish fulfillment; his diction suggests also an unconscious assuagement of anxiety. His phrase of astounding insult and innocence—"almost no head at all"—assures him that the black man should not frighten, being an incomplete creature, possessed, as we would like to believe, of instinct and rhythm, but deprived of intellect. Jim's final hyperbole registers his fear of this alien black face saved from repulsiveness only by a toothy servile smile. To attenuate his portrait of d'Arnault, Jim introduces innuendoes of sexual incompetence. He recognizes d'Arnault's sensuality but impugns it by his image of sublimation: "all the agreeable sensations possible to creatures of flesh and blood were heaped up on those black-and-white keys, and he [was] gloating over them and trickling them through his yellow fingers" (p. 126). Jim's genteel opening phrase connotes male sexuality, which he must sublimate, displace from the man to the music, reduce to a "trickle." D'Arnault "looks like some glistening African god of pleasure, full of strong, savage blood"; but superimposed is our familiar Uncle Tom, "all grinning," "bowing to everyone, docile and happy."

Similarly, consider Jim's entrancing image of the four Danish girls who stand all day in the laundry ironing the townspeople's clothes. How charming they are: flushed and happy; how fatherly the laundryman offering water—no swollen ankles; no boredom or rancor; no exploitation: a cameo image from "the beautiful past." Peter and Pavel, dreadful to any ordinary mind for their murderous deed, ostracized by everyone, now disease-ridden and mindless, are to Jim picturesque outcasts: Pavel spitting blood; Peter spitting seeds as he desperately eats all his melons after kissing his cow goodbye, the only creature for him to love. And Mr. Shimerda's suicide. Jim reconciles himself to the horror of the mutilated body frozen in its own blood by imagining the spirit released and homeward bound to its beloved Bohemia. Only the evocative beauty of Cather's language—and the inevitable validation as childhood memory—can romanticize this sordid death and the squalor in which it takes place. Violence is as much the essence of prairie life as the growth of the wheat and blossoming of the corn. Violence appears suddenly and inexplicably, like the suicidal tramp. But Jim gives violence a cameo quality. He has the insistent need—and the strategy—to turn away from the very material he presents. He can forget the reaping-hook and reshape his dream. And as the novel reveals him doing this, it reveals our common usage of the past as a romance and refuge from the present. *My Ántonia* engraves a view of the past which is at best partial, at worst blind. But our present is continuous with the whole past, as it was, despite Jim Burden's attempt to deny this, and despite Cather's "sad little refrain": "Our present is ruined—but we had a beautiful past."[20] Beautiful to one who recreated it so; who desperately needed it so; who would deny the violence and the destructive attitudes toward race and sex immortalized in this very denial. We, however, have as desperate a need for clarity of vision as Jim had for nostalgia; and we must begin to look at *My Ántonia,* long considered a representatively American novel, not only for its beauty of art and for its affirmation of history, but also, and instructively, for its negations and evasions. Much as we would like to ignore them, for they bring painful confrontations, we must see what they would show us about ourselves—how we betray our past when we forget its most disquieting realities; how we begin to redeem it when we remember.

Movement and Melody:

The Disembodiment of Lucy Gayheart

Red Cloud, Nebraska

ON WILLA CATHER: II

I should like to present this essay with little comment. One of the last pieces in this volume to have been written, it is too recent for an afterword. I shall say, however, that it attests to the enduring fascination Willa Cather has for me, an attraction based, I believe, upon radical differences in our backgrounds, social ideas, and daily ways of life. Of course, I take for granted the great and fundamental difference that Cather is, above all else, a creative artist. As remote as her creativity is from my experience, I think I understand the passion and intensity, the desire *she was always describing, that made her an artist. Perhaps "understand" is inaccurate. Others have helped me understand, but Cather has made me feel the force of desire so strong that in* Lucy Gayheart *it refuses to be defeated by death. To have been permitted by the power of her art to feel so intensely, if only in a vicarious and ultimately insufficient way, places me in Willa Cather's debt.*

Willa Cather wrote *Lucy Gayheart,* an apparently simple but controversial work, as she was nearing the end of a long career. Coming after her famous novels, it seemed at worst a redundant statement of familiar themes, and at best a somber epilogue that reconsidered and sought to resolve the same intractable conflicts. Questions about the worth of *Lucy Gayheart,* raised as soon as it appeared, have been suspended rather than settled, for little more can be said about the novel as merely a recapitulation of Cather's earlier fiction. I would urge its importance on other grounds: that as a late work it brings to light issues usually obscured, and does so because Cather revealed more openly than before her anxieties about the end(s) of writing. These ends were various and at odds: the intention and goals of an essentially Romantic writer;[1] limits to the power of language that made these goals seem unrealistic; and the consuming demands of art which might bring the artist's personal life to an end. Such thoughts of thwarted desires must lead finally to premonitions of death, surely on Cather's mind as she began her novel with Lucy already buried and concluded it with a funeral, having in the interim laid to rest her heroine's sister, father, lover, and villainous adversary. This said, I must add that *Lucy Gayheart* celebrates the joyousness of life and, despite its morbidity, seems a slyly comic book—as though Cather were playing a joke at the end of her serious career.

Early in the novel, Lucy Gayheart snuggles dreamily against handsome Harry Gordon, who is giving her a ride home in his sleigh.[2] Suddenly she feels her heart throb in her throat, a symptomatic agitation familiar to readers of popular romance as the feeling of falling in love. The object of Lucy's desire is not Harry, however, but the evening's first star. From across the sky, this bright signaling star has "overpowered" Lucy with its light—a "flash" which brings the mutual "recognition" and "understanding" missing in her relationship with Harry. Throughout the novel, Lucy yearns to renew her communion with the gleaming stars of the sky and with a glamorous singing "star" first seen on the concert stage. Both distant and unreachable, they represent to Lucy "another kind of life and feeling" to which she aspires. Lucy's dream of living in an "invisible, inviolable world" recaptures Cather's youthful ideal of a "kingdom of art," a realm she had long inhabited.[3] Given her "long perspective" on the yearnings of youth, Cather now wondered what she might make in the novel of a young woman's Romantic aspiration, and how she might distinguish it from the commonplace desire for a man's love expressed by the pining heroines of true romance.

With these questions, Cather approached rather precipitately a murky boundary line between the popular novel and art. There, like her own Lucy, she found herself skating on thin ice—aware, as Lucy was not, that she might fall into difficulties from which there was no extrication. To her credit, I would say, Cather took this risk. She decided to use as a pre-text for *Lucy Gayheart* the conventional love story whose traces she had tried to expunge from her earlier fiction, particularly *My Ántonia* where, she said, it might have belonged.[4] Now she would choose this common genre in order to elevate its base material to the heights of literature. Like an alchemist, she hoped to effect a magical transmutation by turning the popular romance into an allegory of Romantic desire. With her famous novels behind her, Cather may have felt free, or perhaps compelled, to try her hand at a love story. Clearly she was departing from her usual practice of choosing classic literary forms for her prototypes: the epic, ecologue, pastoral elegy, saint's legend. But in giving her art to a vulgar form, Cather was so subversive, killing off characters after cancelling whatever they had said or done, that she seemed engaged in a process of erasure.[5] Paradoxically, the end or purpose of this process was, I believe, to prove the language of literature *in*eradicable. For if the words Cather seemed to be wiping off the page had an intrinsic power to stand, then *Lucy Gayheart* should withstand the impact of clichés borrowed from a debased literary genre.

Perhaps Cather left a clue to this involuted test of her art when she described the power of an aging soprano to inspire Lucy by striving "after excellence" even though her material was trite, her audience "humdrum," and her voice "worn": "There was not much physical sweetness left in it. But there was another kind of sweetness: a sympathy, a tolerant understanding. She gave the old songs, even the most hackneyed, their full value. . . . *She gave freshness to the foolish old words* . . . was tender with their sentimentality" (181, emphasis added). I take this passage as an oblique self-portrait, consistent with the self-referentiality of *Lucy Gayheart*. Cather has often been described as worn and tired when she was writing *Lucy Gayheart,* and the novel's sentimentality has often been deplored; but the artist's attempt to give "freshness" to old and "foolish" feelings and to the "hackneyed" words in which they are expressed has been almost entirely overlooked, as has the "gift of sympathy" which Cather had already proclaimed a writer's finest attribute.[6] By grappling with a genre as stripped of dignity as the common love story and sympathizing (if reservedly) with its sentiments, Cather was putting her career at stake; but in doing so she was demonstrating a bold and unexpected way of confronting her welling doubts about the permanence of (her) writing. *Lucy Gayheart* reveals and seeks to allay Cather's anxieties about her art and about the kingdom of art she suspected she might soon be leaving.

Cather's "plot" for her novel required her to leave its generic origins undisguised. Indeed, she drew attention to them by a profusion of romantic paraphernalia: starlit evenings, dinners for two, breathless moments together, misunderstandings ("It was quite possible that he had not meant at all what she thought!"), reconciliations, ecstasy, despair, jealousy, enchantment, flowers, and music. Moreover, the novel presents several hackneyed versions of Lucy's love affair, involves her in a variety of eternal triangles, and places her in two obviously formulaic plots. In one, Lucy finds and loses a lover; and in the other, the epilogue's subplot, she is lost and miraculously recovered. The characters' versions of these plots include Harry's self-serving story of a young girl's infatuation, Fairy Blair's "story" of her suicide, Pauline's of her jilting, and the townspeople's whispers of her desertion by the man who had "got her in trouble."[7] None of these versions describes the evening star or "Life itself" as the most seductive of Lucy's lovers. The "real" lovers of the novel's eternal triangle—Lucy, Sebastian, and Harry—chase each other compulsively, but their sexual pursuits assume a strange hybrid form as the imperfectly erased traces of romantic eroticism are overlaid with Romantic aspiration.

Having retained the banality of her palimpsestic text, Cather then lifted its love affair above the commonplace by etherealizing her characters. She made their main action consist of breathing: of in-spiring and being inspired; and of aspiration. Her lovers unite through mutual inspiration, each in rhythm with the breathing of the other. When Sebastian first takes Lucy into his arms, his "soft, deep breathing seemed to drink her up entirely" (87); and later, lying against him, Lucy "felt herself drifting again into his breathing" (89). Cather makes Sebastian's breath sensuous and soft, deep, absorbing, and, to my mind, ghoulish. Trite as the image of a lover drinking up his beloved may be, it suggests a dissolution of the body and ultimate disappearance, a potentially dangerous fate to which the lovers are oblivious. Entranced as their "airs" mingle in effable harmony, Lucy is inspired by Sebastian's "wisdom and sadness," and he by her youth. Life has grown stale for the aging singer, but when he thinks of Lucy's "devotion" and "chivalrous loyalty," the "air" in his room is freshened. Drifting into her lover's breathing, Lucy renews her idealism: Sebastian "had unclouded faith in the old and lovely dreams of man; that he would teach her and share with her" (87). Their romance consists thus of a sharing of Romantic aspirations, their breaths, rather than their bodies, coming together. Since their love and their song, as well as their lives, depend upon breath, their fate must be precarious and their untimely death inevitable (though critics have considered it arbitrary). Cather has so contrived her plot that Sebastian's life and art ex-pire together. In the final scene of Book I, when Mockford "locked his arms about Sebastian's neck," his "strangle-hold" brought to an end the baritone's life, love, and song—except as they might be recovered by memory; but Lucy's remembering mind is destined to disappear. Book II concludes with a crucial interval in Lucy's breathing, suspended long enough to determine her death, for in between breaths Lucy moves "a long way near the river bend" where the treacherous ice is waiting (197).

The morbidity of *Lucy Gayheart*, as one character after another dies, reflects Cather's usual anxiety about the ravages of time and her doubt that memory and art, upon which she depended, could make restitution. This was a long-standing thematic doubt she now struggled with visibly and with an irresolution that energized her novel, giving it tension and the excitement of a kind of thrashing confusion. Such residual signs of struggle reveal the difficulties Cather was having with large critical problems involving the power of language, or more precisely, its inherent limitations. Writing about music, Cather released her anxiety about words, not only about their permanence, as I have indicated, but also about their affectivity. She questioned whether words alone could express, or evoke, or create—she was not sure which—the human emotions that she thought music made immediate. In *The Song of the Lark*, the novel to which *Lucy Gayheart* is invariably compared, Cather had made ineffableness seem a test of emotional intensity. Her heroine's feelings, her physical sensations and her emotions, became incommunicable when most exquisite. The voluptuous pleasure that Thea Kronberg experienced through her body's exposure to sun, sky, and stone had "almost nothing to do with words," she declared; it was "not expressible in words." Also the "passion" that welled in her song was "so deep, so beautiful . . . that there's nothing one can say about it."[8] As a great opera star, Thea could both express and evoke emotions through music, an immediately affective art, Cather believed. As a writer, Cather had to make mediating words convey the passion that she believed inspired and constituted art. But if, as her autobiographical heroine had said, this passion was incommunicable and, conversely, language inadequate or irrelevant to its expression, then the writer had the impossible task of expressing the ineffable.

This impasse represents, however, a supernal Romantic ideal to which Cather had long been committed. Her well-known statements in "The Novel Demeublé" had valorized "the overtone divined by the ear but not heard by it, the verbal mood, the emotional aura," in short, whatever had not been named—and could not be named—by words.[9] Perhaps more recklessly than she realized, Cather was making the affect of language depend upon the sensitivity of a reader who must respond to what was not on the page and yet in its absence, by absence, was there to be strongly felt. Cather had thus put herself in double jeopardy, dependent upon an unpredictable reader and upon a presence on the page which she herself called inexplicable: "It is the inexplicable presence of the thing not named . . . that gives high quality to the novel . . . as well as to poetry itself."[10] This view placed great pressure upon a style Cather wished to keep simple and suggestive, an implicatory style that would arouse emotion by means of the "musical" qualities of words, their overtones, moods, auras. Understandably, she might at times have wondered if language could achieve her delicate Romantic ends; if the unheard melodies running through *Lucy Gayheart* could be heard and if words lifted from the pages of the popular love story could resonate with significant emotion.

The novel reinforces Cather's doubts by its self-reflections. Lucy's comments about words would be fatuous if they did not serve the purposes of the text in drawing attention to its language. Until she heard Shakespeare's lyrics sung, Lucy says, she "had never known that words had any value aside from their direct meaning" (95). On the other hand, she knew that some paintings "are meant to represent objects, and others . . . to express a kind of feeling" (101). Looking at paintings and listening to music, Cather's characters point to the priority of feeling in these arts; and by their remarks, displaced from literature but defining (Cather's) literary values, they allude to the novel's own aspiration, as remote and Romantic as Lucy's desire for the star. For like its heroine, the novel longs to become a musical composition, appreciated for its verbal overtones, the elusive and reverberating quality of words that Lucy was learning to recognize as a discrete emotional element of song. At the same time, however, the novel shows the destructive potential of words. The townspeople gossip, Harry cuts Lucy with unkind and insulting remarks, and Lucy blatantly lies. When their "direct meaning" is aggressive, words change characters' lives as radically as the melancholy tones of Sebastian's song change Lucy. Showing that words will become cruel, as well as clichéd, the novel is nevertheless determined to demonstrate their power to produce heightened human emotions and aesthetic pleasure. At the same time, as its large interweaving themes indicate, it would probe for truth, nothing less than the meaning of life.

Understandably, such soaring ambitions, along with ambivalences and anxieties, made Cather an epiloguist, since she was always after words to do more. She said that the long epilogue to *Lucy Gayheart* was its most important section.[11] Resuming the story of Lucy's "life" twenty-five years after her death, this section provides the "long perspective" from which Cather wished the past to be viewed. At the same time, it adds to, amends, or erases—"blots out," as Cather puts it—the words of the text. *Lucy Gayheart* ends inconclusively, with an implicit demand for more words. A lengthy critical afterword to the novel has been the debate that began with the novel's publication, continued over the years, and is renewed here because I believe that something more and something else should be said about *Lucy Gayheart*. A brief review of the novel's critical history may place this claim in perspective.

On Sunday, August 4, 1935, the front page of the *New York Times Book Review* section carried a large handsome photograph of Willa Cather and a kind review of her new novel, *Lucy Gayheart*. The review avoided serious criticism by summarizing the novel's plot and complimenting Cather on the "disciplined art" which imbued her style with "quiet grace" and "distinction." The *London Times Literary Supplement* also claimed "distinction" for the "simply told tale," finding in its "tragic" heroine "the full measure of Miss Cather's art." Agreeing that *Lucy Gayheart* was "a work of art," *Saturday Review* tried to pinpoint Cather's "special glory" as a writer by noting her "fine intelligence," "intuitive insight," and "perfection" of style.[12]

Other reviews were not as kind, and some were peevish, disdainful, dismissive. They called the novel "maudlin"; charged it with "facile sentimentalism" and "hackneyed simplicity"; with "triteness," "banality," "cultivated superciliousness"; and with purveying "morally innocuous feminine reading" in a "pastel-shaded" book that should have been called "Lucy Broken-heart."[13]

Over the years, critics have remained divided. Those who praise the novel agree that it shows complexity, experimental daring, philosophical profundity, and a reassuring understanding of life. *Lucy Gayheart* "contains some of the author's most profound reflections on art and human relationships," says one critic; and another reiterates that it is "complex and experimental" and Cather's "most profound novel."[14] In contrast, others find it "unmitigatedly pessimistic" and vapid, with a "hollow center" formed by Cather's fear of sex.[15] Disagreements on style complement those on mood and theme. If the beginning of the novel seems "tired" and "lagging" to one critic, to another, the ending is listless.[16] This apparent lack of vitality has been explained in sexual terms: Cather's strength as a writer sprang from her "masculine sensibility," we are told, but *Lucy Gayheart*, unfortunately, is a "feminine" novel.[17]

Whatever their differences, various critics agree that Lucy is a "silly" girl who "never comes alive."[18] This is a view I would like to see revised or, better still, discarded. Then, I believe, *Lucy Gayheart* might emerge as an interestingly involuted novel with revelations to make about Cather's art and about the art of fiction with which it is self-reflexively concerned. If there is a silly girl in *Lucy Gayheart*, she belongs to its romantic pre-text; as the heroine of Romance, Lucy is a serious character whom Cather would like to make both allegorical (or disembodied) and sublime. Dismissal of Lucy as a lifeless figure results from an understandably mistaken notion of the kind of life Cather wanted to describe as a writer and to have her character represent. From the first Cather describes Lucy as a girl whose essence cannot be captured by a static art: her "gaiety and grace" would "mean nothing" in photographs. She must be identified as a "figure always in motion"—joyous motion. In Haverford, Harry Gordon picks her out instantly from all the other skaters on a distant stretch of ice. Her movements are "direct and unhesitating and joyous" as she heads into the wind, quick and easy in her squirrel jacket, the tips of her crimson scarf floating in the air.

Clearly this Lucy Gayheart is not lifeless, not if life means immediacy of presence and movement. The kinetic images and the successions of present participles that open and close the novel depict Lucy as walking, dancing, skating, flying, darting, catching step with the wind, and finally, running away. This incessant activity represents life as energy, youth, and joy, qualities associated with Lucy as a person and as the personification into which she is transformed by her running. Lucy runs after Sebastian, Harry, and, finally, an unseen "sweetheart" waiting in twilight's "breathless quiet," a foreboding quiet to which, fortunately, she responds by breathing: "She opened the window softly and knelt down beside it to breathe the cold air" (184). Like an enchanted maiden gazing out of a casement window— and specifically like Keats's kneeling Madeline in "The Eve of St. Agnes"—Lucy is "throbbing with excitement" as she feels herself taken by a "Lover . . . she could not see, but knew!"—someone who was "waiting for her . . . drawing her, enticing her, weaving a spell over her" (183–84). If this is the language of pulp fiction, it belongs also to Romance. With an appropriation, conscious or not, of Keatsian imagery—throbbing star, casement window, warm flushes and wintry cold—Cather was attempting to make

Lucy soar out of the mundane world into her dream. Like the evening star earlier in the novel, "something" wondrous in the winter night has once more "flashed" a seductive signal, and once more Lucy yearns, this time to run towards her consummate lover "Life itself," and to keep running until she is transformed into an abstract state of pure (e)motion. As an abstraction, Lucy would be released from her body and still live on, having become movement and a disembodied power to move or, in essence, music. If this conception of her heroine as a musical composition seems esoteric or bizarre, it was no more so than Cather's analogical ideas, as she herself had described them, for the characters of her famous novels;[19] and if it was unrealizable, Cather had already recognized the artist's constant striving for impossible ends when she had her autobiographical Thea Kronberg, a great artist, declare: "I want only impossible things. . . . The others don't interest me" (243).

In *Lucy Gayheart,* Cather created an impossible dream and then viewed it with an alarmed ambivalence she could not resolve. I shall return to this irresolution, but first I wish to quote a passage which makes explicit Lucy's desire for her own disembodiment:

The grey gulls flew by on languid wings. The air felt full of spring showers. On a morning like this . . . Lucy felt an ache come up in her throat. When she looked off at that soft promise of spring, spring already happening in the colours of the sky before it had come to earth, such a longing awoke in her that it seemed as if it would break her heart. That happiness she had so lately found, where was it? Everything threatened it, the way of the world was against it. It had escaped her. She had lost it as one can lose a ravishing melody, remembering the mood of it, the kind of joy it gave, but unable to recall precisely the air itself. And she couldn't breathe in this other kind of life. It stifled her, woke in her a frantic fear—the fear of falling back into it forever. *If only one could lose one's life and one's body and be nothing but one's desire;* if the rest could melt away, and that could float with the gulls, out yonder. (102, original ellipsis; emphasis added)

Spring, sky, breath, air, joy, melody, mood, memory, transmutation, and the ascension of the soul to empyreal heights—these thematic images converge in Lucy's vision of an impossible escape from the human body binding her to the world, our everyday world of brief and precarious joy. The higher Lucy's unearthly feelings soar, the deeper Cather's language sinks into pulp story clichés: an ache in the throat, heartbreak, frantic fear, suffocation ("she couldn't breathe"), melting into the wide blue yonder. Even with this vapid prefabricated style, however, Cather can evoke a perennial human longing which she both sexualizes and etherealizes as the sensation of soaring. At the same time, she suggests the death wish implicit in Romanticism, the desire for dissolution that otherworldly music seems inevitably to call forth (the most famous example, of course, the poet's wish to fade and dissolve upon hearing a nightingale's immortal song in Keats's ode). Lucy's desire for disembodiment must presage disaster, since realistically if one could lose one's body one would die. Lucy dreams rather of transformation: she desires to become Desire, as though she could be turned into feeling without bodily form, the essential condition of music.[20]

Though Cather had cast Lucy in the role of accompanist, here she gives her the composer's impulse to (re)arrange the material of life, in this instance, her own life. Indeed, if Lucy could have her wish and find for herself another form of being, she would be retracing the creative process that constituted Cather's art as she conflated her memories of the two real young women into the figure of her fictional heroine.[21] The joy that Cather found intense but fleeting in these women becomes recoverable in the novel, where both happiness and fear of its loss are inscribed. In the passage I have quoted, losing and finding, or forgetting and remembering, are Lucy's thematic concerns. Happiness can be lost and ravishing memories forgotten unless the artist arrests a movement towards entropy (loss, forgetting, death) by contriving a permanent form for life's fleeting movements and melodies. In a much-quoted passage from *The Song of the Lark*, Thea had defined such arrest as the end of art: "what was any art but an effort to make a sheath, a mould in which to imprison for a moment the shining, elusive element which is life itself,—life hurrying past us and running away?" (304). If Lucy personifies life by her running, she wishes to prevail against life's fugacity by finding a form other than the human body to contain her movement while keeping it incessant. She longs to become the "ravishing melody,"[22] to use her suggestive phrase, which will live on in memory as a nostalgic mood that can be recovered again and again. In the novel's epilogue, Harry effects this re-

covery by remembering Lucy; but the novel itself creates, dis-
solves, and recreates different modalities of life for Lucy as
though it were searching along with her for the immutable essence of personality that neither time nor death could obliterate.
Rather than ending her story, Lucy's death provides an impetus
for it to continue by implicitly reposing the plangent question
Lucy had asked: "if there were not more than one way of living?" (134). After the body disappears, as hers does when she
plunges into the icy river, is there any way a person or personality can be said to live on as a melody might after the song has
ended?

This seems to be a question that inspired Cather's long epilogue to *Lucy Gayheart,* which I would best describe as a palinode,
since it consistently retracts the assertions that appear on its
pages. In this respect, it epitomizes an action that belongs to the
novel as a form and is thus distinct from the characters' performance. In the epilogue, Cather makes a realistic acknowl-
edgement (which she will try to withdraw) that time eventually
prevails against human efforts to resist its inexorabilities. In
time, the mind that remembers will disappear; the materials
molded into art, even stone, will crumble; and every story will
come to an end. In a brief obituary paragraph, Cather equates
forgetting with death, and both with literary closure as "a chapter [is] closed" and "the story . . . finished" (207). By its own
prolixity, the epilogue delays this closure while, at the same time,
it describes an inevitable eradication of the Gayheart family.
Lucy's father and sister die, the town's memory of her joyous
figure dims, and the Gayheart name sinks slowly into "complete
oblivion."

Harry tries to resist these eventualities by preserving a cement
inscription of Lucy's footprints.[23] Made years ago, these prints
are now a "concrete" sign of movement, of "life itself," as Thea
had defined it, "hurrying past us and running away." But Cather
has made the inscription "baffling." Faintly traced, its prints are
discernible only to someone looking for them, someone like
Harry who wants Lucy re-presented. His doubts about the
"gray-white composition" reflect Cather's concern with her text
and, as frequent references to "composition" suggest, with its
artifactuality, perhaps even its speciousness.[24] Like Harry, Cather
wonders whether living movement must be attributed to a static

form, or whether (literary) form can inscribe this movement. The only certainty emerging in the vacillating epilogue is the human will to prevail against time. Harry reinforces his personal will to save Lucy's (foot)prints with a legal "will" which provides a custodian to care for the delicate inscription. Cather's will in creating, killing, and resuscitating her heroine seems formidable, since she was trying to give an account of both loss and recovery through an impossible transmutation of her heroine as she is shaped by music into music.[25] The tableau that brings *Lucy Gayheart* to an end holds the living figure of Harry in arrest as he looks upon a cryptic inscription of (e)motion left by the dead heroine, now transformed into memory, mood, and disembodied movement.

As last seen, Harry appears outwardly unchanged. He still has a "firm, deliberate tread" and, as town banker, is still a man of facts and figures. However, he seems to have undergone an inner transformation (I say *seems* because like all characters he has at least two different selves, neither clearly normative). Early in the novel, Lucy had prayed to become desire without a body; by the end, a chiastic crossing has turned Harry into a body without physical desires. He loves as though in consecration of the chivalric love Cather valued, for he has no hope of possessing the woman he wants except through memory, as always in Cather, a means of repossession. Through memory, Harry can (re)call Lucy at will and do with her as he will. Once thwarted, he now faces no obstacle—except Lucy's death. But the complex strategy of the epilogue—Harry's long "reflections" and Cather's twists and turns and switches of tense—has been aimed at denying that the death it acknowledges means obliteration of the human personality and the feelings it has evoked. Rather, death becomes analogous to the silence in which song is recovered as an unheard melody playing only to the inner ear, but nonetheless playing. In a convoluted way, death fulfills Romantic aspiration.

The play of Harry's mind, as he remembers and slowly appropriates Lucy, shows the ingenuity of human rationalization and the persuasiveness of Romanticism and romantic fantasies. In order to release Lucy from any serious commitment to another lover, Harry invents a self-serving story that describes her as the infatuated heroine of romance, a "heedlessly young" girl who "would fall in love with the first actor or singer she met" (222), as though the glamorous baritone were anyone. Then, as though to assure his claim, Harry symbolically consigns his rival to oblivion; since he now owns the Gayheart house and all it contains, he takes Lucy's photograph of the singer and drops it into his pocket, in effect, making him disappear. Indeed, he makes the past and his complicity in Lucy's death disappear by a strategic switch to the present tense as he asserts that "Lucy Gayheart is no longer a despairing little creature standing in the icy wind" (224). His negations—"no longer . . . no longer"—imply a *once.* Once upon a time, Lucy was "despairing" and "beseeching" and "standing in the icy wind" where Harry had left her, insulted beyond containment. Now, in his memories, she returns momentarily but "vividly" as for a "flash," Harry catches "the very feel of her . . . [her] breath on his cheek" (227).

As thematic words return and combine in the epilogue—star, flash, breath, spring, youth, joy, movement—the language becomes a web, but though tight and intricate, it cannot contain the Romantic impossibilities the novel tries to realize. The strategic switches to the present tense recall rather than obliterate the past, and the wild joy that Harry remembers indicates Lucy's absence even as it re-presents her to him. As though recognizing that her recomposition into movement and melody has not brought Lucy back to life, Harry (and through him Cather) resorts to the resurrection of a buried child, a perennial Romantic *topos.* This regression is, of course, a familiar ploy in Cather's fiction, which often makes a joyous childhood self reappear just as life seems over for the melancholy adult. I need not recall Jim Burden seeing himself a boy again running through the fields with Ántonia, or the "original, unmodified" Godfrey S. Peter, a "primitive" Kansas boy, returning to the played-out man.[26] These displaced and alienated characters find themselves home again when they replace their depleted selves with the child they believe they were. Harry Gordon's recognition of Haverford as his "home town" coincides with an epiphanic reappearance, not of himself, but of the original Lucy as "a slip of a girl in boy's overalls," the hermaphrodite child whom Cather idealized. This little "slip" will grow up to be a "figure" and find even such slight corporeality burdensome.[27] Harry's affinity for this boy-girl-child, not the usual object of a romantic hero's desire, has been prefigured in Sebastian's attraction to Lucy. Though Sebastian and Harry seem antithetical figures in an eternal triangle, the two men have much in common, including their indulgence in "reflection."[28] Early in the novel when Sebastian reflects upon the past, he thinks of a "talented boy, almost a child," whom he had adopted, loved, and then lost because of his wife's jealousy. Lucy allows him to recover the child of this strange triangle, for when he conveniently defines her love for him as "chivalrous loyalty" rather than "passion," he also redefines her sex: "He had sometimes thought of her as rather boyish" (80). Two aging men in the novel, both overcome by Romantic melancholy, typical Weltschmerz, search through their pasts to find something that will fill the lives they now find "empty" and "barren"—childless. Both retrieve a sexually ambiguous child who gives them a renewed, and I would add platitudinous, will to live. This will cannot save Sebastian, who is already doomed by his ominous dedication to art; nor does it save the "real" Harry, who had wanted Lucy to usher him into the kingdom of art.

Such an aspiration in the novel's man of facts, its only survivor, deserves attention. In his everyday world, Harry lives immured within "a hard case of muscle" penetrable only by the restless young woman who makes his "nerves tingle." Like Marion Forrester in *A Lost Lady*, Lucy seems to possess the "secret" of "ardour": "of ever-blooming, ever-burning, ever-piercing joy."[29] For all his apparent stolidity, Harry finds the wildness of this joy irresistible: "It was a gift of nature, he supposed, to go wildly happy over trifling things—over nothing!" (223). Though he cannot find its reason, Harry wants to share Lucy's wild happiness, a potentially dangerous emotion since it makes his body feel "marvellously free and light," as if it too could be etherealized. Like Lucy, Harry longs for supernal emotions, and he has learned from her, as she has from Sebastian, that music can send one soaring. Attending the opera night after night, Harry enters an other world where he needs Lucy as his accompanist as much as Sebastian does, and for the same inspiring purpose. Through her, he hopes to feel the joy of life that Sebastian, like Cather, associated with youth. Once married, Harry plans to "bring Lucy on for the opera every year," making her his "excuse" for pleasures he considers unmanly. Through a sexual division of labor, he will provide the money and she—as though she herself were music—the means for aesthetic self-fulfillment. But Lucy refuses to let Harry "live through her," even though she imagines herself living through Sebastian. Jealous of "her own life," Lucy feels "trapped" by Harry's proposal of marriage. Instead of entrancing her, his romantic desire to merge his life with hers threatens with its vampirish implications: "I want the life you'd naturally make for youself,—and it's the only life I do want" (109). In the sexual chase of *Lucy Gayheart,* Harry wants Lucy's life, Lucy wants Sebastian's melancholy secret, and Sebastian, Lucy's youth. All aspire vainly for what they cannot have. Moreover, each cancels for the other the possibility for an other life, Sebastian by dying, and Lucy by telling Harry her lie.

Lucy's rejection of Harry seems a typical Cather repression of her character's sexuality. Tall, broad-shouldered, handsome, and rich—a love-story hero—Harry impresses others by his commanding physical presence. Only Lucy discerns, mainly through his voice, a secret "real" Harry who makes her feel "afraid" and yet protective: "It seemed unfair [she thought] . . . to let him take off all his jocular masks and show her a naked man who had perhaps never been exposed to any eye before" (109–10). The almost comic sexual innuendoes that have crept into Lucy's language may have inclined her to the startling lie that she has gone "All the way: all the way!" with Sebastian (111). Ironically, the lie she feels "clubbed" into telling imbues Lucy with the sexuality she wants eliminated from her dream of romance. She resents Harry because his sheer physical presence seems to mock the purity of the "ardour" and "faith" she has distilled as the essence of her love for Sebastian: "It was as if he had brought all his physical force, his big well-kept body, to ridicule something that had no body, that was a faith, an ardour" (112). Lucy has translated love into worship, herself into a chaste page of chivalric romance, and the object of love into a distant flashing star that belongs to a world elsewhere. She is transported there by Sebastian's song, passionate but bodiless, lapsing into silence, but hers to hear again whenever she wishes since it has been recorded in her mind, her soul. Lucy could not foresee the melancholy circumstances in which she would hear Sebastian sing again, and to her alone, as she lay in her orchard in Haverford remembering her dead lover. All she knows now, sitting in a restaurant in Chicago, is that Harry has intruded upon her romance by insisting that facts rather than feelings "are at the bottom of everything." Lucy must protect "her own life" against Harry, because his facts would "manage to prove to her that she had been living in a dream" (96).[30] Not Harry, but this dream requires her dissolution; for though a chivalric code seems idealized in *Lucy Gayheart*, the novel persists in exploring the destructiveness of romance as both a love story and an escapist drama. The lovers die not because of sex, usually a cogent reason in Cather's fiction, but because their Romantic idealism requires a state of rarefication obviously impossible for the human body to attain.[31]

The triangles in which Cather has embroiled her heroine are indeed murky and ominous. Seeking to consummate her strange ethereal union with Sebastian, Lucy must struggle against Harry and, in another triangular configuration, against a more insidious and enigmatic adversary, James Mockford. In this second triangle, Cather plays Lucy and Mockford against each other as if they were (to use her words from another context) "influences and counter-influences, themes and counterthemes."[32] Both are Sebastian's accompanists, one supporting his desire for life (to state Lucy's role simply), and the other his drive toward death, conflicting impulses which the novel has made inherent in the Romanticism of his music. As Sebastian says, Mockford plays German lieder with "genius," but he is "not especially good with Mozart," a composer meant to suggest classical control and order. Everything about Mockford is indeterminate. At times he seems young, at times old, as though without age or beyond time, a figure not completely human. Lucy senses something "uncanny about his fingers," and his lame leg arouses aversion, much as physical deformity did in Cather.[33] Mockford's sinister nature seems melodramatically limned, his red hair, green eyes, theatrically white-floured face and indistinct features belonging to medieval death figures.[34] If Mockford represents a general disorder in life that Cather found menacing and inexplicable, he also personifies more specifically the parasitism of art. He has attached himself to Sebastian, enters his studio as if it were his own, smokes his cigarettes, drinks his tea, and rides in his cab, insolently taking all he can get until finally he has taken life itself. He accomplishes the destruction that in his melancholy moods Sebastian fears will be the end of his art. For having poured his soul into his song, Sebastian sees himself so personally depleted that he has become a martyr to his art, a fate meant to be suggested by his name (as Cather makes clear by having him called "Mr. Saint Sebastian"). Though Sebastian leaves Lucy with the promise that he will return with a new and less noxious pianist, as an artist he cannot drop Mockford because he represents an inextricably sinister side of art. Lucy blames herself for not warning Sebastian against Mockford; but even if she had, she could not have broken the stranglehold of art itself, which for all its glory is dangerous and may ultimately lead one, as *Lucy Gayheart* intimates, to a vision of nihilism. In turning the novel over to Harry at the end, Cather attempts to dispel this vision by displaying a lover's faithfulness, hope, and inextinguishable desire. For even after twenty-five years, Harry still strives for possession of his star, the source of brightness in his life, his aptly named Lucy.

Like Harry, Mockford shakes Lucy's confidence in her dream of "another life" with Sebastian. The supernal happiness she thinks they share might be her fantasy or (so Mockford appropriately implies) a mere mockery, a travesty, of love. After their encounter, she wonders what in her life is real and what "make-believe," the childish term suggesting deliberation as well as play. One *makes* believe; the illusion does not happen but must be created. Lucy's power to make believe (like the writer's power to imagine) cannot protect her from real collisions with other people or from the attritions effected by time and chance. Her most poignant recognition of helplessness follows her aimless walks with Guiseppe as he tells her of Sebastian's imminent departure: "It was strange, to feel everything slipping away from one and to have no power to struggle, no right to complain. One had to sit with folded hands and see it all go" (117–18). At this moment, she recognizes her vulnerability in a make-believe world: "There was nothing sure or safe in this life she was leading" (117). Love was unsafe; and, as she would hardly have time to discover, so was the anger that would impel her to the river Platte's treacherous waters. Music was unsafe because it seduced one to illusions that could not survive in life.

Such bathetic thoughts, an implicit plea for sympathy, make

Lucy seem girlish and helpless, but Cather's heroine has the
strength of her desire. She knows what she wants, and she is
single-minded and willful in pursuit, perhaps even ruthless. She
rids herself of Harry so that she can chase Sebastian with an
obsessive and almost comic assiduity. Though Sebastian believes
that in "her companionship there was never the shadow of a
claim" (81), in her own way Lucy would take all from her lover,
even the rhythm of his heartbeat. She invades his privacy with a
professional detective's persistence as she stalks the singer, following him through the streets and into church, listening to his
telephone conversations, spying upon him in order to ferret out
his "secret." For she suspects that Sebastian has concealed an
"other" person, his "real self," behind an amiable public "manner so perfected that it could go on representing him when he
himself was either lethargic or altogether absent" (49). Cather
has given Sebastian the same duplicitous character as Harry:
these rival lovers both hide a private and vulnerable self beneath
a smiling public persona. Probing beyond Sebastian's mask,
Lucy discovers a despairing man burdened with the premoni-
tion of his death; and without realizing that she may jeopardize
the youthful joyousness Sebastian loves, she takes from him a
precocious knowledge of unhappiness, a "discovery about life"
usually acquired through gradual maturation. Seeking in the
singer the source of art, she finds instead its end. In Sebastian's
personal depletion, she discovers the secret of entropy that the
aging singer embodies (and her own body soon will express).

Cather's terms for entropy in the novel are age, loss, and
laziness. When Lucy returns to Haverford, she finds laziness
pervasive among the townspeople, and she feels herself becoming "lazy" like her father and her sister. The Gayhearts seem
busy, as Mr. Gayheart repairs clocks and rehearses the band
(keeping time in order), and Pauline bustles through house-
work; but both accomplish less than they could, both create disorder, the essence of entropy, and neither strives for excellence.
Lucy turns to Harry because of all the townspeople he alone
seems "alive"; "he was not lazy"; he had "imagination." Ironically, she and Harry have singled each other out as unique in
their town because each seems to the other the embodiment of
life. Almost like vampires, all of Cather's lovers are attracted to
vitality, the lifeblood in another that they want for themselves. In

Haverford, Lucy slinks after Harry in the same way she had trailed Sebastian in Chicago, and for the same reason—to feel alive. Just as she wanted Sebastian's breath to inspire her, now she need Harry's "energy"; "he moved," and his movements could start "her machinery going." This mechanical image seems tired, and odd for Cather, but it suits Lucy's run-down state. Once the personification of Life, now she seems the figure of Entropy. She is still running, but frenetically and in circles, her movements like her emotions in dangerous disorder. She is at once restless and listless, purposeful only in her pursuit of Harry. His bland rejections do not stop her; rather they urge her to run faster and more desperately, for the vitalizing energy which she had once had and now has lost seems deposited in the banker's stalwart body.

In a climactic moment of recognition, which comes as she is once more inspired by a singer, an aging soprano, Lucy realizes that the object of her desire has been neither Harry nor Sebastian but a "Lover" they represent. With her girlishly halting question "What if—what if Life itself were the sweetheart?" (184) who had been calling to her, the novel combines popular romance with the allegorical mode implied by Lucy's wish for disembodiment. If Lucy could be released from her body and still exist, then she would be dissolved into her Lover's being and become a figure inseparable from "Life itself." Cather consistently refers to Lucy as a "figure," as though to signify her heroine's function as both trope and representative type and to make her a metaphor for transformation in a rather tricky chain of symbolic changes. As Lucy transfers her desire from a human lover to "Life itself," an abstract force, she is transformed from a stereotypical small-town girl adventuring in the big city (or from any of the other stereotypes of the novel's romantic plots) into a personification of a powerful though mysterious Energy.

When she feels the surge of this energy, Lucy interprets it as the artist's desire for excellence, the charged energy of all striving valued by Cather as a Romantic ideal. Dismayed by the "humdrum people" of Haverford, Lucy attributes this striving to the teeming crowds in Chicago, and she imagines her return to their midst: she "could think of nothing but crowded streets with life streaming up and down, windows full of roses and gardenias and violets. . . . She wanted flowers and music and enchantment and love,—all the things she had first known with Sebastian" (184). If this is intended as a vision of vigorous "Life" in Chicago, it is obviously indistinguishable from trite and derivative romantic fantasies. Cather was either parodying the love story or else showing Lucy's confusion (perhaps also her own) of timeless and ineffable ideals with a romantic young girl's foolish fancies. She may also have been revealing the limits of (her) language which, to resort to tautology, could not express the inexpressible, though such expression, she thought, was the Romantic writer's aspiration and the achievement of Romantic music.

Lucy's Chicago exists as her own creation (and, of course, ultimately Cather's), for through a willed act of eradication, she has created an artificial city, her "individual map of Chicago": "This city of feeling rose out of the city of fact like a definite composition,—beautiful because the rest was blotted out" (24). Lucy also "blots out" Chicago's volatile and ominous weather, its "dark, stormy mornings." Once she ascends to the "unclouded climate" of Sebastian's studio in the Arts Building—to an empyreal height where setting and symbol neatly converge—then the city, to be escaped as well as sought, is "blotted out." Cather's repetition of this blunt, graceless verb *blotting* begins to suggest a (writer's) duplicitous process of describing and denying, revealing and repressing, the presence of life's "disturbing" aspects. In the studio, Sebastian's song seems to arrest the confusion that Lucy and Cather equate with "time or change." "Shut away from the rest of the world," Lucy sees things take on "their proper relation" as they settle into an orderly and unchanging form. She does not suspect that immutability might be another term for death. She thinks only that the "joyousness" of life will be made "safe" by song. But the song Lucy associates with the studio, Schubert's "Die Forelle," should have given her pause, since its happy trout is in time tricked, captured, and killed. Neither "trivial" nor "disturbing" aspects of life can be "shut out," as Lucy desires, except temporarily and by a deliberate act of will; nor can life by "resolved into something simple and noble," even in the studio. The Mockfords of the world clamor for their place in the design of things; and in Haverford, Lucy's memory of Sebastian singing "Die Forelle" evokes despair.

The songs that Lucy first hears Sebastian sing establish the motif of doubling that resonates through the novel. Schubert's lied describes the twin stars Castor and Pollux as divided but complementary beings, one mortal and the other a god (and both, ironically, protecting men at sea; obviously the stars have failed Sebastian and Lucy, who drown). Another song, "Der Doppelgänger" from Schubert's cycle *Die Winterreise*, divides a fornlorn lover into his present and past selves. All the characters of *Lucy Gayheart* are similarly split and doubled, not only Lucy, Harry, and Sebastian, but also secondary figures like Lucy's father and sister.[35] As a clockmaker and musician, Mr. Gayheart is attuned to two different kinds of time; perhaps that is why he seems "the happiest man in Haverford" (7). His plain daughter Pauline inexplicably conceals an other self: "The plump, talkative little woman . . . was a mannikin which Pauline pushed along before her; no one had ever seen the pusher behind that familiar figure, and no one knew what that second person was like" (168). Perhaps Cather did not know; at any rate, she was not telling. She was suggesting, however, a fear of self-revelation, as though the real self must remain hidden behind mannequins, masks, and manners in order to be protected against violation. For as each character in *Lucy Gayheart* seeks the secret inner self of the other, each puts the other in jeopardy. Perhaps Harry survives because Lucy does not want the hidden (music) lover; nor does anyone else, including his wife. Cather's strategic splitting and doubling of her characters furthered her quest for a way for Lucy to transcend both her mundane and her stereotyped romantic self, a way for her to survive disembodiment. At the same time, Cather was weaving into her own intricate design themes already familiar in the fiction of Hawthorne and of Hemingway which expressed fears that she shared: fear of another who would violate the privacy of the human soul (her personal fear as a woman trying to protect herself as a writer); and fear of words which might "spoil" the way one feels.

Instead of allaying such fears, the novel itself becomes an anxious object. It holds in constant tension opposite and irreconcilable views, as though any statement, once inscribed on the page, must be challenged but not erased, leaving all to exist simultaneously in a state or irresolution. The effect is to induce critical anxiety, since one cannot decide which of the novel's explicit statements have validity; or one may conclude that in the end *Lucy Gayheart* does not intend to establish meaning as much as movement—a pursuit, displacement, and return to themes that is characteristic of music. For example, the novel both affirms and denies the timelessness of human dreams either through a single character who expresses contradictory views or through paired but contrasting characters. In the epilogue, when Harry Gordon summarizes twenty-five years of human history full of violence and change, he declares "the old beliefs of men . . . shattered" (220). At the same time, however, gazing upwards at the seemingly steadfast stars, he nullifies human history by asserting that whatever has happened to people, including those mutilated or killed in war, "mattered very little when one looked up there at eternity" (220). The novel ends with the stars of the winter sky still flashing their seductive signal, which may have deluded Lucy and may now be doing the same to Harry.

While the stars remain steadfast, the seasons alternate rhythmically from winter to spring to underscore a thematic opposition between decay and resurgence. Cather suggests that her heroine might have resolved this opposition. As youth and joy, Lucy seems a living embodiment of the season of renewal: she constantly "refreshes" Sebastian and Harry, touching them lightly and sweetly like spring rain, the novel's recurrent image. When she fronts Chicago's wind, she imagines herself making "an overcoat of the cold" so that she would feel "warm and awake" even in a climate "where roses froze instantly." But though winter exhilarates Lucy, she cannot prevail against the season of death; roses will freeze in winter air, and Lucy finally succumbs to Haverford's "frozen country" and "frozen people," both epitomized in Harry's "insult." Infuriated as Harry leaves her stranded on the icy road, "she was no longer conscious of the cold"; but the anger that enwrapped her like an overcoat and made her very blood hot, blinded her to danger. Seeing "nothing" in the bare merciless winterscape, imagining her escape from its nihilism to another place of "light and freedom," Lucy Gayheart skates to her death.

Sebastian might have predicted this end, for though he desires Lucy because she is young, he has seen youth fade and time bring loss. Looking at the lush flowers Lucy admires, he comments cynically, "Very suggestive: youth, love, hope—all the things that pass" (69). Later, however, Harry insists that "all the fine things of youth . . . do not change" (224) and that Lucy, though gone, has not been lost: that her impression, the imprint left on his memory as well as the sidewalk cement, has the presence of the original, of Lucy herself. But this assertion depends for its cogency solely upon Harry's word(s), since it defies common sense and the realistic plot of the novel which has led to Lucy's drowning. Ironically, when Lucy announced her desire to run toward Life, she ensured her death, for she was committing herself not to everyday realities but to her Romantic aspirations. The impossibility of living in two antithetical modes—as a person and as the personification of an ideal—eventuates in a fall which makes possible Lucy's apotheosis. Through song, Lucy had entered the "invisible, inviolate world" in which she longed to live; through death, she could remain there.

Lucy Gayheart may be read as Willa Cather's testament to the Romantic imagination that had imbued her fiction. Here, however, as in Keats's great odes, the imagination questions its own reality, and the writer wonders whether all she had believed may have been not only delusory but also destructive. Realistically, Lucy Gayheart's dream of living in the "unclouded climate" of an "invisible, inviolable world" evoked for her by music was impossible. Yet with her words, often the banal words of love-story romance, Cather imagined this world into being, a kingdom of art already entered by great Romantic poets. There melodies played on forever, and lovers were forever young, forever in motion. Cather transformed Lucy into a figure on the Grecian urn and into the urn's emblem, but she knew, as she came to the end of her career, that an urn can break. She had seen, she said in a much-quoted remark, her world break in two.[36] In *Lucy Gayheart* she tried to put together its disparate parts: dream and reality, experience and memory, art and life, life and death, music and words. After a lifetime spent in writing, she suspected that language would prove incommensurate to her desire. If in *Lucy Gayheart* she failed, her attempt was revealing, interesting, and, I believe, significant enough to warrant a serious reconsideration of the novel. It may also have been foolhardy. For she wished to capture in the language of love-story romance the elusive ideals of the Romantic imagination. To keep these ideals perennially alive, Willa Cather sa-

crified the body of her heroine and created an "other life" for
Lucy Gayheart as movement and melody.

Epilogue

One last word remains to be said—kindness. This is the single
value that Willa Cather did not blot out in her palimpsestic
novel. On a simple and sentimental level, *Lucy Gayheart* may be
read as a plea for compassion. Lucy returned to Haverford to
ask Harry Gordon if "he couldn't feel kindly toward her . . . and
speak kindly" (174). He knew he was treating the forlorn girl
"badly": "I've not said a kind word to her since she came home"
(218). Sebastian had escaped his wife's "cruelty" by fleeing to
Chicago, where an exchange of favors consummated his love
affair with Lucy. "You were kind to give me this evening," the
great Sebastian tells his accompanist (85). Paul Auerbach, Lucy's
teacher, advises her to marry because she is "too kind" for the
aggressive world of the artist. After Sebastian's death, Auerbach
and his wife care for Lucy, pack her clothes, set her on the train
to Haverford. There, Pauline heeds her distraught sister's plea
that she save the apple trees under whose sheltering branches
Lucy finds her only repose.

Kindness makes their "life sentence" endurable for Cather's
characters, while cruelty and indifference buffet them as merci-
lessly as the winter winds.[37] The novel's insistence upon the
characters' need for mutual support subverts Harry's reconciliation of personal cruelty and mass violence with a vision of eternal cosmic harmony, with the music of the spheres. Whatever his
rationalization, Harry behaved unconscionably when he denied
Lucy a "courtesy he wouldn't have refused to the most worthless
old loafer in town" (220).[38] Cather's characters needed each
other's generosity because they were not sustained by a social
order; and the novel apostrophized Life, an abstraction, because
its vision of society was sterile. The image of Lucy alone on a
treacherous icy landscape epitomized its view of the individual
in a social setting: a vast, empty, dangerous place where one felt
one's isolation and dependence.

At the end of the novel, the wind is at Lucy's back—a wind she
had once headed into and caught step with. The sky is low and
gray, the sun a "glassy white spot." The road is frozen, and

Lucy's foot catches in its hard muddy ruts. When she hears the "singing" of Harry Gordon's sleigh bells, she waits "to beg a ride"; and when she is rebuffed, she runs angrily to her death. Lucy Gayheart might have lived, one would like to think, if she had been given a word.

The Hidden Mines

in Ethel Wilson's Landscape

(or an American Cat

Among Canadian Falcons)

Ethel Wilson

ON ETHEL WILSON

*In 1973, at Lincoln, Nebraska, while participating in a symposium
celebrating Willa Cather's centennial year, I met a young Canadian
scholar. In the course of desultory conversations, I asked him what good
Canadian novels I should be reading. He did more than suggest
titles; when he returned home, he sent me sample works by Margaret
Laurence, Alice Munro, Gabrielle Roy, and Ethel Wilson. This
bundle from Canada marked the beginning of a continuous, pleasurable, and intensifying study of Canadian writers, particularly of
women writers. As critics have observed, the number of excellent women
writers in Canada is remarkable. Explanations for this fact, however,
have faltered; some have been unflattering to women and country,
linking both as second-class citizens in the American continent. That
praise of excellence should be tinged by denigration seems to me
an instance of sexual prejudice. Literary achievement is usually attributed to talent, discipline, mastery of the métier, and vision—in male
writers. Such factors should not be minimized in women, certainly not
in Canadian women writers whose reputations are growing throughout
the world. Indeed, in 1982, Margaret Laurence was one of the
contenders for the Nobel Prize in literature. As an old writer, Ethel
Wilson is less modern and experimental than Laurence, and less
modish than Margaret Atwood. Her writing seems timeless in its
smoothly polished and witty veneer, its perfection of style. Beneath this
surface, however, lies a murky depths that an American reader, accustomed to darkness and violence in the novel, might discern. Wilson's
fiction contains many discrepancies, uncertainties, vacillations, all of
which resist interpretation. Her treatment of women, her major subject,
seems strangely equivocal. She values women in traditional roles
as wives and mothers, even though she approves of wives deserting their
husbands in her fiction and mothers bearing illegitimate children.
Some of her women are nagging, comically so, and mean-spirited, playing petty games of one-ups(wo)manship. But like other woman writers
in this volume, Wilson portrays perennial survivors, heroines who prevail on their own terms. Her women make concessions to society, but
they never concede their essential identity, as they choose to define
it, or their essential dignity. The pettiness they occasionally indulge in*

*turns out to be their way, perhaps their only way, of preserving a
sense of self. I like remembering that my introduction to Ethel Wilson
came indirectly through Willa Cather, an inviolable American woman
writer whom she admired and took as an inspiration.*

"I had handled dynamite," Frankie Burnaby thinks at the
end of Ethel Wilson's novel *Hetty Dorval:* "I had handled
dynamite, and in so doing had exploded the hidden mine of
Mrs. Broom to my own great astonishment. . . ."[1]
     I start with this image of a hidden mine in Ethel Wilson's
fiction because I am an American reader, accustomed by my
literature to explosions of violence in the novel and also to abundance, to the presence within a vast and varied landscape of rich
deposits—the inexhaustible resources of art. Canadian critics, as
they describe the abundance contained in Wilson's fiction, its
richness of natural and social detail, have praised the surface
serenity of her art: the detached tone; the compassionate and
comic insights into the foibles of the great human family; the
faith that remains unshaken even when these foibles, our seemingly innocent but obsessive meddling with each other, turn into
destructive or coercive acts, violations of each other's freedom. I
wish to excavate to a depth hidden beneath the surface sustained
so beautifully by Wilson's style and tone and the seemingly
casual meandering of her form; I wish to dig for the dynamite I

In her essay "A Cat Among the Falcons" [*Canadian Literature*, I (Autumn 1959),
10–19], Ethel Wilson avers that she is not a "qualified critic," not one of the
"falcons [who] cruise high above and search the literary plain." Rather, as a
country cat, she remains indoors, keeping her literary convictions safely private
while she watches the sky where the "formidable and trained"—and contentious—falcons soar. Having been invited to give an American perspective upon
Ethel Wilson's fiction at a conference distinguished by Canadian critics immersed in Wilson's work, life, and milieu, I recognize my affinity with the country cat. If I venture out with the falcons, I do so in the hope of making criticism
"interesting" and perhaps even "amusing," the effects that Wilson valued in
diversity of critical opinion.

suspect she has concealed. By her own image she has alerted us to the possibility of hidden mines and so validated the process of excavation, which I take to be the critic's essential act. First of all, I want to extract from Wilson's fiction the violence that lurks beneath its serenity. In these dangerous depths, I expect to find also abundance—a rich subterranean treasure of motives and meanings that constitute the source of Ethel Wilson's art.

To the critic, surface and depths evoke complementary images of light and darkness, the contrast integral to Wilson's art and to her vision of the duplicity of life which allows us brilliant evanescent moments whose meanings are shadowy and elusive. In a striking passage, Wilson describes a fluidity of light flowing over the landscape of British Columbia and defamiliarizing the "daily look" of mountains and forests. Falling obliquely upon mountain slopes, light "discloses new contours"; in forests, it "discover[s] each separate tree behind each separate tree."[2] Then it fades, leaving us with unforgettable images. The light I hope to bring to Wilson's landscape is also oblique, slanted by an American perspective, but I hope its illumination, coming from an unfamiliar direction and moving into an unexplored darkness, can discover aspects of Wilson's art—images of hidden violence and of abundance—that will be remembered long after the critic's light fades.

Obviously, violence in Wilson is much more muted, much less shocking and perverse, than in the fiction of William Faulkner and Ernest Hemingway, not the most brutal but the most famous male American novelists writing as Wilson's contemporaries. American women writers also shed blood more unsparingly than Wilson. Murder, rape, mob vengeance, and war erupt in Flannery O'Connor and Katherine Anne Porter; and in Willa Cather, violence assaults the peaceful Nebraska landscape with the suddenness of locusts. In Wilson's novels, a child can slip into a turbulent ocean in one unobtrusive sentence, a beloved mother die almost parenthetically, a wife submit to her husband's "hateful assaults" as a nightly aside to daily life, and a war, or two wars, fit incidentally into the unimportant gaps within a family's continuous life. If in these wars, a man's hand should be "blown off," neither he nor his family "look upon this as anything out of the way."[3] Nor do we, for Wilson somehow disposes of the violence she has released, tucking it away among the details of daily life which resumes its ordinary course after an explosion; or else she separates us from violence, as Frankie is separated from war-torn Vienna, by a convenient "wall of silence." In Wilson's stories, however, the violence contained within the beautiful Canadian landscape cannot be concealed by silence, hardly allowable in the short story's urgent form, or by dense details that attract our attention in the novel, distracting it from hidden dangers. The "humped" body of a murdered woman lies exposed on the dyke in "Hurry, hurry"; the blood of an innocent Chinaman flows from repeated stab wounds and a gunshot in "Fog"; blackness and the sea pour into a reeling boat that strikes a reef and splits, spilling four people into death and causing the suicide of a pregnant woman in "From Flores"; and in "The Window," a would-be murderer stands with "a short blunt weapon in his hand," arrested in his deadly assault only by the shocking image of his own imminent violence.

Violence held in arrest by its own image seems to me a stunning effect of Wilson's art. At the moment when the would-be murderer sees himself, his hand is halted, perhaps (to use one of Wilson's favorite words) only temporarily, but long enough for Mr. Willy's life to be spared. Violence thus allows for providential rescue, common in Wilson's fiction; and rescue influences our perception of life, of its indifference to human needs or its concern, its accidental nature or design. With these polarities we plunge to the depths in Wilson's fiction, reaching her bedrock thematic issue. Has human life ultimate meaning, or is it simply—like Topaz Edgeworth's life—a succession of "sparkling dots" uninscribed in a "significant design"? Nihilism and belief struggle for supremacy in Wilson's fiction, which, like the darkened window of her story, reflects the interior space of the mind—or perhaps it is the soul—where significant human action takes place. When the murderous thief brings violence into Mr. Willy's living room, the consciousness where life is centered, he cracks the darkness that is slowly enveloping Mr. Willy; he allows in an unexpected slant of light that can show Mr. Willy where meaning may exist in an apparently meaningless life. To recognize the danger of irrational, unpredictable, undeserved violence seems in Wilson's fiction a necessary preliminary to believing in providential design. Such recognition, however, brings one precipitously close to the Abyss, the empty darkness that Mr.

Willy sees outside and within his window when night effaces the day's stirringly beautiful Canadian landscape. However abundant and variegated external nature appears in Wilson's lavish descriptions, human reality enacts its drama in an interior private living room—in the heart and head, as Nell Severance tells us in *Swamp Angel*.[4] Any human being isolated in this room, cut off from significant relationship to others, must find his or her thoughts mined (or undermined) with dangerous elements: a fear of nihilism, a suspicion of life's ultimate meaninglessness, a sense of the fortuity of encounters that may end in death or in permanent scarring such as Ellen Cuppy will suffer in *Love and Salt Water*. If we dig deeply enough into Wilson's fiction, we strike against the Void, and when Nothingness lies below us, leaving us unsupported, then life and fiction may catapult us into a violence as sudden and meaningless as that which engulfs the odd assortment of men who drown together in the death-drenched story "From Flores."

Like the waters into which a Wilson character may at any whimsical moment sink, the desert represents an endless Void. Thus *aridity* recurs as Wilson's thematic term for deprivation of meaning, an invidious form of violence that can enter a room impregnable to a thief. In "Tuesday and Wednesday," Victoria May Tritt (who has more of a name than an identity) lives "in a parched way," lost in a "desert of loneliness" created by time— "the desert between now and sleep." Water and desert sand, both vast, elemental, and seemingly empty, both dangerous for men and women to traverse, especially alone, stretch before the reader as irradicable images of a cosmic Void. "Do we always live on a brink, then," Nora asks in *Love and Salt Water* (192). Wilson's fiction shows us that "we do," while every urbane aspect of her style and tone tries to pull us back from the Void, providing us with a calm or comic or collected perspective that diverts us from the emptiness of spirit into which anyone, particularly anyone of our modern world, may fall. If oblique means of preventing an explosion of the hidden mines of nihilism, means of formal control, seem inadequate, then Wilson openly moralizes against despair, insisting upon the "beautiful action[s]" of which human beings are capable, acts of compassion, performed by Maggie Lloyd in *Swamp Angel*, of loyalty and love, exemplified by Morgan Peake and George Gordon in *Love and Salt Water*, of self-discipline developed by Lilly in her story, and of miraculous rescue produced by "dirty, old" men like Mr. Abednego.

A profound fear that man may be an island, a desert island, the fear that leads Mr. Willy to despair over the "aridity" of his isolated life (rather than exult over his freedom) makes Wilson insist, I believe, upon the integrity of the human family. This insistence, however, raises my anxiety, and like Lilly, I grow afraid of unforeseen "Trouble." For since we are all related, enmeshed though we cannot know how in each others' lives, I worry about effects upon my own life that may come from gratuitous and unfathomable causes. I feel myself treading over hidden mines, any one of which may accidentally blow up in my face and leave me, like Ellen Cuppy, scarred. How can I tell what "arrangements of circumstance" have been prepared for me by those nebulous agents of causality in Wilson's fiction, "life and time," which are fusing all of us into one continuous family, relating me to generations past or distant whose effects I can neither know or avoid? Occasionally the long-range fortuitous effects of family ties will be amusing. In *The Innocent Traveller,* Rose attends the theater (and develops "a taste for . . . the deceits of beauty") because ten years earlier her Great-Aunt Annie and a famous actor had met as shipmates in an encounter arranged by chance. But when chance becomes causality, linking together a chain of events that is incongruous but destructive, I fear its vagaries. If they affect my life—as they effect Mort's death in "Tuesday and Wednesday"[5]—then life itself seems random, without intrinsic order. Wilson tries to mollify the fear of chaos she arouses by showing how families maintain order as they transmit from one generation to the next a pattern of manners, traditions, and beliefs. Families provide a context of relationships which give a woman (in particular) a meaningful role in life as mother, wife, daughter, sister, cousin. *The Innocent Traveller* celebrates these roles, but also undermines them, I believe, by showing Rachel as a woman held in perpetual if loving servitude, and Topaz as a "youngest child" held in perpetual helplessness. Always cared for by her family, Topaz seems extraordinarily lucky in her hundred years of cheerful idle life; but even she may not have escaped the explosions of hidden mines. Triviality may be one; helplessness, another. The loving family that pampers Topaz also infantilizes her, I believe, by accepting (if not fostering) her helplessness; in her comic way, she remains forever helpless, a child even when she reaches venerable age. Though family ties are tenuous in "Tuesday and Wednesday," they do hold together Myrtle's ego, but also they bind Myrtle forever to her cousin's lie. If in this novella Wilson parodies family life, creating an aunt who is a "kitten" and a "conveniently anonymous" cousin, she nevertheless reveals its profound ambiguities which her most serious fiction cannot resolve. In *Swamp Angel,* Maggie Lloyd's surrogate family focuses the heroine's new identity, but also infuses it with new anxieties and problems; and in *Love and Salt Water,* Nora Peake's loving sister nearly wrecks Nora's life.

Wilson also celebrates and undermines marriage, which stultifies characters to whom it brings the only fulfillment possible. Married men and women run away from each other in *Swamp Angel,* "The Window," "Beware the Jabberwock. . . . ." Wives dream of freedom, and husbands of "slugging" or even murdering their wives. In "A drink with Adolphus," Mr. Leaper notes in his secret diary that a man "is undergoing trial for the murder of his wife. The thing that impressed me [he writes, thinking of his own marriage] was that he and his wife had *seemed* to live a devoted and harmonious life together."[6] I emphasize *seemed* because appearances conceal the truth of family life in Wilson's fiction; or the fiction itself conceals the truth it makes us suspect, hiding it beneath the surface of serenity so that we see the Edgeworths or Cuppys or Forresters as "ideal couples," much as Vicky May saw that irascible pair, Myrt and Mort. In *Swamp Angel,* Maggie experiences marriage at its best (but death ends her happiness) and at its most crimping. In the same novel, Nell Severance understands that her marriage, never sanctified by law, only by love, required her to hurt her only daughter. This daughter, at first fearful of marriage, finds in it her fulfillment; but happiness demands her submission to another, and Wilson's women typically say they wish to be free. Thus family relationships involve so many complexities they elude understanding or judgment. They become mysterious though ordinary; and mystery engenders fear. If a woman, in a moment of carelessness, might cause her nephew's death, then sisters and aunts, no matter how loving and well-intentioned, have ominous potential. Wilson never lets us forget the harm we might do each other within the family; and since she insists that family bonds (the

commonplace phrase implies imprisonment as well as security)
somehow connect all of us to each other, she implies that the
invidous effects of human relationships are general and inescapable. Within the great human family are hidden subterranean
links that no one can discern because they are buried like an
enemy's mines where one would least suspect their presence and
where one would be sure to tread.

The enemies to human happiness are often coincidental circumstances whch defy rational explanation. How can we find
meaning in life, the "belief" that Mr. Willy seeks to rescue him
from the aridity of his desert island, the faith that Nell Severance magisterially declares in *Swamp Angel,* when we see that at
any moment coincidences may spring upon us as the hoodlums
sprang upon old Mrs. Bylow, precipitating her death in the aptly
named story "Fog"? Coincidence, sheer coincidence, brings together Eddie Hansen, Mort Johnson, and Victoria May Tritt at
the corner of Powell Street, from where the men march to their
accidental death and Vicky to her unexpected apotheosis as a
teller of tales. What I call accident other readers may consider
providential design, a view we can justify when we see fortuity as
part of a comprehensive plan to educate characters to their responsibilities and to love. In *Love and Salt Water,* family members
meddle with good intentions in each other's lives, but the results
are almost disastrous. Though she is a strong swimmer—
Wilson's repeated metaphor for a self-reliant, courageous
woman—Ellen Cuppy nearly drowns, and worse, she nearly
causes the death of her beloved nephew Johnny. From this experience Ellen learns that "She had better mind her own business.
Everyone had better mind their own business" (188). But in a
family where everyone's business is inherently connected, bound
together by inextricable and untraceable human ties, letting
others *be,* an allowance that is surely one equation of love, may
prove impossible. Acceptance of others does lie within one's capacity. Ellen learns to value Morgan Peake and to trust George
Gordon's love which her terrible accident could not jeopardize.
We learn a lesson I find frightening: that the "circle of life is
extraordinary," including relationships among people widely
separated in space and time whose lives touch by coincidence, by
accident (or design?, what design?), in ways that many affect
them "perhaps temporarily," Wilson equivocates, "or perhaps

permanently and fatally" (133). Wilson's uncertainty catapults me into an unknowable world where, I suspect, only caprice rules. We may be trapped: we may escape. We may be rescued: we may die. Whatever happens seems beyond control and beyond reasonable prediction. We do not know where the hidden mines in life are buried and which will explode when.

If I were to imagine Edith Wharton taking over Wilson's novel *Love and Salt Water,* I would feel certain that fate would be cruel. Once Ellen and Johnny fall into the sea, I would expect them to drown[7] For again and again Wharton shows that life is so constituted that rescue never comes when we need it, when we are trapped by the capacious web woven by circumstance, by small choices, weak mistakes, fortuitously untimely encounters, by a lapse in manners, a break in traditions that Wharton, like Wilson, fastidiously portrays. No one rescues Lily Bart in Wharton's inexorable novel, cruelly entitled *The House of Mirth.* Lily dies, probably by her own hand, and Selden arrives, when he arrives, too late. Only death releases Lily from the despair which time makes inevitable. Sometimes Wharton will not allow even death to give her characters respite from pain. They live on in *Ethan Frome,* caught in an incredible web woven of human passion and irrational accident. Perhaps I am saying that for all the similarities between them as keenly observant novelists of manners, Wharton as an American has a vision of life somehow inaccessible to Wilson. Providential rescue from seemingly inescapable dangers, like those besetting Oliver Twist, belong to the tradition of the Victorian novel with which Ethel Wilson's fiction seems to me continuous. Though Wilson creates for her readers (and for an American reader especially) a magnificently highlighted Canadian landscape, her vision of life seems as unconditioned by this landscape as her famous travellers who retain in the new world an "innocence" they acquired in the old—whose innocence consists precisely in their preservation of English traditions in the new Canadian city of Vancouver where they come to live with family connections intact. In *The Innocent Traveller,* when Sister Annie looks at the vast Canadian country passing elliptically outside the railroad window, she says, "We shall have to try and learn new ways . . . and I for one am quite ready."[8] But almost immediately, as she sees the "same sheep, same cows, same horses as in England," she dispels thoughts of a new life and thinks instead, "I am rather old . . . to be able to assimilate great change" (111). But her daughter Rachel is not too old. Yet though Rachel falls in love with the Canadian landscape, responding mystically, ecstatically, to its "dark endless prairie," she lives in Canada the traditional life of filial responsibility she would have led in England. We all know that the Canadian landscape figures in Wilson's fiction as a constant source of wonder and beauty, giving to her themes of nihilism and faith, isolation and love, randomness and providence a richly symbolic representation through abundant indigenous detail. Moreover, her characters need the space of the Canadian continent, both to effect their escapes from confinement and to discern "the miraculous interweaving of creation—the everlasting web" that engenders their faith in God's boundlessness. Ultimately, however, Wilson uses a uniquely Canadian setting to universalize human experience, to arrive at truths that transcend place or time. To say this is not to diminish her stature as a Canadian writer but to praise her as she praised "great" writers—for being "both regional and universal."[9]

Willa Cather, the American writer with whom Wilson would inevitably be compared, also sought for universal meanings, those expressed in the cycles of nature and the passage of time. But when Cather dealt with time, she focused on change—upon development, maturation, and decline; upon history. She recalled, with nostalgia, a past associated specifically and uniquely with the transformation of America from an inchoate land— "the material out of which countries are made"[10]—into a country. In *A Lost Lady*, a novel to which *Hetty Dorval* bears almost startling formal resemblance, the fate of a beautiful woman melds inseparably with the fate of the American West. Marion Forrester disillusions young Niel Herbert as Hetty Dorval does Frankie Burnaby; but the American woman's betrayal of the ideals of honor with which, Niel (and Cather) believes, a great country was created represents a crisis in history, the passing of an old chivalric order to make way for a new crass society represented by such grasping men as Ivy Peters. When the "lady" of Niel's visionary dream of the West becomes "lost," an entire community dependent upon her civilizing force suffers. Mrs. Forrester understands her cultural role, that she personifies a dream and must purvey grace, beauty, and manners to a crude primitive people living through a time of historical transformation. Even when she is depleted, without money, friends, or honor, Mrs. Forrester tries with her dinner party to bring civilization to the impervious stolid young men of Nebraska. Like Ántonia in *My Ántonia* and Alexandra in *O Pioneers!*, Mrs. Forerester's destiny intertwines with the future of the American West, and as time diminishes her brilliance, it also fades the dream that, Cather believes, imbued the American past with heroism. Hetty's fall from grace carries no such historical connotations. Frankie's changed perceptions of Hetty invite no thoughts about the destiny of Canada. The context of Wilson's drama is a moral world in which chance arranges for the convergence of two lives that momentarily flow together, like the cojoined Fraser and Thompson rivers, and then separate, leaving a young woman to ponder the unfathomable mystery of human relationships. Hetty's amorality remains unattached to historical or even psychological causalities (though we might infer that her fatherless childhood, which she thought also motherless, may have conditioned her to the sense of isolation that becomes merely selfishness). Hetty appears gratuitously in Lytton and later in London as a wanderer who brings disorder because disorder is inherent in life and will make its presence known even when it is hidden behind the face of beauty. Marion Forrester belongs to her particular time and place; and when she suffers displacement, her loss entails the loss of Captain Forrester's heroic dream of the future, of Niel Herbert's romantic dream of the past, and of the pervasively shared American Dream. Even Hetty's end in the novel seems adventitious as she disappears into a country where she is a stranger. But Marion Forrester remains an irrefrangible part of the land in which her husband and her honor lie buried. She survives in Niel's consciousness as "a bright, impersonal memory"[11]—the memory of the glorious "promise" that life extends to youth and to young countries. Hetty Dorval, like Topaz Edgeworth, both sharply defined but atomistic characters, can be forgotten.

In her own wrong way, Hetty seeks freedom and security, the goals of all Wilson's women, incompatible goals perhaps and perhaps not susceptible to clear definition. By freedom, Hetty means a life without "complications," a term immediately familiar to the American reader because it recurs thematically in Ernest Hemingway's famous collection of short stories *In Our Time*. Unlikely as a comparison between Wilson and Hemingway may at first seem, it discloses contours in Wilson's landscape that perhaps the oblique light of an American perspective can best reveal. Both writers were consummate stylists who used style to curb meanings too turbulent to release. Both were masters of understatement: of irony—each creating a discrepancy between tone and meaning; and of elision—each leaving narrative gaps implicit with meanings, often terrible meanings, we must infer. Both sense the tension between natural beauty, which endures, and human vulnerability: "You are walking along through the grass on the cliff top, admiring the pretty view, when—crack crack."[12] Either could have written this sentence (though "pretty" would have had a special ironic intonation in Hemingway), for both have been alerted to the profound insecurity of human beings who may at any moment be surprised by violence. Their unsurpassed fishing scenes dramatize a concern with surfaces and depths, as well as a love of the art of fishing, of nature, and of the possibilities for self-possession in solitude. Like Hetty Dorval, Nick Adams in "Big Two-Hearted River," the greatest of American fishing stories, seeks to escape human "complications," but unlike her, he has already felt the world "crack" beneath him, literally shatter as the bombs of war have exploded. The wounds he suffers end his innocence as a young traveller. A traumatized hero, hurt physically and emotionally, he wants to be alone so that he can be *let* alone and perhaps recover the balance he has lost. He needs to hold himself "steady," like the big trout in the depths of "deep, fast moving water" that resists the current which could sweep him away. Hetty's avoidance of complications is different, an effect of laziness, indulgence, or egoism. She wants to be alone to do as she pleases because she considers herself an island, free from any intrinsic connection with others who share her human state. She desires only sensuous ease, at least superficially; perhaps beneath this desire lies fear of the possibly dangerous currents of life. Like Nick, though for different reasons and to a different degree, she feels the tenuousness of her control over her own destiny. How little it would take to throw her off balance—only some shipboard gossip. "I want security," Hetty says, "I want it badly"; and though Frankie and her mother suspect Hetty of artfulness, they believe that her plea for security is real, that Hetty is truly "frightened" (52). She does not know, of course, all that she has to fear, the war that "life and time" are arranging. After Nick crawls inside his tent, "the good place," he thinks "Nothing could touch him." Eventually, however, inevitably, he will have to enter the swamp and fish in its "tragic" waters. Neither he nor Hetty can remain safe. *Hetty Dorval* ends in uncertainty, the milieu that, I believe, Wilson, like Hemingway, finds as natural to us as rivers, forests, mountains, and sky.

"We have no immunity," Mrs. Severance tells Maggie, saying in effect that life cannot be ordered and that in its disorder, it allows no one to remain secure. Though Wilson's characters travel and run and hide, trying to escape from "Trouble," they can never rest at "the good place." Where is it to be found, her women ask, the place where they can be secure? Is it by the Similkameen River, where Maggie hides from the meanness of her husband only to be threatened by the jealousy of Vera Gunnarsen? Is it at Comox on Vancouver Island, where Lilly remains isolated with the Butlers, or in the Fraser Valley, where she merges into the order of the matron and her well-run hospital? But here, inexplicably, a strand of her former life as a hunted creature reappears, woven fortuitously into the web no one can elude. The Chinaman Yow arrives in the Valley, and once more Lilly is on the run, seeking in the anonymity of Toronto the security now imperilled by this figure from her past. Love and marriage seem to promise security; but the happiest of marriages, like those of the Cuppys in *Love and Salt Water* or the Burnabys in *Hetty Dorval* or the elder Edgeworths in *The Innocent Traveller,* may be terminated abruptly by death. Impersonal forces as well as people threaten any woman's security at any time. So do one's own emotions, especially the welling of loneliness. Even Vicky May Tritt recognizes the danger of "insupportable" insights into one's isolation, insights that threaten the security she tries so carefully to create through the meager "arid" routine she calls her life. Like Lilly, like Hetty, Victoria May wants to be safe. But "at unexpected times" (chosen, one guesses, by chance), she cannot help catching a "frightening" glimpse of "something vast" that is usually "concealed," something always "there"—like "the sorrow of humanity."[13] To protect herself against the pain of "revelation," Vicky May "averts her gaze" and waits until what she cannot bear to see is once more concealed. But she cannot deny this revelation of human sorrow, and neither can Wilson's fiction, though it persuades us also to avert our gaze from the suffering it reveals. Like Wilson's women, we want security and see it jeopardized by life's hidden mines. How can we avoid them—the destructive emotions of others, jealousy, meanness, the will to oppressive power, and the accidents of chance?

What little protection we have comes, it seems, from an innate human impulse towards order; and when we share the order we create, we perform the beautiful act of charity. It occurs almost always in Wilson's fiction in a clean well-lighted room, to use one of Hemingway's famous phrases. Again and again, Wilson shows that we may find safety in an interior made comfortable by human hands, though when this safety remains unshared, it seems pathetic if not simply ludicrous. Vicky May's room, illuminated by one small naked bulb, is not a well-lighted place, but when Vicky is there, reading her old newspapers or her movie magazines and munching on her apple, she feels "safe": "Here in her room she was at home and secure."[14] In her diminished way, she has found the good place for which all the homeless, alienated characters of American fiction yearn. Perhaps because I have so often identified myself with these homeless insecure Americans, I particularly appreciate the recurrent image in Wilson of a small protected world that human hands create. If a "room lit by a candle and in a silent and solitary place is a world within itself,"[15] it is one that the human being makes and offers as a refuge to other members of our oddly assorted chaotic human family. When Vera, near death, enters Maggie's room, Maggie thinks that warmth, not words, should communicate between these two estranged women: "it seemed to her the least important thing that she should speak and make words, and the most important thing that a fire should burn and warm the cabin and then there would be, somehow, a humanity in the room" (147). Maggie warms Vera as she has warmed Mr. Cunningham, rescued by her hands from death. She instructs Angus "to start the fires everywhere" when they return to open up the camp. She understands that a clean well-lighted place offers us the only security we can expect in a vast impersonal complicated landscape that could overwhelm us with its immensity as well as its indifferent beauty, its inevitable darkness, its dark waters, its fog. Earlier, alone in a cabin, she had retrieved her own life. At Chilliwack, Maggie repossessed herself in a room that she had first to hold private and inviolate so that later she could share it with others who come to it ravaged by the sea and by life. "The cabin was a safe small world enclosing her"—this image of security is appealingly regressive. It takes Maggie back to a former and authentic identity; to a place still untouched by time; to a primitivism that historical change will challenge and in time destroy; to elemental needs, like the human need for warmth, touch, food. Maggie cooks, and Lilly cleans; and both women, by responding to elemental needs, create order in a world that can fall quickly into chaos. "It seemed as if order flowed from her fingertips," Mr. Sprockett thinks, watching Lilly straighten out his hotel room.[16] Intuitively, he feels she will bring order into his life, disrupted and left in confusion by his wife's death. Making Mr. Sprockett comfortable becomes Lilly's equation of love as she earns her right to respectability and marriage through years of self-discipline spent in creating a clean well-lighted place for others. If the world were not intrinsically chaotic, asks the American reader, why would we delight so in women who bring order? If it were not so menacing, so full of imminent "Trouble," why would we seek refuge in a solitary warm room; why would women who can bring order into others' lives be on the run, seeking for themselves a security that has been denied? If the world were not indifferent to our needs, why would we turn again and again to another for comfort and compassion, so highly valued in Wilson's fictional world?

As an American reader who is also a woman, I respond ambivalently to Maggie cooking at camp and Lilly making Mr. Sprockett comfortable, though I celebrate their ability to care for others. I like the desire of Wilson's women for self-possession, and I am not always pleased at their acquiescence to a servant's role, no matter how much I admire the order they bring into others' lives and, by this means, into their own. Guiltily, I enjoy Myrtle's merciless domination of her employer; but at the same time I am annoyed at simpering weak Mrs. H. X. Lemoyne who "was terrified by Myrtle's eyelids, and could be disciplined any minute that Myrtle chose."[17] What an invention—those formidable drooping domineering eyelids and those outlandish soap-opera instantaneous lies! Wilson makes me laugh, and for the sheer pleasure of laughter I am grateful. Laughter may also instruct us, and Wilson's funny satiric treatment of Myrtle sets into perspective for me the serious impelling need almost all her women have for freedom. Myrtle does not want anyone to dominate her—but neither do other characters. Ellen Cuppy initially refuses George Gordon's proposal of marriage in *Love and Salt Water* because she did not "want to be controlled by him or by anybody" (108). As soon as he proposes, freedom becomes essential to her, and marriage seems, mistakenly as it turns out (or so we imagine), "a prison far away with a stranger." Mrs. Emblem, though "formed for" male companionship, resists another marriage, having discovered that one of "the joys of privacy" is that "she now owns herself." For a hundred years, Topaz Edgeworth has remained irrepressibly herself. Oddly, of all the characters in *The Innocent Traveller*, only she sees Canada as offering its immigrants freedom. She suggests a quintessentially American theme—that of a new life in a new land. "This is a free country, isn't it," Topaz asks insistently, as she crosses the prairies on her way to Vancouver; "We've come to a free country, haven't we?" (109). But Topaz's idea of freedom (she is here defending her right to enter the gentlemen's smoking car) is comically skewed. For freedom means to Topaz being her idiosyncratic self—obsessively loquacious, basically idle though busy, dependent upon others and yet detached—a likeable and occasionally admirable woman who might fill one with dread at the ultimate inconsequentiality of a human life. Having always been treated lovingly, Topaz responds to life with a continuous interest which effects nothing. On a few crucial occasions, she shows generosity of spirit and exquisite manners—when she defends Mrs. Coffin in danger of being blackballed, and earlier, when she withdraws from Mr. Sandbach's dinner party. I like her best when she curses Mr. Sandbach aloud in her bedroom, but that may reveal my secret wish for release from gentility rather than the novel's moral high point. If Topaz remains a free spirit through the Family's financial and moral support, other characters like Maggie Lloyd and Lilly struggle towards freedom through the murky circumstances of desertion, betrayal, jealousy, moral meanness, isolation. Both undergo a "rebirth" in which they act as their own midwives. In her cabin in Chilliwack, Maggie

Vardoe is reborn as Maggie Lloyd. In the beauty shop of Miss Larue, Lilly Waller becomes immutably Mrs. Walter Hughes, an identity which permits her a new life as Lily [sic] Sprockett. Wilson tells us that fitting Lilly with a wig and advising her on wardrobe, "Miss Larue, on a fine creative spree, was assisting at the rebirth of a free woman, Mrs. Walter Hughes." "But will it change me?" Lilly thinks, "Shall I be safe?" (255). Perhaps she can never be safe, but she has become free of feckless Lilly Waller.

Wilson's free characters are also fugitive, running like their American relatives to a territory ahead where they can elude repressive men like Edward Vardoe, Huw Peake, or Yow. They need the space of the Canadian landscape to effect their escape. But while Wilson's sense of spaciousness suggests to me the American theme of freedom (for space and freedom are often synonymous in American fiction),[18] her manner seems alien to American writers, insofar as we differentiate them from the British. Occasionally, Wilson reminds me sharply, and with pleasure, of Virginia Woolf, whose consummate novel *To the Lighthouse* she recalls to me with a work that apparently I like much more than her Canadian critics. In *Love and Salt Water*, Wilson shows the passage of time through elision, as Woolf does in the central section of her famous novel. Like Woolf, Wilson evokes the menace of the sea and the world of nature that makes the warm safety of home essential to the human community. She too describes how the fulfillment of a child's wish—to see the seals, to go to the lighthouse—brings unanticipated realizations and unanticipated terrors. Also like Woolf, Wilson mentions the death of her character in one quick sentence; then she moves on to the business of life. In *Love and Salt Water*, Ellen learns to let her sister Nora *be*—and letting others be (as Maggie Vardoe thinks, her husband "would never have let me be") emerges as the essential equation of love that Woolf had worked out in *Mrs. Dalloway*.[19]

As I read Wilson, I enjoy her evocation of English literature, her command, her deftness, certainty, and lightness of tone, her confidence in the quixotic phrase, the wry aside, the moralizing moment. Her work has both the fastidiousness and the insouciance that belong to one who possesses a native tongue as her birthright. But I miss the struggle contained within American writers like Theodore Dreiser, Sherwood Anderson, or Gertrude Stein. Bereft of a language of their own, they laboriously invent a style that turns out polyglot, awkward, cacophonous, colloquial, confused, but also powerful; a style that confronts, without possibility of easy evasion, the profoundly difficult and unanswerable questions of life. I find Wilson's use of John Donne as a kind of last resort for coping with ultimate problems uncomfortably facile. I brood with Dreiser, whose work is impressed indelibly upon my American imagination, over the possibility that man or woman *is* an island, a person essentially alone and adrift in life, like Hurstwood or Carrie in Dreiser's ponderous and imponderable novel *Sister Carrie*. Perhaps, as Dreiser shows, we are creatures driven by chemic compulsions that nullify our pretensions to personal freedom. In Dreiser, great economic forces, as well as hormones, determine not only an individual's fate but also the evolutionary direction of a vast society. When Wilson described the growth of Vancouver, she made it seem, by her simple cartoonish description, almost comic: "Down came the forests. Chop. Chop. Chop. . . . The forests vanished, and up went the city."[20] Wilson does note that "men of the chain-gang" were doing the chopping, but she quickly disposes of their plight and of the implications of power and powerlessness, and of tremendous historical transformations that effected radical social reorderings—of the entire drama of growth, industrialization, urbanization, and their consequences. She sounds merely three words now rather terrible for modern ears attuned to cries of ecological depletion and economic greed: "Chop. Chop. Chop." Because Dreiser could not be fluent, lacking a literary language and tradition as an American writer, because he could not reach into a bag of past poets and pick out a consummate line that would epitomize a world view—"no man is an island"—because he had to struggle in his life and in his work, he became enmeshed in the endless web about which he wrote, a web woven by desire, irrational chance, coincidence, natural forces, evolutionary drives, social designs. He cared about his characters in ways that could not allow him to be detached or superior. Never could I imagine Dreiser describing a woman or man as Wilson describes Victoria May: "Insipid," "unimportant," "anonymous," "stupid." Wilson is "cool," Dreiser heatedly compassionate and committed to his characters.

Though obviously unlike Dreiser, Willa Cather shared Dreiser's absorbing interest in characters, no matter how humble. In *One of Ours*, half-witted illiterate Mahailey emerges as loving and lovable, worthy of the esteem given her by the family she faithfully serves. None of Cather's women is "insipid." Each is potentially a creator of life, is herself alive, and finds life interesting. A minor character in *Sapphira and the Slave Girl* epitomizes this interest: "Mrs. Ringer was born interested." Though Mrs. Ringer is poor, unendowed, alone, "misfortune and drudgery had never broken her spirit. . . . She had probably never spent a dull day." If her days were never dull for Topaz, they seem so to us; but all the days of Cather's women belong within a large significant pattern in which, whatever they do, they sense themselves a creative part. Nell Severance would have been quelled by them, I think, for they could have articulated fully and precisely the faith she asserted in vague incomplete terms. Even when they lived in Canada, like Cécile Auclair in *Shadows on the Rock*, they sensed themselves part of a process that was creating out of individual and inchoate efforts a whole way of life, creating by preserving and by making anew, by continuing and beginning again, as Cécile continues the French traditions her mother transmitted to her and makes them pristine and permanent by transferring them to Quebec. Unlike Wilson's women, Cather's seldom seek security; rather, they provide it as they make a home and a great nation. A hidden mine that Cather describes explodes with life, as we know from the famous image in *My Ántonia* of children bursting out of a subterranean storehouse— "a veritable explosion of life out of the dark cave into the sunlight" (339).

Perhaps I am saying that in American novels the sense of the new—of a new land, new pulsating cities like Chicago, pristine prairies of color-drenched grass, new railroads, new openings, new beginnings—stirs us deeply because we are also concerned with a new American language and a new style. We must create a style that expresses our perennial sense of discovery, dream, and disillusionment. Dreiser could not rely upon what was said before because the city he describes had not existed before, and even as he wrote, he saw it grow, develop, and change. He was driven by the historical urgency of capturing a kaleidoscopic scene that would not stay still long enough to be memorialized. Wilson feels neither this urgency—the typical sense of rush that

Americans experience as their daily lives—nor Cather's nostalgia over what has been and will be no more. Her anecdotal ease in dealing with the past in *The Innocent Traveller* seems inaccessible to American writers, who invariably regret and long for a past that has disappeared. Think of Cather's *A Lost Lady* or F. Scott Fitzgerald's quintessentially American novel *The Great Gatsby*. Not without reason, our most popular book is entitled *Gone With the Wind*, and the greatest Southern writer, William Faulkner, shares with the most widely read, Margaret Mitchell, a passion for the past to which American readers resonate as they typically feel loss and separation as their real experience. In Vancouver, Wilson's characters find continuity: as Annie noted, correctly or not, "the same sheep, same cows, same horses as in England." Beyond the city, in mountains, lake areas, woods, Wilson's characters can recapture their own past, or at least exorcise a present they find oppressive; in unchanged places (of which we have few in America), they can retrieve a pattern of peace they once knew. They cannot "escape" from life, as Nell Severance tells Maggie in *Swamp Angel*, but they can recover—recapture the past and recuperate from the present. Nick Adams knows that a wounded American can hope only for a temporary stay against chaos before he fishes in "tragic" waters that Maggie may not have to enter. Maggie will not escape Vera Gunnarsen's jealousy, but Nick will never escape himself. Nor will he find refuge with others, even temporary or turbulent refuge, as Lilly found with the Butlers, and Maggie with the Gunnarsens. Like Wilson, Hemingway turned to Donne for a definition of human relatedness, for directions on how to deny his own bleak vision of life, one which I believe he found, finally, both inviolate and intolerable. Much as he wishes to deny it, he saw that man was an island—separate, alone, adrift. In *For Whom the Bell Tolls*, Hemingway's hero tries to link himself with others in a concerted effort to make shared ideals prevail, but the occasion of his union is war, and the outcome is death. Robert Jordan dies alone, merging himself in lyrical rapture and in terror with the earth. Hemingway's vision of life is ecclesiastical: it contains the vanity of human wishes—even the wish for love, marriage, family—and the eternality of the earth upon which, with an order denied to chaotic human affairs, the sun rises. As a reader of American fiction I feel buoyed by Wilson's way of tucking war, chaos, and violence into the parenthetical asides of her novels; but unlike Maggie, when she thinks she can swim about obstacles, I feel insecure on surfaces, accustomed as I am to the inevitability of depths. Even while I delight in reading of a happy but thoroughly inconsequential life, like that of Topaz Edgeworth, I cannot help remembering other characters to whom nothing happened. I remember Marcher in Henry James's "The Beast in the Jungle," and then I feel my pleasure adulterated as I consider the life of a woman to whom nothing happened—though everything in the world was happening—and who made nothing happen, who in effect was powerless. Powerlessness, fear of isolation, alertness to violence and acts of violation, the vagaries of chance and indifferent if not malign forces, as well as the urgencies of economic and social inequality which must lead to conflict—so I learn from *The Grapes of Wrath*—how could I not be conditioned by all this which I encounter again and again in American fiction? Abundant as it is, American fiction is deeply mined with skepticism and uncertainty. Its landscape is vast, beautiful, and bleak. I have travelled in it for many years, and to deny its influences, to say I am still innocent and can enjoy without wryness the surface skimming of a waterglider or even the complex skill of a juggler (juggling a weapon of destructive power) would be to deny the power of literature.

Wilson celebrates this power by consciously drawing attention to the creative act of storytelling. Her characters tell stories—are unabashed liars; and sometimes by withholding their stories, they assert their autonomy, their possibility of eluding facts and consequences by refusing to acknowledge that they exist. In *Love and Salt Water,* Ellen Cuppy tries to keep her mother alive by not telling that she had died, and her sister Nora tries to keep her son whole by not telling that his hearing is impaired. Frankie collaborates in the fiction Hetty Dorval creates by not telling what she knows about Hetty; and Hetty herself remains somehow inviolable because she has not told the truth about herself, by this withholding making herself inaccessible even to Frankie in whose consciousness she lives. Frankie knows she is inventing the story of Hetty Dorval; this act frees her of Hetty's influence and at the same time, since stories last, makes the influence of Hetty's distinctive beauty and power permanent. Through the art of storytelling, Frankie both dispels the trance in which Hetty has placed her and captures it for all time; and she becomes a force powerful enough to cause an explosion in which another story, Mrs. Broom's version of the past, will be released from the depths of silence in which it lies buried. Frankie makes Mrs. Broom tell the story she has withheld, and we cannot minimize the power she exercises in forcing, without forethought, another's confession. In "Tuesday and Wednesday," characters make up stories all the time. Mort and Myrtle lie unconscionably, and by their lies, they subdue others, sometimes each other, and so exercise their wills. The stories that give them momentary victories cannot save them, however, from the fate that coincidence has laid in store; but rescue does come from a most unlikely source, from the story of heroism that reticent, neurotic Victoria May Tritt invents. By telling her story, Vicky frees herself, if only for the moment, from the prison of shyness, insecurity, silence, and a sense of worthlessness; from the inconsequentiality of her life; from powerlessness. She effects a change in how Mort will be remembered, in how Myrtle will feel, and in how an inexplicable accident will evermore be described. She changes her own behavior, her very identity from a silent and withdrawn woman to a purposeful, active storyteller, the focus of rapt attention. In *The Equations of Love*, Lilly's lies become the truths of her life, the means by which she can possess herself and give a happy useful identity to her daughter. Through her own fictions, she learns how to serve others, and though she seeks isolation, she belongs to a community that includes the matron, the hospital, and finally the wide world where she may, perhaps, live as a free woman with the man to whom she brings comfort.

This confusion of lies with truth celebrates the storyteller's power to convince us of the reality of fiction; it also dramatizes the mysterousness of life whose essence we cannot know with certainty. As Wilson's stories show, we cannot know each other because we present, in everyday life, social faces that conceal a real identity shown only to a friend or lover. Though Mrs. Forrester smiles and talks and entertains in the story "Truth and Mrs. Forrester," her reality exists thousands of miles away from the room where people come and go and where all her familiar things are placed—thousands of miles away where her husband lies ill, possibly dying. The "true Mrs. Forrester" is the loving wife, not the charming hostess who lies out of politeness and boredom or the helpless employer "in thrall" to her garrulous maid. "Truth is so hard to tell," says Mrs. Forrester, "while fiction is the easiest thing in the world."[21] Certainly, Ethel Wilson makes fiction seem easy, though the truth of her women is hard to define—whether they are utterly traditional creatures finding happiness only in caring for others, cleaning, cooking, creating comfort, yielding compassion. Is Family their essential need, and marriage, though initially avoided (as by Ellen Cuppy and Hilda Severance), their ultimate fulfillment? Is Mrs. Emblem, in "Tuesday and Wednesday," with her pink boudoir and her pink complexion and golden hair and her three husbands, truly an emblematic Woman as the story insists? "Vicky Tritt does not know what it feels like to be a woman," the story tells: "Mrs. Emblem knows nothing else" (56). "Truth is so hard to tell," Ethel Wilson might answer, and she enacts the difficulty in her equivocal style. She shows us complexities, gains and losses within a single situation, and generosity and withholding within a single person: "I knew I was in the web," Mrs. Severance says, explaining her desertion of her daughter; "I did the best I could in the web, and it takes God Himself to be fair to two different people at once" (151). One must juggle one's responsibilities, as Mrs. Severance, a skilled juggler, knows; and one must distinguish between the symbol and the essence, deciding finally for the essence, though one has become attached to the symbol as though its glitter were real. Perhaps the truth is that, like Wilson's characters, we are all storytellers. When we tell our own story, we come into possession not of objective truth but of a reality we imagine, that of the person we would wish to become, like Mrs. Walter Hughes, or to retrieve, like Mrs. Maggie Lloyd. Perhaps our own power of invention is the truth about us, and those who possess this power strongly imagine a person into being, becoming in fact their own fiction, as Lilly becomes Mrs. Walter Hughes. Naming one's self represents a quest for one's own truth. Topaz Edgeworth never changes her name in her hundred years of life, and her reality as a person becomes evanescent, forgettable—except in the story that Wilson tells. Lilly changes her name several times, and in the end accepts the name of a stranger in order to become the self whom she has imagined into being. Kind as he is, her future husband takes possession by reiterating the name he will impose—"LilySprockettLilianSprockettLilySprockettLilianSprockett." The name delights him, and with it he makes Lilly a character in the story of his life. "Would you mind me calling you Lilian?" he asks, and Lilly, either entirely secure now in her achieved identity or else willing to relinquish it for another that promises love, does not mind losing a name that gave her "self-possession." Is Wilson mocking Lilly when she has her confess her secret at the end of her story—that she wears an "adaptation"—or is she rejoicing in the erasure of Lilly's past, once so full of "Trouble"? The truth is hard to tell, though the fiction, "Lilly's Story," is easy to read. "Perhaps" or "perhaps not," "I think," "it was impossible to say," the omniscient narrator says again and again in Wilson's fiction, implying that even the all-knowing storyteller does not know the truth. Sometimes we as readers have a choice, because the narrator, uncertain of the truth, offers two exclusive possibilities, two adjectives or nouns linked together by *and* though they require *or*. Perhaps we need faith because we cannot know the truth. This, at least, is what I think when I read Wilson's fiction, but of course I cannot be sure. Her fiction makes me certain and uncertain.

Of her descriptive powers I have no doubt. Her effulgent images of the Northern Lights, of the perfect V of flying wild geese, of indigenous creatures, changing landscapes, sky and space, are famous. Her short short story "Hurry, hurry," to which I referred at the beginning, is charged with natural scenery which seems to me translucent. Mountains, trees, slanting rays of light, fog, birds, dog, hawk, heron, bushes, blackbirds, steep grassy dyke—all take on a brilliant and unforgettable urgency, a cosmic meaning whose truth might be so terrible that it eludes us as the image of the "hunched" hawk gives way to that of the "humped" corpse of a woman. Human life and animal life seem internecine. The hawk "with its sharp beak and tearing claws . . . would have mauled the terriers, and they would have tormented it." The hawk stares brightly, and so does man the murderer, compelling the woman to hurry away as "he held her eyes with his eyes." She escapes, running. The murderer shows her mercy, or perhaps only indifference. The woman he has killed lies "beside the salt-water ditch." His tears must be salty as he stumbles along "sobbing, crying out loud." Does he cry in regret or for love lost? Are love and salt water inseparable in Wilson's world? If some lucky ones escape the salt water, if they are rescued from drowning, is it at the sacrifice of others, like the drowned boy in *Love and Salt Water* or the murdered woman in "Hurry, hurry," characters linked with the living in Wilson's great web of life? Meanwhile, the light falls obliquely on the mountains. Each tree stands out separately. We see each clearly. We see each fade. "The light is gone"—the story is over—"but those who have seen it will remember." The memory of Ethel Wilson's stories lies deeply buried in our consciousness, our imagination. It is a hidden mine that we might at any moment of recall explode with terror and delight.

Gone With The Wind and

The Impossibilities of Fiction

Margaret Mitchell

ON MARGARET MITCHELL

Writing about the impossibilities of fiction I was, ironically, finding it impossible to bring the essay on Gone With The Wind *to an end. I thought I understood why it was begun: to show that covertly* Gone With The Wind *was a text about the American thirties—about dispossession and loss, homelessness, hunger, the collapse of a society and its miraculous recovery. The restoration of Tara, though never to its former glory, promised a future to millions of readers in despair over a disheveled present. Somehow this theme became muted in the moiling essay, which like the novel itself, grew out of bounds. I felt I was dealing with a fabulous work, though I had only a popular romance. My mind, as I wrote, was divided, beset by doubts that a best seller warranted serious analysis. Literary value could not be gauged by popularity, no matter how massive and lasting, I had been told. Nevertheless, the novel seemed a repository of important literary secrets, among them, a relationship involving women, the theme of survival, and popularity. Today, critics are discovering that Scarlett O'Hara is a heroine of great independence—an exemplary survivor. At the same time, undeniably, she is a dependent creature, always running to the same man for help. Her double nature—both as a divided character and as a duplicitous woman—makes her elusive and unexpectedly modern and complex. For this reason and others,* Gone With The Wind *is now receiving considerable critical attention. A collection of essays on the novel and film has recently appeared; two more collections are in print; and a new biography of Margaret Mitchell presents the legendary as well as the mundane aspects of her life. Such serious critical discussion of* Gone With The Wind *may continue, for a consideration of what appeals to the public, and why, seems difficult and undesirable to bring to an end.*

E ver since its publication on June 30, 1936, critics have tried to uncover the secret of *Gone With The Wind*'s inexhaustible popularity, the appeal of a novel loved by millions of readers throughout the world. To this day the reasons for this appeal remain a mystery, even a matter of wonder; for *Gone With The Wind* has become a legend in publishing annals—the best-selling American novel of all time.* Attempts to explain its extraordinary sales—sometimes 50,000 copies in a single day—have simply been inadequate to the immediacy, power, and universality of its appeal. We cannot accept the argument that *Gone With The Wind* attracted bargain-hunting women who found a three-dollar book cheaper than library copies lending at five-cents a day; or that it capitalized upon a war close to American hearts, since other Civil War novels—*Marching On, So Red the Rose, Bugles Blow No More, The Fathers*—never approached its sales; or that it mindlessly reinforced a magnolia-and-honeysuckle plantation myth, when in fact it exposed Southern men as feckless, and Southern belles *as hard, resistant,* and *tough* (the author's words); or that it reduced American history to a simplistic story, a view refuted by the experience of the novel; or that it renewed old-fashioned melodrama, which would hardly explain its tenacity as a modern best seller; or that it was so atrociously bad that people loved it, public taste being execrable.

Margaret Mitchell, the diminutive author of this giant book, found herself at first baffled and then distraught by *Gone With The Wind*'s popularity. Like secessionist Atlanta, she was placed under seige, her personal life ravaged by invaders she could not repel, strangers who telephoned incessantly, sent her bizarre letters, involved her in crank lawsuits, autographed her novel in bookstores, stole its title for a striptease act. In August 1936, Mitchell could still write calmly about her success to Harold Latham, the man responsible for it: "How did you know six months ago that 'Gone With The Wind' would be a success? . . . I do not see how you anticipated the enormous sales which have been so unexpected and bewildering to me." By October, her questions to Herschel Brickell, the *New York Post* reviewer, were almost comic in their incomprehension:

*In hardback. As a bestselling paperback it was superseded by *The Godfather.*

Herschel, sometimes, when I have a minute I ponder soberly upon this book. And . . . I can not figure what makes the thing sell so enormously. . . .

There's no fine writing . . . no grandiose thought . . . no hidden meanings, no symbolism, nothing sensational. . . . Then how to explain its appeal from the five year old to the ninety five year old? . . .

Reviews and articles come out commending me on having written such a "powerful document against war" . . . Lord! I think. I never intended that! Reviews speak of the symbolism of the characters . . . Lord! I never intended that either. Psychiatrists speak of the "carefully done emotional patterns" . . . Good Heavens! Can this be I? People talk and write of the "high moral lesson." I don't see anything very moral in it. I murmur feebly that "it's just a story" . . . just a simple story of some people who went up and some who went down, those who could take it and those who couldn't.

The novel began to make history even before publication when its advance sales broke all records at Macmillan. Within a month they had printed 200,000 copies; within two months, they were selling 6,000 copies a day; within six months, 1,000,000 copies were gone with the wind. In August 1936, two printing presses worked continuously around the clock in three eight-hour shifts, while two binderies fastened sheets day and night. Macy's filled its famous display window with staggering columns of the book; and Macmillan converted its sales figures into astounding graphic images. *Gone With The Wind* would tower above Manhattan, rising to fifty times the height of the Empire State Building if all the books sold were stacked back to back; and if laid end to end, they would wind about the equator almost three times, as though to show how, by a universal popularity, *Gone With The Wind* embraced the world. By 1940, twenty-four countries, aside from England and Canada, had printed their own editions, countries as diverse and far-flung as China, Latvia, and Chile, as Norway and Cuba. During the war, totalitarian nations recognized *Gone With The Wind's* popularity by such strict censorship that the penalty for its possession, according to an American journalist, was death. Nazis and communists officially condemned it because its individualistic ideals, its expression of one's love for home, subverted loyalty to the state. Ironically, radical leftists in America also found it subversive, contrary to democratic ideals because its characters were stereotypes rather than individuals, and its attitudes racist. These political heresies apparently eluded millions of readers throughout the world who read *Gone With The Wind* for entertainment, confirming Mitchell's view that it was just "a simple story," a clean story shunning sex and "degeneracy" and extolling the old-fashioned Victorian virtue of *gumption.*

Mitchell's statements about the simplicity of *Gone With The Wind* invite us to overlook the complex involutions within it that critics have regularly overlooked, as though the mystery of why or how a novel entertains us were entirely solved. If we try to explore the mystery—and no novel suits this purpose better than *Gone With The Wind*—we discover, ultimately, an impossible union of opposites. Our pleasure at this reconciliation, which fulfills fantasies of omnipotence and total gratification, may explain a secret of the novel's appeal—of this novel in particular and of novels generally. Secrets are *Gone With The Wind's* explicit concern—hinted at, withheld, hunted, and exposed. The story begins with the Tarleton twins telling Scarlett their secret, and ends with Rhett telling her his, that he has always loved her. Love is a mystery that Scarlett has skirted but never solved, one of many mysteries in the novel, all of them sexual, and all hidden behind the novel's *closed doors,* a detail of setting which appears so recurrently that it becomes an obsessive symbol, autonomous and dreamlike rather than incidental. Reality in the novel is frequently transmuted into dream or so confused with it that finally Scarlett asks, "Was she dreaming again or was this her dream come true?" Her sleeping dream—the nightmare of a child who is lost in the fog—seems impossible to reconcile with her heroic accomplishments. But the reconciling of irreconcilable desires is, I believe, the ultimate secret of *Gone With The Wind*—a secret it shares with great fiction, which accomplishes this same end in muted and much more difficult ways. *Gone With The Wind* fulfills the reader's irreconcilable desires openly, again and again, in a manner that makes gratification immediately accessible. For this reason it remains our most popular novel. It may also prove one of our most complex—crude, undoubtedly, and styled by clichés, but nonetheless intricate and relevant to our understanding of the mysterious motives of fiction.

Of course, every reader can find in *Gone With The Wind* a simple but compelling story of survival. When it first appeared,

Americans could enjoy its immediacy and distance, seemingly incompatible qualities. Dealing with social collapse, the novel immersed contemporary readers in poverty, struggle, dispossession, and loss, problems immediate to the thirties but displaced to a historical past in which they had already been resolved. *Gone With The Wind* showed that survival depended upon *gumption,* the novel's homely word for courage, a word that evokes childishness and difficulty as it makes us gulp—as though we were swallowing a sticky gumdrop. Strained swallowing, however, is better than choking, as an old survivor, Grandma Fontaine, tells Scarlett at her father's funeral. Facing the loss of her father— "one of the last links . . . to the old days of happiness"—Scarlett needs the strength to swallow a grief that would choke her if she weakens. Others have weakened—Cathy Calvert for example, once a Southern belle like Scarlett, and now "white-trash." Grandma Fontaine attributes the difference between survival and defeat to *gumption,* courage that enables "flattened out" people "to rise up again." Having suffered and survived the South's turbulent history from early Indian raids to the present war Grandma Fontaine speaks with authority, and as another survivor, Scarlett confirms her message. Looking at what has become of Cathy, she states the novel's "moral": "There but for a lot of gumption am I."

Survival seems a clear unequivocal theme in *Gone With The Wind,* until we move into the murky circumstances surrounding Scarlett's survival. Then we stumble upon a dark mysterious figure inevitably there. Whenever Scarlett's gumption fails, when she needs money, rescue, consolation, or challenge, one of the novel's closed doors opens and Rhett Butler appears. Only Rhett, a man she "hated," can save her from "doom," Scarlett thinks, as Atlanta falls to the enemy. The Yankees are coming; rebel defenders have set the city aflame and are fleeing; it is "the end of the world." Now that the excruciating ordeal of helping Melanie through childbirth is over, Scarlett's self-control collapses. Fear overwhelms her, turns her into a hysterical child who wants "to bury her head in her mother's lap. . . . If only she were home! Home with mother!" She summons Rhett Butler, who appears magically to lead her through the burning city and the dangerous countryside until she can go on safely alone. As always, Rhett supports her when she is helpless, but encourages her to be strong—so that her victories in the novel involve an interesting combination of dependence and self-reliance.

When Scarlett arrives at Tara, she is a survivor (though she left as a child), and she makes an appropriate if unexpected literary allusion to shipwreck. "Tara might have been Crusoe's island," she thinks, "so still it was, so isolated." Unlike Crusoe's lush island, however, Tara is a ruin that reinforces in Scarlett the sense of helplessness that had her crying for her mother on the long journey home. "Mother! Mother!", she called, wanting "the kind arms of Tara and Ellen." Like the red soil of Tara, Ellen Robillard O'Hara, the novel's *great lady,* provides Scarlett with an unfailing source of comfort. Indeed, mother and earth were intertwined in many early images of the novel, so that Scarlett's desire for Tara becomes almost naturally both double and indivisible: "I will go home!" she cries, "I will! I will! . . . I want my mother!" Will overrides common sense and Rhett's objections because it is impelled by fantasy as well as realistic fear. Returning home means being in Ellen's arms again, resting her head on Ellen's breast, telling her mother, "I'm always your little girl." This is a perennial appeal for which a child longs; and *Gone With The Wind,* like *Robinson Crusoe,* appeals to the child who survives in us all.

Unconsciously, Mitchell may have been suggesting this appeal when she described her novel as a "simple story of some people who went up and some who went down." Children would respond readily to such a nice clear-cut movement (like that of a seesaw), but mature readers might suspect that this simplicity is superficial; they already know that beneath its simplicity, *Robinson Crusoe* is complex. So, I believe, is *Gone With The Wind,* which appeals to us on several different and contradictory levels, gratifying our wish for fact with American history; for moral improvement, with examples of personal courage; and for escape from reality and moral constraint, with fantasy. The fantasy underlying *Gone With The Wind* can be traced back to early feelings of helplessness and omnipotence, strong but irreconcilable feelings which every child experiences and later usually forgets—or, more precisely, remembers in the most disguised ways. *Gone With The Wind* revives these childhood emotions, once so intense and dangerous, and makes them safe to recall; not only safe but deeply pleasurable because we can suspend judgment of our self while we indulge in fantasies that belong to another, to a helpless but yet omnipotent woman who is reliving for us the child's divisive drama of growing up within a family.

Throughout the novel Scarlett O'Hara maintains an inviolate sense of family, manipulating others to maintain herself as either the child of the family or the mother. Her childishness is reflected in her dependence, a continual reliance upon Ellen, Mammy, Melanie, Will Benteen, Archie, and of course, Rhett: "How wonderful to be a man and as strong as Rhett, she thought. . . . With Rhett beside her, she did not fear anything." At the same time, she knows men would be wise to fear her power, for she can make them do whatever she wants: make Charles Hamilton and Frank Kennedy, both promised to others, marry her; make Ashley Wilkes betray Melanie by declaring his love, and make Rhett Butler lose his proud imperturbability. She can manipulate men, but her real adversary is hunger, and to fight this grim and implacable foe, she needs the magical power of metamorphosis, a power that belongs to women in fairy tales. Only by changing herself—from a helpless little girl, or a flirtatious Southern belle, or a hapless victim of war—can she survive the vicissitudes of change that have swept away her security and broken her family. Scarlett transforms herself constantly, playing the different and conflicting parts which allow her to care for her ruined father and her sisters, Careen and Suellen, for Ashley's family as for her own, for Mammy, Pork, Dilcey, and Prissy, for Aunt Pittypat and all her aunts in Charlestown who would starve to death discreetly without her help. Like Robinson Crusoe, she is essentially alone, for at Tara she finds her mother dead, her sisters sick, and her father "a little old man and broken." Out of necessity—her own and her family's—Scarlett becomes simultaneously a child and mother at Tara: like little Beau who nurses at Dilcey's breast, she lays her tired head on the "broad, sagging breasts" of her Mammy; but she cannot rest there. With Ellen gone, Tara needs a strong woman, and on the night of her return, without hesitation, Scarlett takes up the maternal duties she will keep for the rest of the novel. "Now you're going to take another drink and then I'm going to take you upstairs and put you to bed," she tells her father, talking to him as Ellen might, as though he were a child. In this way, she enters into an involuted relationship prepared for her by her

parents when Ellen Robillard, a girl of fifteen, married Gerald
O'Hara, a man twenty-eight years older than she, old enough,
we are told, "to be her father."

When Scarlett catches the roving eye of Rhett Butler, who is
almost twice her age, she is sixteen (only fourteen when she falls
in love with Ashley Wilkes). Women married young in antebellum Georgia, a historical fact that becomes evocative of fantasy
in the novel—a fantasy of incest and doubling, of forbidden or
impossible relationships. This fantasy revolves around childlike
women, epitomized by Melanie Wilkes (originally intended to be
Gone With The Wind's heroine). Melanie is introduced as "a tiny,
frailly built girl, who gave the appearance of a child masquerad-
ing in her mother's enormous hoop skirts." She remains a frail
girl, her breasts undeveloped, her body unable to deliver a child;
and yet she mothers everyone, taking care of those who ostensibly protect her—Ashley, Scarlett, and Rhett. "She's like mother,"
Scarlett thinks as Melanie lies dying, a convenient time for un-
welcome revelations; "Everyone who knew her has clung to her
skirts." Melanie's death, like Ellen's, unmasks the novel's disguised characters, the paternal husbands who are children to the
child-wives who constantly mother them. In effect, *Gone With
The Wind* relies upon surprise; the delight and terror of children
who like to dress up as adults and who like to see adults un-
dressed. Trouble unmasks characters who cry and run for comfort to mothers and fathers, but parents are also childish, like
blustering, helpless Gerald O'Hara and genteel Ashley Wilkes.
Without Melanie, Ashley lapses into helplessness and is rele-
gated, like Gerald without Ellen, to Scarlett's care. Marriage in
the novel, especially the exemplary marriages of Gerald and
Ellen, and Melanie and Ashley, involves a complicitous relationship between a helpless loving child and an omnipotent parent.
This is the relationship Rhett Butler tries, at times desperately,
to duplicate.

"There, there, darling," Rhett comforts Scarlett: "Don't cry
. . . my brave little girl . . . blow your nose like a good child."
Holding Scarlett in his arms, Rhett emits "comforting" male
smells of "brandy and tobacco and horses" that recall her father.
Rhett soothes Scarlet as she will soon comfort Gerald, so that she
is the child, mother, and lover of two fathers. Like Gerald, Scarlett is "headstrong" and "insensitive" (Rhett's words), and yet so

helpless that, like him, she needs a wise parent. Loving this "brave, frightened, bullheaded child" (Rhett's words again), Rhett gives Scarlett everything she wants, except Ashley. A "stock figure of melodrama"—Mitchell readily admitted—Rhett Butler embodies the novel's fantasy of love as something secret and forbidden and ultimately impossible—though for a while, he achieves an impossible identity as Scarlett's father and lover. Every reader takes comfort when he murmurs paternally, "There, there, darling . . . don't cry"; and every reader responds with erotic pleasure when he drives Ashley out of Scarlett's dream: "By God, this is one night when there are only going to be two in my bed." While Scarlett enacts her sexual fantasies of Ashley by sleeping with Rhett, Rhett enacts his fantasy of Scarlett by sleeping with Bonnie, his little girl. Knowingly, Rhett substitutes a real child for an unattainable daughter, later telling Scarlett, "I liked to think that Bonnie was you, a little girl again . . . and that I could pet her and spoil her—just as I wanted to pet you." When Rhett cradles his frightened daughter in his arms, Scarlett remembers jealously that "Rhett had comforted her in much the same manner he comforted Bonnie." In time, Bonnie actually replaces Scarlett in Rhett's bedroom (while Scarlett locks herself behind closed doors): "Bonnie was removed from the nursery to the room Rhett now occupied alone. Her small bed was placed beside his large one." The novel sees to it that we question the innocence of this shifting of beds, though obviously it reflects a father's concern for his frightened little girl. We know that "the town buzzed when the story got about. Somehow, there was something indelicate about a girl child sleeping in her father's room, even though the girl was only two years old." If we are expected to snicker at the town gossips, we meanwhile share their titillations as we peep through bedroom doors with mixed feelings of approval and prurience.

I am not suggesting that *Gone With The Wind* is simply a disguised story of incest; that would be as reductive a reading as those I have questioned. Nevertheless, I do wish to point out facts made absolutely explicit in the text. Rhett Butler has fallen in love with a child and knows it; Scarlett has rejected her husband as a lover and accepted her father as her son, in this way replacing her mother; while Melanie has mothered her husband, with whom she cannot have sexual relations, and willed him to Scarlett's maternal care: "Look after him, Scarlett [Melanie whispers before she dies]—but—don't ever let him know." This whisper lets Scarlett into the secret of Southern women—a secret that Ellen has kept in pampering Gerald; and it obligates her to replace the mother-figure she has tried to dispossess with "insane obstinacy." This is Rhett's phrase for Scarlett's passion for Ashley, a passion that dies when Melanie dies and Ashley bcomes available. Then Scarlett sees that the man she has loved is a child with whom she will be burdened forever: "As long as I live I'll have to look after him and see that he doesn't starve and that people don't hurt his feelings. He'll be just another child, clinging to my skirts. I've lost my lover and I've got another child."

Scarlett's loss is doubled when Rhett leaves. Now that she loves him, his passion is spent, having died with Bonnie. He says that "when she went, she took everything." For him, *everything* means a little girl who constantly eludes him, first when Scarlett rejects his love, then when Bonnie dies, and again when Scarlett awakens from her nightmare and begins to grow up. As soon as Scarlett understands that in her dream she has always been running "home to Rhett!", he says, "I will not be pursued." Controlling "childish wild tears," she respects his demand for a dignified parting. Her moment of maturity is brief, however, only long enough for her to behave like a woman and lose the lover who desired a child.

These unexpected twists and transformations bring us the pleasure of surprise, a childish pleasure, perhaps, but one never outgrown. At the same time, they fulfill narrative expectations of which we must have been aware, since they bring also a sense of satisfaction, of appropriate resolution to knotty complications in the novel that no single action could completely unravel. Four possible endings succeed each other in the last section of *Gone With The Wind*, each irreconcilable with the other. However, we need not choose among them: we can have them all, since each is validated by a logic of its own and by the logic of impossibility that prevails in the novel to effect a repeated reconciliation of the irreconcilable. First, Melanie's death allows a "happy ending" to the story of Scarlett's love for Ashley. Now they can marry, as Rhett points out, and Scarlett's fairy-tale version of romance—her "childish fancy" of a golden prince—can come true. But we have seen this prince tarnished and the novel's "pirate" enhanced, so that a happy ending to Scarlett's romance would violate our sense of reality be denying Ashley's real weaknesses, Scarlett's mistakes, and Rhett's patience and love. In another possible "happy ending," Scarlett recognizes this love and at last runs willingly to Rhett: "this time she was not running from fear. She was running because Rhett's arms were at the end of the street." In this ending, dream and reality coalesce. Scarlett is still in a dream, still running through a mist, but this time the mist belongs to "Peachtree Street, Atlanta, and not the gray world of sleep and ghosts." Peachtree Hill means home; but if Scarlett is a lost child seeking a home she deserves, she is also a scheming woman, as Rhett reminds us by his amused review of her past—which includes "murder, . . . husband stealing, attempted fornication, lying and sharp dealing and . . . chicanery." Punishment for all this comes when Scarlett arrives home breathlessly to claim a love that Rhett tells her is *gone:* "But, Scarlett, did it ever occur to you that even the most deathless love could wear out?" Though this had not occurred to Scarlett, clearly stunned by the question, it has occurred to readers who wonder how long an astute man like Rhett can pursue a woman who rejects and exploits him. To Scarlett's question "If you go, what shall I do?", Rhett gives the succinct reply that has become famous: "My dear, I don't give a damn." This ending is modern and tough, recognizing that love will judge selfishness and insensitivity, and that time will wear away love. Final rejection of Scarlett satisfies the reader, since we have envied her victories over men, deplored her tactics, felt belittled by her ability to transcend disaster. Now we can feel smug—self-righteous and superior; and also disappointed: a reaction pleasingly resonant in its complexity and irresolution.

After all, we must admit that Scarlett has been heroic in the novel showing more than *gumption* by achieving *gallantry.* Ashley, an expert on Southern virtues, had discerned this gallantry, though it was often disguised—like the red velvet curtains resewn into the dress Scarlett wears to Atlanta. Scarlett is off to save Tara. Like the heroine of melodrama, she must pay the rent and she can't pay the rent; but she does not wait helplessly for the hero's rescue. She sets out alone with a style that stuns Ashley: "he had never known such gallantry as the gallantry of

Scarlett O'Hara going forth to conquer the world in her mother's velvet curtains and the tail feathers of a rooster." This gallantry has murky (as well as comic) aspects, for Scarlett plans to bargain with Rhett over her only commodity—herself. But she will sacrifice anything for Tara, the home that as the novel's mother she must hold intact for her family, and that as its child, she must find when she is frightened and lost. As Scarlett imagines Tara and its red earth, her final vision in the novel, the figure of Mammy emerges, and once again earth and mother become one: "Suddenly she wanted Mammy desperately, as she had wanted her when she was a little girl, wanted the broad bosom on which to lay her head." Return to the earth's broad bosom satisfies conflicting desires that *Gone With The Wind* evokes—a desire for renewal and continuation (promised by its *tomorrow*), and a desire for rest, for ending (promised, indeed, by narrative form). Scarlett's renewed vision of home shows her still a helpless child and still a survivor, both identities in tension with each other, irreconcilable and yet inseparably merged within her single determination to return to Tara. The thought of going home comforts her, especially since she has made a vow to get Rhett back, a vow which may be impossible to keep. How can she make Rhett yield to her once more when she knows he is "strong, unyielding, implacable"? With its fourth and last ending, *Gone With The Wind* stops, but like a modern open-ended novel, leaves its story inconclusive. The novel has imagined many endings for us and yet left us free to conclude whatever we please, to shape tomorrow to our own desires.

Gone With the Wind's last ending gives an impression of decisiveness through Scarlett's single-minded determination to get Rhett back, but actually it is profoundly ambiguous, describing a child's regressive longing for home and mother that resonates to longings for death. Scarlett's final vision of earth and mother intertwined removes us from her practical everyday world of schemes for survival to her enduring fantasy in which irreconcilable images merge. In fantasy, the red earth of Tara is both a mother, a source of life, and a grave; the mother, a nurturing but dangerous figure whose indulgence keeps a child from growing up; and home, a haven where the helpless child can withdraw and an indomitable woman find new courage. We cannot escape these ambiguities—that is one reason why the novel is compelling; we cannot resolve them; and yet the novel allows us to find satisfaction in coping with their irreconcilable oppositions. We manage to reject a regressive fixation on home by distancing ourselves from Scarlett, adulterating our admiration for her courage with condescension towards her childishness. Her promise to "get" Rhett, daring as it is, may strike us as puerile; her reassuring last words—"After all, tomorrow is another day"—as merely tautological. Still the vow does appeal to us, for we have become that impossible reader Mitchell could not imagine—a survivor, "a ninety five year old," combined with a child. Like a child, we fall into fantasies of home when defeated, while as survivors, we try to transcend our own mistakes and history's disorder.

During the war, Scarlett longs for the order that Tara represents not only to her personally as her childhood home, but also to a society that still remembers its emergence from the wilderness of Georgia. This memory is evoked at Gerald O'Hara's funeral, where his achievement in life is simply stated: "He had made a big plantation out of the wilderness." *Gone With The Wind* retells an archetypal creation myth as it describes Tara rising out of chaos, first when Gerald builds it on a land recently devastated by fire, and again when Scarlett restores it after the war. Their efforts to create order out of chaos give them a heroic dimension that the novel sustains by its epic scale. A civilization is at stake in *Gone With The Wind:* not only the style of life of the South, imperiled and indeed destroyed by the war, but the *idea* of civilization as an ordered way of living maintained tenuously, since the forces of disorder always threaten to break loose from the restraints imposed by men and women of heroic vision. Though Gerald O'Hara blusters and bungles and depends utterly upon his wife (and his slaves), he is a visionary character, seeing a civilization where chaos prevails. Chaos has preceded him to Clayton County; fire has destroyed the house, and seedling pine and weeds have overrun the fields that Gerald gambled for and won at a poker game (a nice touch, this winning, which makes Gerald a typical American hero, a "self-made" man who has luck as well as pluck).

Where Tara is to rise to antebellum splendor, Gerald sees in miniature the ruin that war will soon spread throughout Geor-

gia: "blackened foundation stones . . . uncultivated fields . . .
pines and underbrush." Beyond fields that men had worked to
clear, waiting to reclaim the clearing, looms the wilderness, implacable and dark. Throughout the novel, this primordial wilderness keeps threatening the South as relentlessly as Sherman's
troops. Both have encroached upon land cleared for cotton
fields and country homes and left it devastated. Both represent
forces of disorder. The war is a historical event fixed in time; but
the wilderness is timeless, a force always opposed to civilization,
as its primal darkness is to light. Tara is set in "a land of contrasts," in the north country of Georgia where "brightest sun
glare and densest shade" balance each other as tenuously as the
forces they represent—clearing and wilderness, order and
chaos. In the opening description of Tara, *Gone With The Wind*
introduces the wilderness, its timelessness and its threat to civilization:

The plantation clearings and miles of cotton fields smiled up to a warm
sun, placid, complacent. At their edges rose the virgin forests, dark and
cool even in the hottest noons, mysterious, a little sinister, the soughing
pines seeming to wait with an age-old patience, to threaten with soft
sighs: "Be careful! Be careful! We had you once. We can take you back
again."

Oblivious to the forest's warning, sixteen-year-old Scarlett sits
on the front porch of Tara overlooking the "endless acres of
Gerald O'Hara's newly plowed cotton fields [that stretch] toward
the red horizon." Beyond the horizon gather clouds of war that
Scarlett, thoroughly self-absorbed, refuses to see. In the novel,
war releases an enemy more ancient and tenacious than the
Yankees, for it allows the wilderness, until now held in abeyance,
to advance upon the South with its atavistic design: "In another
year [Scarlett later sees] the woods will take over the fields
again. . . . we country folks will go back a hundred years like the
pioneers who . . . scratched a few acres—and barely existed."
The obstinacy that Scarlett had shown in love when she pursued
Ashley becomes heroism when she stubbornly "fights" the wilderness in a struggle to save Tara: "This whole state can go back
to woods . . . but I won't let Tara go." Just as a child cannot let
her mother go, Scarlett cannot relinquish Tara, her security, her
one certainty, "the *indestructible* red earth on which she stood (my

emphasis)." Scarlett's passion in *Gone With The Wind*, the passion of a woman frigid in sex, is not for Ashley, nor for Rhett, but for Tara:

> Her love for this land with its softly rolling hills of bright-red soil, this beautiful red earth that was blood colored, garnet, brick dust, vermilion, which so miraculously grew green bushes starred with white puffs, was one part of Scarlett which did not change when all else was changing. Nowhere else in the world was there land like this.

By the end of *Gone With The Wind*, Tara has become "the best farm in the County," but still it is "only a farm, a two-mule farm, not a plantation." The great working plantations of Scarlett's childhood are gone with the war, the Yankees having helped the wilderness reclaim them: "Plantation after plantation was going back to the forest, and dismal fields of broomsedge, scrub oak and runty pines had grown stealthily about silent ruins and over old cotton fields. . . . It was like moving through a *dead* land (my emphasis)."

Two irreconcilable adjectives—*indestructible* and *dead*—now describe Scarlett's vision of the South she loves, of its land and its past. *Gone With The Wind* makes immutability and change, indignous themes of Southern fiction, simultaneous—as they have become in the great novels of William Faulkner. Like Faulkner, Mitchell shows the ravages of time and then denies them; her novel is caught in the tension between the two generic forms—literary romance and historical war novel—that it strains to combine. As escapist literature, a romance, *Gone With The Wind* tries to elude the historical fact implied by its title and stated in its text: that the South's "ordered world was *gone* and a brutal world had taken its place, a world wherein every standard, every value had changed (my emphasis)." The characters who have adjusted their lives to historical change deny its irreversibility. At the end of *Gone With The Wind*, even Rhett Butler lapses into nostalgia over "the old times" in Charleston (where he had been ostracized): like Scarlett he goes home again to seek "the genial grace of days that are *gone* (my emphasis)." Like her, he wants the impossible.

Gone With The Wind gives credibility to its inherent contradictions by presenting history as a cyclical pattern of loss and recovery, and by emphasizing courage. Courage becomes an obstinate refusal to accept loss, an implicit demand for recovery. Mitchell said her mother impressed this demand upon her as a little girl, and later it inspired her novel: "every sixty years or so," her mother had said, "there is an upheaval, and only the things that people can do with their heads or with their hands stay with them." Scarlett can add figures in her head (to her husband Frank's chagrin) and hold a plow in her hands—abilities that allow her to prevail. Still, like Tara, her "two-mule farm," she ends diminished, and so does Rhett. Last seen, he is no longer "a young pagan prince on new-minted gold but a decadent, tired Caesar on copper debased by long usage"; and Scarlett is a woman who has lost her "soul" but insists she will get it back. This belief in recovery denies the permanence of any loss, in effect denies our common sense of history. The past is *gone* (with the wind), but courageous characters will demand recovery; and those who find recovery impossible are weak and defeated and, like Ashley, merely dreamers.

In its extremity, refusal to relinquish the past may become a form of madness eliciting horror and admiration, as in Faulkner's great story "A Rose for Emily." This story, like much of Southern fiction, expresses a human longing for the impossible: for the permanent arrest of time that must pass into history; for the immutability of all that must change. Faulkner's Emily refuses to admit the passage of time; she denies death by sleeping with her skeletal lover night after night. Her intransigence is macabre but heroic, maintained with a purity of vision so extreme it has turned into madness. *Gone With The Wind*— obviously more limited, prosaic, and compromised than Faulkner's fiction—presents a view of life that appeals to ordinary people, those who commonly believe that history offers possibilities, that after "everyone loses everything . . . everyone is equal" and anyone has a chance to "come through." Rhett's plain words (repeating those of Mitchell's mother) articulate an ideal implicit in American democracy. History may have tarnished this ideal, but as a fiction, *Gone With The Wind* reaffirms it by combining realism and romance. Scarlett is realistic in facing day-to-day problems, heroic in defending Tara against the forces of chaos, and otherwise unaccountable except as a romantic figure. She changes with time and yet, like Faulkner's Ike McCaslin, remains the same, running through the dimensionless mist of dream; there a child may be lost forever and still reach a secret haven impossible to find except through fantasy. At the end of *Gone With The Wind,* Scarlett denies the historical changes she has lived through by reentering her fantasy of childhood. Once again she goes home, where Mammy waits, representing to Scarlett the endurance of an Old Order, Ellen's "ordered world," which has not endured, and the promise of gratifications which cannot be fulfilled.

Early in the novel, when Mammy stuffs Scarlett with yams and hot cakes before sending her to the Twelve Oaks barbeque (where ladies are not supposed to eat), Scarlett announces the impossible desire of all children: "Some day I'm going to do and say everything I want to do and say, and if people don't like it I don't care." Later she thinks money will buy her this license—Rhett's money. With it she builds an ostentatious house in Atlanta intended "to make everyone who's been mean to me feel bad." "Oh, Scarlett, you are so young you wring my heart," Rhett exclaims as she grabs the green bonnet he has smuggled through the blockade. Like an indulgent father, he delights in her youngness, letting her have whatever she wants. On their honeymoon, he laughs as she stuffs herself with New Orleans gumbo, shrimp, and pastry, and he himself feeds her "as though she were a child." He buys her satin slippers, brocade dresses, embroidered chemises, and encourages her outrageously "to speak her mind." Scarlett tells him that he is the "only man . . . who could stand the truth from a woman . . . who didn't . . . expect me to tell lies." She offers this as her reason for marrying him, but she knows that she does not really understand why she accepts Rhett, whether for his money, his reliability, or his rascality; for his similarities to her or his differences. Other than her strongly articulated desires to feed her family and keep Tara, she does not know what she wants except to do whatever she wants with impunity. This childish wish is obviously unrealizable and, in fact, Scarlett is always punished. Success in Atlanta leads to social ostracism, love for Ashley to disgrace and guilt, desire for Rhett to frustration.

Turning upon the mystery of desire, *Gone With The Wind* is an involuted novel that pursues one of the great themes of modern American literature. Desire impels the characters of Theodore Dreiser, F. Scott Fitzgerald, and Saul Bellow, whose gargantuan

Henderson reiterates the phrase dear to Scarlett's heart: "*I want, I want!*" The mystery of what she wants, however, remains hidden behind the novel's *closed doors,* within *secrets* Scarlett feels compelled to discover:

> "If you'll promise, we'll tell you a secret," said Stuart.
> "What?" cried Scarlett, alert as a child at the word.

This childish exchange at the beginning of *Gone With The Wind* initiates Scarlett's plot to "get" Ashley (which soon entangles Rhett), for Stuart Tarleton's secret entails Ashley's engagement to Melanie. To Scarlett, this social ritual is also a secret rite preparing for intimacies between a man and woman that Scarlett does not understand. She needs her mother to explain, but Ellen is off on her own secret mission which Scarlett discovers by eavesdropping: she stands outside her parents' bedroom door and, like a child of an imagined primal scene, overhears them whisper about sex. "Curiosity" is "sharp" in Scarlett, as in any child, and sustained because she cannot find out what she wants to know. Ellen's genteel code prohibits mention of sex (though it hints at a married woman's mysterious trials); and Scarlett herself represses sexual desire by imagining Ashley as a shining knight to be adored romantically from afar. Nevertheless, his appeal is profoundly sexual, for he embodies the titillating mystery of the *closed door.* The language that tells us this is explicit if clichéd, the cliché resonating with sexual overtones: "The very mystery of him excited her curiosity like a door that had neither lock nor key." At Twelve Oaks, Scarlett draws Ashley into a "semidark room" from behind a "partly opened door" that "automatically" he closes. "Who are you hiding from?" Ashley asks, not oblivious to her sexual excitement, "a tenseness about her, a glow in her eyes . . . rosy flush on her cheeks":

> "What is it?" he said, almost in a whisper . . .
> "What is it?" he repeated. "A secret to tell me?" . . .
> "Yes—a secret. I love you."

To Scarlett, love is both a secret to tell and *secret*—hidden, inaccessible, beyond understanding. However, someone else hidden in the room seems to understand love—Rhett Butler. Concealed in semidarkness, he is the real secret locked from Scarlett behind closed doors (had she understood that, *Gone*

With The Wind might have moved swiftly to a single "happy ending"). "Eavesdroppers often hear highly entertaining and instructive things," Rhett teases an enraged Scarlett, but she uncovers clues she never understands. She has sneaked into Melanie's bedroom and "secretly" read Ashley's letters, only to find them unfathomable. She has listened when Ashley speaks—"excited . . . as if on the brink of discovery"—and felt disappointed, like "a child who opens a beautifully wrapped package and finds it empty." That emptiness *is* Ashley's secret she discovers only upon Melanie's death when "she really understood him for the first time"; and then she wishes herself rid of him. Throughout the novel, Scarlett's love for Ashley has been sustained by mystery—engendered along the "secret bridle paths" they rode together, renewed by their secret trysts, symbolized by the "secret guerdon" she gives him in Atlanta. In the end, it is spoiled by disclosure; but by then another secret binds her to Ashley—her promise to care for him and "never let him know."

Like Ashley, Rhett fascinates Scarlett by his mystery—the indefinable sexuality that makes him "glamorous" to Atlanta's gossiping matrons and innocent girls. Rumors of a "bad reputation" enhance his appeal with "the titillating element of the wicked and the forbidden" (Mitchell's words, however innocently meant, are insinuating). Rhett radiates a male vitality that none of the women, not Scarlett, nor Melanie, nor Aunt Pittypat, dares mention, though in its presence all feel strangely "discomposed." Just as Scarlett could not fathom Ashley's secret, she cannot find "a clue" to Rhett's "inscrutability," the "smooth dark blankness which had baffled her so often." She cannot understand the waiting watchful look in his eyes—eyes that "read her like a book," that "found her transparent as glass."

This transparency relieves Scarlett of the constant necessity to lie, a demand placed upon Southern ladies, but it places her in Rhett's power. From the first, he knows her secret and diminishes it by mockery. "Fear not, fair lady!" he hisses when they meet again in Atlanta, "Your guilty secret is safe with me!" But though he laughs and encourages her to "tell me everything"—"You should have no secrets from me"—on their honeymoon he curses her for the secret love she takes to their bed. "May God damn your cheating little soul to hell for all eternity," he shouts into her dream of Ashley, and his "heavy arm," turned to "iron," tightens into a threat. On the night that Scarlett's secret becomes a public disgrace, Rhett's hands form a vise about her head where fantasy perdures:

Observe my hands. . . . I could tear you in pieces with them . . . if it would take Ashley out of your mind. But it wouldn't. So I think I'll remove him from your mind forever, this way. I'll put my hands, so, on each side of your head and I'll smash your skull between them like a walnut and that will blot him out.

But Rhett finds a better way to *blot out* Ashley: he forces Scarlett to an *ecstasy of surrender.* Trite phrases which have become devoid of reference conceal the sexual event they describe, so that Scarlett's *wild mad night* remains the secret of clichés that tell us what we already know about sex (especially from popular fiction), tell us of the *hard hammering* of the heart, the yielding *soft flesh,* the *wild thrill, joy, fear, madness, excitement, surrender,* of *sweeping and primitive* emotions climaxing in *rapture.* Rhett is *bullying and breaking* Scarlett, releasing his secret passion through rape.

Rape is a secret whispered throughout Atlanta. Scarlett is shocked when Rhett says the word aloud, but his function in the novel is to reveal the secrets locked behind Southern manners. "No use getting mad at me for reading your thoughts," he tells Scarlett when he knows she is thinking about rape; "That's what all our delicately nurtured and pure-minded Southern ladies think. They have it on their minds constantly." War fixes rape on their minds, for it makes women vulnerable to Yankee soldiers and roaming blacks. Scarlett escapes these dangers barely: she shoots a Yankee on the loose and eludes a Shantytown "nigger." In each instance, rape calls forth a rescuer. The Yankee brings Melanie with a sword in her hand, its appearance signifying her secret courage, described as a "thin flashing blade of unbreakable steel." The "nigger" produces Big Sam, the largest and most formidable-looking black man in Georgia. As they struggle in the dark shadow of the woods, rapist and rescuer are united momentarily in their conflict. Big Sam calls Scarlett's assailant a *black baboon,* for any sexual man in the novel is a *gorilla* or a *black ape.* Even Rhett fits into this stereotype when aroused to sexual desire. His silhouette in the doorway conjures up an image of a dark apelike creature: "He looked huge, larger than she had

ever seen him, a terrifying faceless black bulk that swayed
slightly on its feet." Always Scarlett's rescuer, Rhett is driven by
jealousy and frustration to sexual violence that the novel
legitimizes: after all, Rhett is Scarlett's "wronged husband," he
loves her desperately, and at least for one *wild mad night* he
makes her love him. When Rhett carries Scarlett off to the bedroom—as when Big Sam merges with Scarlett's attacker in the
woods—rapist and rescuer become one, an impossible coalescence made possible in fiction by the oxymoronic power of language. Scarlett tries to escape Rhett, to get to her bedroom and
"turn the key in the stout door," but he captures her, running
silently like "an Indian," the savage in the American imagination. He takes her in a darkness where, finally, the secret of sex is
penetrated:

She was darkness and he was darkness and there had never been anything before this time, only darkness and his lips upon hers. . . . Somehow, her arms were around his neck and her lips trembling beneath his
and they were going up, up into the darkness again, a darkness that was
soft and swirling and *all enveloping.*

In night's *hot swirling darkness, Gone With The Wind's* secret
fears converge: fear of the black race *(darkies),* fear of sex, and
fear of death *(all enveloping darkness).* Associated with a primordial swirling chaos, sex is a violent energy released by rape,
prostitution, and white-trash adultery. For Scarlett, it is the secret that civilized people keep in the dark; the morning's bright
"sunlight" makes her "ashamed. . . . a real lady could never hold
up her head after such a night." For Scarlett, sexual passion
recalls other "sweeping and primitive" emotions—the fear she
felt when fleeing burning Atlanta, the "dizzy sweet" hatred when
she killed a Yankee. Dense as Scarlett is about her own feelings,
she links sex to rape, murder, and death; and so does the novel.
Gone With The Wind's wild night, its climactic scene in every
sense, ends in disorder and death. Scarlett loses the child she
had conceived in darkness, and she too almost dies—Rhett has
taken her to a "darkness . . . darker than death." Ultimately,
death prevails over love in *Gone With The Wind,* its optimism
overcome by the dread of dissolution that is thematic to the
novel. War between the states makes dissolution actual. Waged

to preserve a culture, war releases the dark forces that will destroy it—wilderness, apelike men, and primitive emotions of fear, hatred, and sexual desperation. Rhett struggles against the darkness that he has come to represent when he calls for lights, "lots of lights," to burn in Bonnie's bedroom, but he cannot protect anyone associated with his passion. His unborn baby dies; Bonnie dies; and Scarlett survives only to find love dead— her love for Ashley and Rhett's "deathless love" for her. "I stood outside your door," Rhett says, "hoping you'd call for me, but you didn't and then I knew . . . it was all over." Had she unlocked her door, Scarlett might have been lost to Rhett anyway, for a woman who lets sex into her life invites death. Melanie had "sped" into the bedroom "when Ashley opened the bedroom door." "Overcome with some frightening emotion," but also "shyly happy," she had wanted sex with her husband; and in the same bedroom where she had made love, she nearly dies in childbirth. Melanie can live as long as she abstains from sex, and when she does not, her death becomes inevitable.

Melanie slips into Rhett's bedroom with remarkable ease (and in Atlanta allows him into hers with "no surprise"). After Scarlett's miscarriage, she enters his room, closes the door, and takes him into her arms, holding him like a child with unbearable secrets to tell: "he began speaking rapidly, hoarsely, babbling . . . secret things that brought the hot blood of modesty to her cheeks." "You don't understand," Rhett persists when Melanie tries to silence him, "She didn't want a baby and I made her." Bonnie's death brings Melanie once again to Rhett's door: "it opened quickly . . . he pulled her into the room and shut the door." Whatever secrets they now share as she soothes him are private, locked behind a closed door. The two secret encounters that transform Rhett into Melanie's child are separated by a third in which he plays his usual paternal role, proposing a "secret" that will protect Melanie's marriage. But though Melanie listens and agrees, she needs to disavow all secrets because they tell her what she does not want to know. "I have never kept anything secret from my husband," she says at the same time that she seals a secret pact with Rhett. As for Rhett's secret confessions, she has converted them into the "babbling wild fantasies" of a man "drunk and sick from strain": "the awful things he said . . . could not be true." Melanie remains "a great lady" by denying her experience; she refuses to acknowledge the sordid secrets in which she figures—Scarlett's infatuation with Ashley, his lust for her, and Rhett's desperate sexuality. To know and yet not know is an impossibility Melanie tries to achieve; and her efforts end in death. For in life, innocence and experience cannot be synonymous, nor change and changelessness simultaneous. Only the oxymoronic language of fiction—phrases like *Gone With The Wind*'s "timeless time"—allows this.

Like Melanie, Scarlett refuses to recognize the truth before her—that Ashley belongs to Melanie, that the bedroom door opens only for her, Ashley's flushed and happy wife:

> The door closed behind them, leaving Scarlett open mouthed and suddenly desolate. Ashley was no longer hers. He was Melanie's. And as long as Melanie lived, she could go into rooms with Ashley and close the door—and close out the rest of the world.

Once more, Scarlett seems a little girl watching outside her parents' bedroom door. Doors close frequently during Ashley's brief furlough in Atlanta, and Scarlett—in a passion that is "violent" because "repressed"—waits for them to open. She wants to be alone with Ashley, to whisper her secret again: "I love you. . . . I've always loved you. I've never loved anyone else." Scarlett tries to evade the impossibility of this love, but it is forced upon her by the delicate secret of Melanie's pregnancy: "Then there suddenly leaped to her mind the closed door of Melanie's bedroom and a knifelike pain went through her, a pain as fierce as though Ashley had been her own husband and been unfaithful to her."

Of course, Ashley is never actually unfaithful; nor, for all her willingness, is Scarlett. As Mitchell noted, her novel shunned seduction, infidelity, and perversion, the prurient appeals (she thought) of Southern fiction and American best-sellers. Her statement, like her portrayal of sexual fidelity, rests upon a technical nicety, for *Gone With the Wind* manages to make infidelity exist without being actual. Infidelity is imagined so vividly that Scarlett finds Ashley unfaithful to her, and Rhett knows she is unfaithful to him when she lies in his bed, in his arms, dreaming of Ashley. Rhett says that he would not have cared if Scarlett *had* given her body (rather than her imagination) to Ashley: "I know how little bodies mean—especially women's bodies" (especially, one might add, in a slave society). Bodies are commonly for sale in *Gone With The Wind*'s Georgia, a practice no one questions except gentle, hesitant Melanie. Before Rhett buys Scarlett at Dr. Meade's charity auction. Melanie stammers, "Don't you think it's—it's just—just a little like a slave auction?" In a novel that accepts slavery, even bodies of white women will be bought and sold as commodities. When Scarlett needs money for Tara, she offers herself for sale. With unintended irony, Ashley praises the "gallantry" that Scarlett frankly calls "prostitution." So does Rhett when he accuses her of "pouting and frisking like a prostitute with a prospective client"; as a steady patron of Belle Watling's whorehouse, he should know. Nevertheless, he buys her in marriage, her second marriage for money. Later, when Scarlett asks flirtatiously, "Do I mean so much to you?", his reply is not irrelevant: "Well, yes. You see, I've invested a great deal of money in you, and I'd hate to lose it."

Rhett has invested also in Belle Watling, a more profitable venture in many ways than marriage. With her flaming red hair, Belle is the novel's authentic scarlet woman, a "hussy" in whom Scarlett recognizes herself when she accepts Rhett's money. Unlike Scarlett, Belle sells herself openly and gives full satisfaction. Moreover, she satisfies the novel's moral demands: she helps the Cause and the Klan (imperiled by Scarlett); she recognizes Melanie's fine mettle; she supports Rhett with a protective "motherly" love. Though she is *Gone With The Wind*'s "bad woman," Belle seems more virtuous than Scarlett. As the whore with a heart of gold, Belle belongs to a sentimental literary tradition, which in the novel allows for a moral inversion we would usually condemn. Belle turns prostitution into an innocuous, even benign, form of buying and selling—as innocuous as slavery in the novel. Belle sells her body but keeps her heart of gold. Dilcey, the only slave we see sold, is bought by Mr. O'Hara so that she can live with her husband, Pork, at Tara. Dr. Meade auctions Southern ladies for charity; and Rhett buys Scarlett to rescue her from the inanition of widowhood. If, as Rhett says, women's bodies mean little, then the novel has devalued them, has even led us to condone the sale of human beings by trivializing it or disguising it as charity, social responsibility, or marriage. In this way, the novel allows our imagination to betray our moral ideals while we can claim actual fidelity—as Scarlett does in her marriage to Rhett. "I know you have been physically faithful to me," he says; but his condemnation of her moral dishonesty eases our conscience as we read. We share his indignation at Scarlett's infidelity while vicariously we enjoy her confused illicit desires.

Victorian in its adherence to sexual fidelity, *Gone With The Wind* exposes the other side of Victorianism: its prurience. The novel titillates the reader with sexual secrets that titillate its well-bred ladies—pregnancy, prostitution, rape. Melanie nearly swoons when Rhett notices her "condition," and Scarlett tries to hide hers by smothering under a lap robe. She is "horrified" when Rhett says the word *pregnancy:* "I'm not a gentleman to have mentioned the matter. . . , [but] pregnant women do not embarrass me as they should. . . . [I] treat them as normal creatures. . . . It's a normal state and women should be proud of it, instead of hiding behind closed doors." When Dr. Meade gets beyond Belle Watling's closed doors, his wife plies him with questions (which the reader now shares): "What did it look like? Are there cut-glass chandeliers, . . . red plush curtains, . . . full-length gilt mirrors? And were the girls—were they unclothed?" These avid questions leave Dr. Meade "thunderstruck" at "the curiosity of a chaste woman concerning her unchaste sisters," a "*devouring*" curiosity shown by matrons and "innocent and well-bred young women" like Scarlett. In Atlanta, Scarlett is "curious" about Belle Watling as she had been about Emmie Slatterly in Tara. Sexual curiosity vies with sexual fear in the novel, producing an ambivalent desire for exposure and concealment, the essence of Victorian prurience.

As in a Victorian novel, the men of *Gone With The Wind* are punished for their sexuality, for the passion that Scarlett insinuates into their lives. Her first two husbands die. Her third, worn out by marriage, becomes "a swarthy sodden stranger disintegrating under her eyes." Ashley is demoralized. Always good at calculation, Scarlett adds up her ruinous effects upon him: "She had wrecked his life, broken his pride and self-respect, shattered that inner peace, that calm based on integrity . . . [and] alienated him from the sister he loved." In devastating both Ashley and Rhett, Scarlett becomes the novel's *deadly woman*, a green-eyed Lamia whom we must reconcile with Scarlett the lost child. This *femme fatale* represents sexual fears so profound that they exceed the novel's private and cultural fantasies to underlie universal myths; but impossible though it may seem, *Gone With The Wind* overcomes even primal fears. Deadly as she can be, Scarlett is finally thwarted when she loses both Ashley and Rhett, her divided lovers who have merged two opposite and mutually exclusive mythoi in the novel into one.

When Ashley first appears to Scarlett on his beautiful horse, he is a "Perfect Knight," well-bred, well-mannered, well-tuned to his times. Rhett, on the other hand, is rude and disruptive, a swarthy swashbuckling unscrupulous pirate. Grandson of an actual buccaneer, he has inherited a pirate's lithe strong body and rapacious face—a "hawk nose," "animal-white teeth," "black mustache." How prince and pirate, antithetical figures, achieve the same identity as Melanie's little boys and Scarlett's lovers seems impossible to explain, but Ashley understands that "Rhett and I are fundamentally alike. We come of the same kind of people, we were raised in the same pattern, brought up to think the same things." Rhett, on the other hand, sees that they want the same woman in basically different ways: "He doesn't want your mind . . . and I don't want your body." If this Victorian version of love is true—and body and soul can be separated—it is also untrue; for surely Rhett wanted the body he ravished behind closed doors. Love and lust are made distinct and then indistinguishable in the novel—as are all antinomies: prince and pirate, wife and whore, prurience and purity. The grand design of *Gone With The Wind* traces a union of opposites—which is, of course, the essence of the Civil War, its embracing theme.

As a study of war, *Gone With The Wind* shows that reconciliation between opposites is impossible: irreconcilability is the meaning of any war, and in particular of civil war. Symbolically, the Civil War in America was a family affair; brother fought against brother, as we know; but if separation, and even opposition, within a family is inevitable, its union, a union of blood, is irrefrangible. Just as loss demands recovery in *Gone With The Wind*, division eventuates in union. American history supports *Gone With The Wind* as a fiction of inevitable reconciliation by showing us that opposites are not only reconcilable but in fact already united. The novel goes further by making victory the sequel to defeat (and perhaps history confirms this, too, now that a citizen of once-vanquished Georgia has been a president of the United States). Mitchell was always proud of the authen-

ticity of her war scenes; its battles are unmitigated in their violence, the devastation to the land and the appalling loss of life
unromanticized. But a strong sense of victory emerges from the
novel, for the more brutally the South is defeated, the more
triumphant its characters and readers can feel in its recovery. We
are reconciled to horror because we see that it is transitory, that
it can be transcended in the long and durable flow of history that
the novel traces. While Stark Young's Civil War novel, *So Red the
Rose*, ends with a vision of "the darkness and the field where the
dead lay," *Gone With The Wind* ends with Scarlett's renewed hope
in *tomorrow*. That hope does not obliterate the waste of war,
which we recover every time we read the novel, but it does
release us from a haunting image of death.

If *Gone With The Wind* makes our worst fears manageable,
fears of war, rape, chaos, hunger, death, it also gratifies our most
infantile wish, the one Scarlet expressed—that we get everything
we want. As a fantasy of total gratification, the novel shows us
how, in addition to all the reconciliations already discussed, even
an inviolate division between races can be reconciled with union—the union of mother and child, as it exists between Mammy
and Scarlett, and of husband and wife, as in disguised form it
exists between Aunt Pittypat and Uncle Peter, a relationship
worth looking at. Scarlett's Aunt Pittypat has lived with her black
servant, Uncle Peter, in a relationship of mutual dependence
and support. She provides him with a home and purpose, and
he watches over this sixty-year-old woman as though she were
sixteen. Her fears are foolish, her cowardice an occasion for
comedy in the novel. Comedy, however, provides a way of coping with fears, of exorcising the menace of darkness that the
novel constantly evokes. In Uncle Peter, the ever-present *darkie* is
transformed from a threatening *ape* to an aping protector; a
man as insistent upon decorum as any Southern white aristocrat.
Uncle Peter keeps order, though he becomes comic in his efforts,
for in the novel there is something ridiculous about black men
who become *monkeys* and *small children*, their common epithets.
Scarlett describes the blacks as "childlike in mentality, easily led,"
and led to mischief when freed of parental control. Big Sam,
who has killed a man and struggled with a *black baboon*, cries to
be sent home to Tara where Master will care for him again. *Gone
With The Wind* shows Big Sam, Uncle Peter, and Pork sharing

Scarlett's fantasy of regression, her longing for home, her impossible wish to return to a past that pampered and pleasured its children. The reader's pleasure in seeing Georgia's biggest "nigger" (the novel's potential Bigger Thomas) transmogrified into a lost child epitomizes the childlike appeal of *Gone With The Wind* as a text on the impossibilities of fiction, for only in the language of a text can oppositions inherently irreconcilable be brought together for our possession, can division become synonymous with unity.

Beginning with division—with Scarlett poised between the Tarleton twins, divided men about to fight in a divided nation—*Gone With The Wind* ends with doubling. We need not choose between contrarieties because we can possess them both in our imagination where they have become one. Scarlett herself personifies a union of opposites. As a divided woman, she is both a peasant and aristocrat; lost child and Lamia; victim and survivor; hussy and heroine; country girl and city woman; earth goddess ("like Antaeus," Rhett says) and entrepreneur; child and mother. Unlike the Tarleton women, whom she envies for their "single-mindedness," she is fated to conflict by the mixture within her blood of "Irish peasant" and "overbred Coast aristocrat"; her character epitomizes her times, both in a state of internal conflict. Because her conflicts seem impossible to resolve, she is confused, uncertain, and unpredictable; but also resilient and fascinating. She wants *everything,* and is everything to her readers—child, mother, and elusively sexual woman, all of these aspects of her being and more in irrepressible conflict. That she should divide others as she herself is divided, is inevitable. She alienates Atlanta by precipitating "a feud that would split the town and the family for generations." The order she tries to establish is inseparable from disorder; and both are pleasing to us as readers. We share her chaotically conflicting impulses and safely enjoy seeing them gratified and punished. Sympathizing with her, we also repudiate her, so that we too become divided characters. We give Scarlett our emotional allegiance, but we overlay it with intellectual disdain.

When Rhett calls Scarlett "a child crying for the moon," he means of course that she wants the impossible; but the impossible has become more and more difficult for us to define, while our desires for the moon have become less outlandish. Because

Scarlett reaches for the moon, she is forever attractive and forever dangerous. She keeps unfulfilled dreams alive, while she shows that dreams which do come true may bring death. She does in fact make Rhett's dream come true—the dream that she will someday love him; but by the time she loves him, his "deathless love" has died—and so have their two children. Only the intensity of their mistimed desire for each other lasts and becomes our memory of their romance. Sexual desire, the secret that, with Scarlett, we seek behind closed doors, is not only prurient in the novel but proper, for desire sustains its characters and makes their survival possible. When survival seems impossible, as recurrently in history it does, we find it imagined for us in fictions which fulfill the wishes that reality denies—a wish for the moon, a wish for romance, a wish for romance to merge indivisibly with history, a wish to feel the impelling intensity of desire that makes Scarlett O'Hara so immediately and permanently alive.

Another famous novel of desire, *The Great Gatsby,* suggests differences between art and popularity. Like Scarlett, Jay Gatsby believes in romantic clichés, and his impulse like hers is regressive. But Fitzgerald's language so far transcends cliché that his style seems the impossible achievement of his fiction. We could not have imagined his language (nor that of Faulkner), but we might have anticipated his social vision. Fitzgerald saw a *pandered* American dream that contained divisions by which it was irreparably split, so that the impossibility of reconciling dream and reality was as intransigent as the impossibility of foregoing one for the other. These impossibilities kill Gatsby. He cannot live without Daisy and he cannot live with her; unlike Scarlett he runs out of tomorrows and schemes for retrieving what is gone. We want to know how to survive impossible conflicts, not to die of them. This is Scarlett's secret and, I believe, a secret of *Gone With The Wind's* popularity. Gatsby dies into the language of *The Great Gatsby.* His dream becomes inseparable from Fitzgerald's style; and this, I believe, is the secret of its art. We can say what Scarlett wants; we can never say what Gatsby desires. Only the totality of the novel expresses a desire which exceeds Daisy to become coterminous with America. Having said that, one must read *The Great Gatsby* again. One may quote its poetry, whereas one quotes, as I have, *Gone With The Wind's* clichés. *Gone With The*

Wind's popularity depends upon language that is familiar and transparent, as Margaret Mitchell intended, language that as cliché is almost non-present. But such language constitutes another impossibility of the novel, for clichés are notoriously inert, and yet they become charged with vitality in *Gone With The Wind*. They create, sustain, and propel a narrative of such compulsive force that people of all ages and nationalities sat up all night reading and then cried when they finished its thousand pages. *Gone With The Wind* demonstrates the creative and coercive power of language, and if this seems impossible given its clichéd style, then we must deny that power relates to effectiveness in making people read. Millions have read *Gone With The Wind*, and rather than arousing critical disdain, the interest and curiosity it constantly renews in the reader should be renewed in the critic. *Gone With The Wind* is a novel that revolves around secrets, and one of them may be the secret of fiction. The clues point, as clues invariably do, to the child and its devouring curiosity about life's closed doors. I am not propounding a theory of voyeurism, but of impossibility. The child fantasizes impossibilities that the adult knows are unattainable— as I know that my wish to penetrate the secret of *Gone With The Wind*'s popularity can never be entirely fulfilled. Residual mystery is the critic's pleasure, exciting him or her with the promise of new discoveries tomorrow. The reader's pleasure is a fulfillment of impossible desires. *Gone With The Wind* united child and adult into one reader, and then by the divisions in its form and its characters, divides and at the same time doubles the reader's response, doubles his or her pleasure. As fiction, it achieves the child's impossible desire for everything, and if this gratifies us, it also makes us ashamed of our childishness, ashamed of enjoying a novel that is not "great," only compelling and indelible, only uniquely and universally popular.

Sister to Faust:

The City's "Hungry" Woman

as Heroine

Flatiron Building

ON THE CITY'S "HUNGRY" HEROINE

Years ago I wrote a book about American urban fiction that noted, in a desultory way, how the city as setting affected the lives of women. For some, like Theodore Dreiser's Carrie, the city—New York—was the scene of glittering success; for others, like Edith Wharton's beautiful Lily Bart, of thwarted desire and of death. While in the book I considered the fate of individual women characters, as they happened to appear, I did not think of women generally. I did not see their success or failure in the city as essentially different from that of men. At the time one was not looking for generic characteristics that could be linked to gender. When, in recent years, I began to reread urban fiction, focusing upon women's fate, I was prepared for victims, suicides, madwomen—characters described as prototypic in modern feminist criticism. Such women appeared. Some were brutalized as men beat and raped them. Some killed themselves in despair. Others found oblique methods of revenging themselves on men by becoming devouring mothers, wives who sapped their husbands' strength, demanding and destructive mistresses. These urban vampires were as unsurprising as the victims. But another character was appearing recurrently, someone I had often encountered in life, but was unprepared to find in urban literature or see so deeply and comfortably entrenched. She is a woman "hungry" for knowledge; she frequents libraries; she works and attends school. Often she is an immigrant or the child of immigrant parents. Usually she shares her dreams with her mother. This relationship between mother and daughter, common in everyday life and increasingly significant in feminist critical inquiry, also seemed surprising. For Dreiser's Carrie has no mother in the novel; neither do most of the women characters I had been reading about years ago. Lily Bart's mother in The House of Mirth *is dead and has left as her legacy a set of values that helped kill her daughter. Now I was discovering mothers who nurture their daughters, creating a bond between them that enhances the strength of both. I liked these characters and was to discover that others liked them too. When in various lectures I described the hungry heroine, women in the audience reacted personally, said they were hearing the story of their own lives. They were academic women, professors and students, and yet in images of hard-working, idealistic, and often lonely characters—many of them poor immigrants in the city—they saw admirable reflections of themselves.*

A s Eugene Gant sets out for the "shining cities" of the North, in Thomas Wolfe's novel *Of Time and the River,* his sister stands beside him in Catawba's little railway station. Soon the paths of brother and sister, once connected by family ties, will diverge, never to reunite. The outbound train will take Eugene on a "road to freedom," away from the "mournful" South to the North's "golden cities"—ultimately to Boston, to Cambridge, and Harvard, where Eugene will discover the university's "enormous library with its million books."[1] All of these books, which he tries madly, obsessively, to read, prove incommensurate to his *hunger,* a furious and relentless hunger—"literal, cruel and physical," he calls it—and insatiable: a desire "to devour the earth and all the things and people in it." Driven by this "ravening appetite," Eugene tries to "read everything that has ever been written about human experience." He wants to "know it all, have all, be all." Real life, no matter how crammed with experience, cannot satisfy this epic craving; nor can realistic fiction, limited as it is to the usual, contain the impossible fulfillment it demands. Eugene's hyperbolic hunger, by ordinary standards egotistical if not simply mad, requires for its full expression literary forms that will enlarge life: those of legend and myth. Not surprisingly, in the first three books of *Of Time and the River,* Eugene's story is subtitled "The Legend of Man's Hunger in His Youth"; and Eugene himself is called "Young Faustus." Later he is simply Faust.[2]

After his father's death Young Faustus returns home briefly, to hear of the hungers still unappeased in the sister he left behind. "*'You're* the lucky one!'" she told him at the railway station; "*'You* got away! . . . to Boston—to Harvard.'" No one had imagined an equally "incredible escape" for her. No one had thought of buying her a ticket to "freedom" and including her in the city's "enchanted promise" by paying for her education. Unlovely and without charm, though enormously charged with life, she remains unenhanced by legend. If anything, legend diminishes her stature by emphasizing her deficiencies. For this frenzied Helen, a woman strikingly misnamed, lacks beauty. Her gaunt tormented face will inspire neither love nor poetry nor heroic strife: it will launch no ship.[3] Still, she has known supernal longings. Like her brother, she too has hungered for fame, has longed for adventure, voyages, cities, and the power of artistic expression. Recalling her "grand ambitions," Helen says wearily, "But that's all over now"—over for her, but not for Young Faustus, whose appetite she will try comically, lewdly, to keep aroused. Seeing her brother disconsolate, she promises him a huge dinner, enacting with sexually insinuating gestures a mock temptation scene meant to stir his ambition, lust, and gluttony. For in her frenetic monologue Helen shrewdly presents fame, women, and food as interchangeable male gratifications. Meanwhile she gratifies herself, appeasing her own hunger as she feeds her brother. By this act of displacement, she can merge martyrdom with seduction and sustenance. Ludicrous as she is, she pursues a purposeful strategy, comic and convoluted but effective in dramatizing herself as the eternal woman. In a typically feminine way she gives and demands love by offering a man *southern fried chicken, mashed potatoes, string beans, stewed corn, asparagus, steak, sliced tomatoes, deep dish apple pie and apple cobbler topped with cheese.*

Remarkable as she is as a literary character—with her tics and grimaces, her frenetic outbursts, her martyrdom—as a *woman*, Helen Gant represents a reality one wishes to repudiate. For we suspect that her persistent sacrifices to her family, always reviewed with resentment, disguise a debilitating fear of independence. Somehow she manages to tighten every constraint imposed upon her by her circumstances, her time, place, and sex; and yet she expresses, again and again, her passionate desire to be free. Crying for "peace and privacy," to be let "*alone* for five minutes," she abhors solitude and fears separation; unlike Eugene, she would never leave home because she has woven her own sense of identity about the members of the family she says she wants to escape. Perversely, but to a purpose, she makes them dependent upon her, in this way avoiding a potentially dangerous pursuit of her own desires. Satisfying her hunger for life vicariously, she urges her brother to flight while she remains at home, constrained by a familiar domestic routine that precludes difficult choices. Her words emphasize Eugene's freedom: "'Now, it's up to you,'" she says; "'Well, you do exactly as you please!'" Doing as one pleases, she implies, is the man's prerogative. While Faustus wanders through the world, his sister must stay at home and cook.

I choose Helen Gant as a point of departure because I consider her a character we should know and, as Eugene did, leave behind. I want to argue that Faust has other sisters in American fiction radically different from Helen, women who share her hunger and her tremendous energy but transcend her fear. These women will dare to leave home, following a lonely and frightening "road to freedom" that leads them, as it did Eugene, to the library—"the citadel of the self," as one heroine called it. Once within this citadel, each woman reiterates the same belief: that her real self, repressed by life, will somehow be released by literature. Like the enchanted figure of fairy tale, she keeps wishing for this release, feeling herself constrained by forces she cannot always name, though she recognizes their effects in her unhappiness, her sense of inauthenticity, her stultification. Attracted to martyrdom and self-mockery, this heroine refused the consolation they offer Helen; she lacks Helen's sense of farce but also her grotesqueness. She values maturity, but believes in the magic that children love—a transforming magic that can vitalize Sleeping Beauty and turn her into a woman. Unlike the child, however, she refuses a fantasy of helplessness; she dismisses the prince from her dreams—and her life. She sets out alone to find for herself, within her self, the power of transformation. Like Faust, she believes that books will give her power, and so she reads—compulsively, looking for ways to change her life. Seeing herself as an inchoate woman, or if formed, then somehow deformed, she wants to become a fully realized "person," someone she defines vaguely but succinctly as free.

She is an urban character. For reasons I shall discuss, the city evokes her desire for freedom, and by its disorder—all the confusions of urban life usually considered devastating—promises her fulfillment. A recurrent figure in fiction written by women about women, she appears also in other novels, classic and con-

temporary, where her features may be disguised or distorted or
else so familiar that we seldom re-view their expressions. Because the underlying pattern of her life seems invariable, her
impulse, purpose, and course of action the same, I consider her
a generic heroine—one not yet subsumed by our usual stereotypes (or archetypes). As contemporary readers we should not
overlook her presence, for she suggests to us the possibility of a
woman's dignified survival, and in so doing, she points to a way
out of the impasse reached by oppressed heroines who become
self-starving, suicidal, or mad—heroines currently receiving
much critical attention.[4] I call this generic figure a sister to Faust
because she is embraced by the heroic aspects of his legend—his
hunger for knowledge and autonomy (rather than his damnation)[5]—more closely than by any other, including those centered
upon women. Like Athene, she represents intellect, but unlike
the goddess, she is not born easily and full grown. On the contrary, she labors long to become herself, undergoing a slow ar-
duous birth. Though sometimes blamed for the troubles of the
world she inhabits, she is not Pandora, a woman impelled idly by
curiosity.[6] Like Eve, she reaches towards the tree of knowledge
(and her metaphor also entails orality, eating), but her city, with
its artifactuality and disorder, seems the very antithesis to Eve's
garden. Nor is she simply a female version of Faust, for, as a
woman, she has modulated desire in ways inconceivable to him;
and yet the family tie is as undeniable as that between Eugene
and Helen Gant. Essentially, she is a sister—to the legendary
brother whose hunger she shares, and to all the women in the
cities of America whose drive for knowledge and freedom she
personifies.

If this heroine seems naive in her belief that literature can
transform life, the books she will read teach her sophistication
through one of two possible lessons: either that literature and
life reveal the same secrets, literature inducting the reader into
life's mysteries; or else that they are separate and irreconcilable,
the truths of literature being in reality the fictions of life. As I
shall point out, doubts may await the heroine (and the critic) at
the end of her road to freedom, but she sets out—as perhaps all
serious readers do—confident in the powers of literature.
Standing in New York's great public library, one contemporary
protagonist, a woman in her thirties, speaks for many others

when she says: "If I were systematically to attack these volumes, one by one, reading from beginning to end, I could solve my life."[7] Her language clearly tells us that she has found her life problematic, in need of *solving,* and that by *attacking* books she has chosen to move to a solution actively, even aggressively. In another contemporary novel, an older woman continues to read on her deathbed as she has been reading all her mature life, methodically, compulsively, searching through the encyclopedia, book by book, for "labels" that would name "the point of life, and of having lived."[8] As still another modern heroine feels herself losing the point, she gives up reading great books, finding them "unbearable" because they made her "think . . . and . . . to think involves thinking about her own life."[9] Later, when she can face thinking, she resumes her education in Harvard's library, where we have already seen its million books linked to man's illimitable hunger.

I am proposing that in American novels women's hunger reveals itself in unexpected places and in unexpected ways. We are accustomed to seeing fictional heroines in a bedroom, hungering for love, but we have conveniently overlooked their regular appearance in a library, wanting knowledge. Reasons for "neglect," as we are realizing, are socially rooted, though they may manifest (or masquerade) themselves as purely literary matters pertaining to the canon. Since the canon excludes popular novels, and since many popular novels are written by women for women, the heroines who emerge in them, serious and instructive as they may be, fail to engage our critical attention. But in neglecting them, I believe we neglect also significant, perhaps crucial, aspects of women characters who appear in important contemporary novels (like *The Crying of Lot 49*) or in American classics (like *Sister Carrie*). For the paradigmatic heroine of popular fiction outlines clearly a literary pattern that can help us understand complex and enigmatic characters whose meanings, however much they have been explicated, remain inexhaustible. Theodore Dreiser's Sister Carrie is a mystery still. She hungers, as we know, but not for a man's love, and not for anything we can clearly define. She dreams and desires, epitomizing finally an indeterminate and ineffable desire which can never be fulfilled. In the novel's two brilliant restaurant scenes, Carrie consumes food that increases her hunger, for as she eats she is reading a text whose theme is insatiability. Carrie learns to want "more" as she becomes a reader of the urban scene before her, glittering and yet ominous, pulsating with an energy to which she can respond only by wanting. Changing her name, her walk, her clothes, her expectations, she wants, like every hungry heroine, to be transformed. For her (as later for Oedipa Maas in *The Crying of Lot 49*), the city itself is a vast text, a coded system full of signs and significations whose meanings, once deciphered, would, she believes, change her life. So Carrie studies—she is always studying: the streets, the crowds, other women; the lines of a play; and finally, when last seen, a great book, Balzac's *Père Goriot*. How can we explain the novel's incongruous conclusion: that it ends with unintellectual Carrie, known not for her brains, nor even for her beauty, but for her expression of hunger, sitting alone, ruminating about life, and reading? I wish to suggest that more heroines read than we realize, to more serious purposes than we have noted, and more texts, real and symbolic, than we have analyzed.

While critics may have overlooked the hungry heroine, other characters find her provocative: she arouses them to sympathy or else to anger, and sometimes to violence. All see her potential for subversiveness. She refuses to stay where she "belongs," and by leaving home and abandoning men, she destabilizes the family. Though she will claim her acts are private, concerning only changes in her self, others perceive them as assaults upon society; and when she acts publicly, engaging in the radical politics of the sixties, for instance—as in *The Women's Room*—she may be killed, co-opted, ostracized, or driven to doubt her sanity. Indeed, if the hungry heroine could learn all she hungers to know—the secret of identity (pursued by great heroes like Oedipus Rex)—then she would achieve the ultimate "revelation" that such an oddly and aptly named heroine as Oedipa Maas seeks in Thomas Pynchon's *The Crying of Lot 49*.[10] To understand the end of life, its ultimate meaning, would make the generic heroine truly Faustian in her knowledge—and (unlike Faust) truly free. It would also transform a secular quest, with revolutionary implications for society, into a religious pilgrimage. In *The Crying of Lot 49*, a parodic novel with serious religious overtones, Oedipa journeys to a mysterious and ominous city that she tries to read in much the same way that Carrie reads

Chicago: by deciphering meanings encoded in its surface streets and its labyrinthine underground. She wants to become so keenly "sensitized" that she will possess the "Word"; and though she seeks "It" in copies of a parodied Jacobean play (a corruptible text she discovers, and one that may be variant, illegible, or destroyed), she believes, like the paradigmatic hungry heroine, that when she reads the final Word she will become the executrix of her own will—an autonomous person. As we know, Oedipa ends in a locked room where she may find revelation or death. There she waits.

I am suggesting that complex and indeterminate novels about women in a city may be illuminated by the relatively simple explicit works in which I trace the configurations of the generic character I have been calling a "hungry" heroine. The name is suggested to me by a book of stories I hope to see more widely read: Anzia Yezierska's tales of immigrant women in New York entitled *Hungry Hearts.* "I'm crazy to learn," Yezierska's nameless heroine cries in the final story: "I need school more than a starving man needs bread."[11] She is, in fact, a starving woman working for starvation wages in a clattering sweatshop she describes as "hell." Fantasies of escape transport her to "heaven"— "to the schools of America." Hungry heroines share this aberrant vision of heaven as a place replete with books. In *The Promised Land,* another immigrant, Mary Antin, finds libraries a "paradise" where "one could read and read, and learn and learn."[12] Even as a girl in Russia, she recalls, "I was so hungry for books that I went at them greedily." America intensifies this craving: here she falls upon books "as a glutton pounces on his meat after a period of enforced starvation." In the public library of Williamsburg, little Francie Nolan of *A Tree Grows in Brooklyn* follows an orderly plan to read "all the books in the world."[13] To her, the shabby old library is a "beautiful" church; its books, sacred objects; its smells redolent of "burning incense at high mass." If Francie shows more control than Mary Antin, who pounces on her prey, she is no less hungry for "books . . . books . . . books." On the fire escape where she sits and reads, she imagines herself high in a tree called in Brooklyn the "Tree of Heaven." There she could spend eternity with her bowl of candy and her books.

Such young heroines read with an avid hopefulness shared by

older women, especially middle-class women who want to escape a daily boredom often indistinguishable from despair. Asked by her English professor to describe "an important experience" in her life, Ella Price, a suburban housewife, writes in *Ella Price's Journal:* "Nothing important has ever happened to me."[14] She has married the football player who was her high-school sweetheart, kept house in the suburbs of San Francisco, and brought up a pretty daughter. Now, at the age of thirty-five, she attends Bay Shore Junior College, advised by her doctor to find "new interests" after she has suffered a desolating attack of panic because she "couldn't locate myself." She plods through novels with "female protagonists" who may help her find a self hidden behind the Barbie Doll face that conceals her real features. Typically, she goes to the library with a reading list in hand, directed there by her professor. Methodically, she searches through book after book for a way to release "something in me": the woman who feels. Unlike the fictional heroines she encounters, passionate women who "go after what they want," she has always hidden her feelings. Now books imagine for her a release of emotions she could not have imagined expressing herself. As she reads, a door begins to open:

the door of a closet where I'd hidden a lot of things that didn't seem to fit into my life, a closet stuffed so full that once I'd opened the door just a crack, I couldn't push it closed again, and things started tumbling out. . . .
    I guess I'm afraid that if I let that stuff out it'll make a mess of my nice, neat little house. But it's too late now.(63)

Ella Price discovers "freedom" only because no one, she thinks (mistakenly), has further plans for her. Since the plans for her "first lifetime," designed by "other people, or outside forces," have been fulfilled by marriage and motherhood, she can create a "second" life by releasing the "person" repressed until now. The books she reads in slow succession warn her against the woman she might become: someone invisible like Catherine Sloper in *Washington Square;* or trapped into a dull routine like Carol Kennicot in *Main Street;* or swept to passion and suicide like Emma in *Madame Bovary* and Anna in *Anna Karenina;* or independent but powerless like Anna of *The Golden Notebook;* or ambivalent like Candida. Each fictional heroine enacts a part of the entire process of transformation she is undergoing, teaching her to avoid helplessness, futile rebellion, and spurious freedom, and to develop strength, though she is loved for her weakness by a husband who says, "Lean on me, hon, I'll take care of you." Words which have always seduced her as expressions of love now seem to urge her into permanent helplessness. She sees her marriage as a contract in which she agrees to be "sick and neurotic" to please her husband. In *Androcles and the Lion,* she admires Lavinia's "guts"; and in *Antigone,* the transcendence of a woman who refuses to be "trapped in sex." Such examples lead Ella finally to abort the new life growing within her—the baby she feels manipulated into conceiving—in order to give birth to her self. Like all hungry heroines she wants to become a person born of her own desires and needs, her own feelings: that is what she means by autonomy. She ends with a simple assertion: "I feel." Then she stops, without a final period, so that her journey can continue even though her journal has come to an end.

As an exemplary text, *Ella Price's Journal* shows clearly how the hungry heroine can transform herself by transforming literature into life. But while Ella demands of art its highest function, that of shaping life, she reduces it to didacticism by turning each novel she reads into a textbook. Meanwhile, the novel in which she appears, the novel she creates as she writes her journal, becomes a series of explicit lessons. In a textbook, clarity is a virtue; and in her journal, Ella pursues this virtue necessarily as she tries to understand and revamp her self. But her personal needs conflict with those of the work of art, which requires the complexities and tensions that make the novels she reads "great." In comparison with great novels—a comparison forced upon the reader by its references—*Ella Price's Journal* lacks literary distinction: its didacticism seems banal, its colloquial language flat, and its characters one-dimensional, figures in an allegory that Ella describes as her life. Moreover—if more can be said in criticism without devastating a novel I consider interesting and instructive—Ella remains a naive reader, unquestioning because she desperately needs the answers she finds. Perhaps one should not expect from her the sophistication (and cynicism) of a Ph.D. candidate studying literature at Harvard, from someone like Mira in *The Women's Room.* Mira suspects that the great books she studies contain "lies" because they stop short of the "real endings" life concocts. "Suppose Antigone had lived," Mira thinks, jumping to a startling possibility unimaginable to Ella: "An Antigone who goes on being Antigone year after year would be not only ludicrous but a bore." Ella desperately needs Antigone to be as she has defined her: "the hero in a story about loyalty and integrity and courage and freedom"; and if this definition is unexamined and simplified, still it motivates readers to act courageously. Perhaps courage will prove ineffectual in a society that punishes those who try to change it, but to submit to such pessimism at the beginning of the heroine's journey—as Mira submits at the end—means impassivity, hopelessness, and death. In *Ella Price's Journal,* as in other novels, the heroine not only avoids this fate: she achieves a positive goal. She becomes articulate. She expresses what she feels and she feels herself becoming an integrated whole person. For a woman who could not "locate" herself, this is not a negligible accomplishment.

I have already mentioned a recurrent character in whom the heroine sees her ideal person mirrored: the professor who complicates her life with longings for love. In Yezierska's story "Wings," when Shenah Pessah is with a young professor, she becomes ambiguously aroused, imagining her "person" in his as both an erotic and intellectual fulfillment. *Ella Price's Journal* describes going to bed with the professor as an obligatory initiation rite for a woman reentering college. But physical union, passionate (or disappointing) as it may be, involves a symbolic identification which, once made, allows the heroine to go on her way alone. Jane discards five farewell notes in *The Odd Woman* and could have written more, simply to tell her professor, "I decided to leave." Sometimes he is the one to leave, for once he initiates the heroine to the ritual of reading, arousing her desire for books—and life—he has fulfilled his function and can disappear. He may leave the heroine mystified, wanting more, as Carrie wants more from Ames. He may show her the difficulty (or impossibility) of ever reading correctly, as does Professor Emory Bortz, that strange unpredictable character who gives Oedipa an illegible text: " 'I can't read this,' Oedipa said. 'Try,' said Bortz." The heroine's male mentor need not, of course, be an actual professor. As in *A Tree Grows in Brooklyn,* he may be a more advanced student than the heroine, or else a more sophisticated, intellectual interlocutor, someone who can teach even by his negative example. In *Brown Girl, Brownstones,* Clive says prophetically to eighteen-year-old Selina: "Look, how would you like to take lessons from me—so that when you're my age [twenty-nine] you won't be like me."[15] And she won't, for already she is "grabbing [at] life" as she gazes beyond his body to the books stacked on his kitchen shelf. Like Francie in another part of Brooklyn, Selina spends her girlhood summers in the public library and dreams of going away to college.

Such dreams isolate the hungry heroine, who pays a high "price" for the city's free education. As another of Yezierska's heroines says in the novel *Bread Givers:* "Knowledge was what I wanted more than anything in the world. . . . And now I had to pay the price. So this is what it cost. . . . No father. No lover. No family. No friend. . . . I must go on—alone."[16] Because she defies her father and her sister's husband, parasitic men who have ruined her sisters, Sara Smolensky becomes an outcast; but as she learns "to love being alone," she converts her isolation into freedom. Later she chooses solitude over marriage, refusing a wealthy lover who excites her with his passion while he remains unmoved by hers: "You're only books, books, books," he shouts, having already told her that "only dumbheads fool [with] . . . education and books and all that sort of nonsense." Like James Joyce's fabulous artist as a young man, the young heroine must fly by all the nets that would confine her: duty to parents, sexual passion, marriage. In some ways her flight is more perilous than his, since in giving up love, she loses her timeless identity as a woman, suffering a kind of death so that she can live her new life. Eventually, if she is lucky, a man may come along and love the self-created "person" she has become. Most novels end before he can appear.

In her total isolation, as she starves and freezes in her rented room, someone does visit Sara, coming as if by magic to bring her warmth and food—a feather quilt and pickled herring—and love: "selfless, dark, pleading love." Sara's mother, a poor oppressed immigrant woman, who represents above all the person Sara wants *not* to be, travels through the cold night, from New Jersey to East Side New York, to help her daughter. Lurking in the background of most heroines is a helping mother, usually a poor illiterate woman who struggles and schemes for the daughter whose hunger she herself may arouse. In the novel, mothers transcend the divisive differences in American life. Whether they are Chinese, black, or white, living in San Francisco, Harlem, or Brooklyn, working in laundries or factories, all share the dream of a better life for their daughters. In Louise Meriwether's novel of Harlem, *Daddy Was a Number Runner,* the mother says:

> "You don't have to do no domestic work for nobody, Francie." We was in the kitchen fixing dinner. "You don't be no fool, you hear? You finish school and go on to college. Long as I live you don't have to scrub no white folks' floors or wash their filthy windows. What they think I'm spending my life on my knees for? So you can follow in my footsteps? You finish school and go on to college. Somebody in this family got to finish school. You hear what I say?"
> "Yes, Mother, I hear."[17]

This little Francie growing up in Harlem might have been named after the heroine of *A Tree Grows in Brooklyn,* a girl who inherits the legacy of hunger from her illiterate Irish grandmother. When Francie Nolan was born, Grandmother Rommely had told her daughter Katie, a poor ignorant janitress, the "secret" of how to make "a different world" for her child:

> The secret lies in the reading and the writing. . . . Every day you must read one page from some good book to your child. Every day . . . until the child learns to read. Then *she* must read every day. I know this is the secret. (74)

Francie's "library" originates with Aunt Sissy's christening present, a twenty-five-cent "worn-out copy of Shakespeare" and a "swiped" Gideon Bible. Years later as Katie Nolan tries to save her children from the "filth and dirt" of Williamsburg streets, she rediscovers her mother's secret. Suddenly, she sees that the difference between vulgarity and fineness comes not from money, as she might have thought, but from education: "It was education that made the difference. . . . That's what Mary Rommely, her mother, had been telling her all those years. Only her mother did not have the one clear word: education!" (185).

Desire for an education may force the heroine into open conflict with her mother, whose strength she finds inspiring but overwhelming. If she is to become her own self, she must escape a bindingly intimate relationship. In *Brown Girl, Brownstones,* Selina Boyce affirms her kinship with her mother as she leaves home: "you see I'm truly your child. Remember how you used to talk about how you left home . . . as a girl of eighteen and was your own woman? I used to love hearing that. And that is what I want. I want it!" Thousands of miles away from Brooklyn, in San Francisco's Chinatown, another daughter defies the mother she emulates:

I'm smart, and I can win scholarships. I can get into colleges. . . . I know how to get A's. . . . I could be a scientist or a mathematician if I want. I can make a living and take care of myself. . . . I'm not going to be a slave or a wife. . . . I'm going to get scholarships, and I'm going away.[18]

To this ringing pronunciamento, with its traditionally male motif of "going away," the mother replies that she already "knows about college": "What makes you think you're the first one to think about college? . . . I went to medical school. . . . I don't see why you can't be a doctor like me." But though the heroine may be like someone else, and may consciously seek someone else to show her who she is, she must establish her difference from the women whose values she assumes. The mother who in China had been Doctor Brave Orchid, an honored "Lady Scholar," now sorts dirty clothes in a Chinatown laundry, but she bequeathes to her American-born daughter timeless stories that celebrate women's courage, intelligence, and will. These qualities inspire the heroine to imitate and also defy her mother and, by leaving her, to answer the question she had once asked: "Which would you rather be? A ghost who is constantly wanting to be fed? Or Nothing?" Ghost or modern woman warrior or both, the heroine knows she will never be nothing, for she has learned from her mother that work gives a woman an identity: "Don't worry about me starving," she says, "I won't starve. I know how to work." Like Brave Orchid, who left China to create a new life in a new land, the Dragon daughter of a Dragon mother must "go away."

Inevitably, the heroines of immigrant background evoke the perennial legend of America as a Golden Land. They see a new Canaan where "learning flows free like milk and honey." With this glowing if clichéd hyperbole, Shenah Pessah presents herself as a new Columbus in a story called, appropriately, "How I

Discovered America."[19] Like Columbus, Shenah explores an unknown territory, a new world opening upon "visions upon visions" of freedom: "I saw before me free schools, free libraries, where I could learn and learn and keep on learning." Shenah sees these glorious possibilities in Manhattan's Lower East Side, a neighborhood scarred with poverty, struggle, violence, and waste. In the slums of great cities, successive waves of immigrants have always renewed the dream of America. Even when the heroine is native-born, she emanates from an immigrant tradition, being spiritually and filially related to women like Brave Orchid, who braved the Pacific to reach San Francisco, and Irish Grandmother Rommely, who crossed the Atlantic to settle in Brooklyn.

In Brooklyn, Francie Nolan goes to the neighborhood library every day for years, and day after day the librarian fails to recognize her. To this indifferent woman, Francie is faceless and nameless, no one in particular. Before she leaves for college, Francie deliberately forces the librarian to look at her, disrupting an established impersonal routine by demanding recognition: "'I've been coming here since I was a little girl,' said Francie, 'and you never looked at me till now.'" The fretful librarian complains that "there are so many children," their sheer number evokes indifference, a buffering mask that protects city people. Urban density, the incessant pressure which shapes the social forms of city life, envelops Francie in anonymity. At once dangerous and liberating, anonymity annihilates her identity, but also it allows her to choose her own name. Like the novel's symbolic tree, which grows out of arid soil, Francie emerges from the dense crowd of anonymous city faces to insist upon recognition of her presence; and every aspect of city life commonly considered invidious seems to strengthen her desire that she be seen as her self. Desire expressed in the physiological metaphor of hunger becomes elemental, synonymous with life itself. The hungry heroine believes that she can live passionately, even in the city's slums and skulking back streets; and that she will live as a person who is free. Freedom seems to her inherent in a fluid if disorganized urban society, one that by its disorder and indifference has released her from the roles assigned to women by history and myth. Inevitably, the city severs a traditional relationship between nature and women; the heroine no

longer need act as earth-mother, the woman who, like Willa
Cather's famous Ántonia,[20] satisfies herself by nurturing others.
In a city throbbing with dreams and desires, the heroine learns
to identify her own needs; and living among strangers, she has
privacy in which to cultivate personal desires usually condemned
by family and friends as "selfishness." Anonymity releases her
from the traditional constraints of small-town life, from constant
surveillance, gossip, and public censure, all outlined in *Main
Street,* a novel that helped educate Ella Price. Enjoying physical
and social space in the city, the heroine moves about freely and
experiences movement as freedom. For her, the territory
ahead—the essence of freedom in male myths of the West—lies
around the corner, a few streets away, in another neighborhood
where nobody knows her and where she alone will say who she
is. Like Sara Smolensky, she needs only enough courage to move
a few blocks away. She may never escape the traps and
confinement inherent in life itself, but she can escape a tyrannical father or a debilitating husband and their imprisoning
definitions. Joe Price has defined a wife as a neurotic and helpless woman, and that is what he wants; and Mr. Smolensky has
defined a daughter as submissive and self-effacing, a slave. The
hungry heroine can reclaim herself from these definitions by
renting a room of her own. Even if she wants to remain at home,
home itself has become temporary in the city, family ties tenuous, traditions of family loyalty demolished as easily and irrevocably as the tenement destroyed overnight to make way for a
new building. Excitement of the new, of a new self and a new
life, can modulate the sense of loss and transform it into libera-
tion. The hungry woman in the city shares with the immigrant a
hope that displacement means opportunity.

Social indifference, considered the bane of city life, also liber-
ates the heroine from constraints, particularly those that seem to
her, perhaps mistakenly, inseparable from love. She wants a love
that leaves her free and intact, a vision she may have learned
from men. In the novels she has read, the hero flees from a
devouring woman, an archetypal figure who projects his fear of
engulfment. Similarly, the heroine runs from love that disguises
possessive desire. She prefers solitude to loss of self, and in the
city she can be alone without seeming eccentric, deficient, or a
failure. Solitude does not mean isolation, a fate that has driven

rural characters to desperation or madness. The heroine compares herself with and differentiates herself from others in the
city, strangers and friends, learning from them who she is. Asserting her own identity, choosing her own name, she resists the
forces of urban anonymity and indifference, turning them into a
test of her own will. Devastating as the city can be for any individual—its violence and destructiveness need no documentation—its illimitable possibilities excite passion.[21] The hungry
heroine feels passionately alive, even to pain. Hunger of course
is painful, but also elemental and driving. Unlike heroines who
deny themselves as a way of denying their society, suffering
silent women, the hungry heroine does not choose pain; she
rejects masochism and madness as foils in a sexual power play;
she would never starve herself like the anorexic heroine, or
make her own inanition and death a form of passive resistance.
She starves because she is poor, but like Sara Smolensky, she will
spend her last pennies for bread so that she can sustain herself
and survive. She chooses action over passivity, pursuing knowledge as a direct access to power.

What knowledge can achieve for a woman may remain uncertain in the novel, for it ends often with the heroine's declaration
of independence rather than with her tangible accomplishments. The Woman Warrior announces her plan to go as far
away as China, where she hopes to discover her roots and the
truth about the stories by which her mother has shaped her life.
When she returns home, a self-created person, she will establish
a new life so far only vaguely defined. In an earlier memoir of a
Chinese-American girl growing up in San Francisco—Jade Snow
Wong's (now highly criticized) Fifth Chinese Daughter[22]—a less
vehement but no less hungry heroine outlines more specific
plans for a new life: having been transformed from an obedient
Chinese daughter into an American woman, Jade Snow opens a
shop which will support her while she writes. San Francisco is
essential to her plans, as are all cities to the heroine seeking
independence, for there, as the Woman Warrior said, "she can
work." Sara Smolensky returns to the East Side to earn her living
as a school teacher: "Home! Back to New York!" she cries, "Sara
Smolensky, from Hester Street, changed into a person!" Like
Cinderella, Sara celebrates her transformation with new clothes,
a new home, and a new union—a "honeymoon with myself."

Eventually, she does find a prince, in fact the principal of her school who recognizes the affinity for which every hungry heroine longs—that she and a learned man "are of one blood." Having been recognized as a sister, she can become a wife.

While such transformations evoke a happy ending, they also define the limits of the hungry woman's imagination and of the social world in which it has been shaped. Young or old, immigrant or native-born, each woman suffers, struggles, and works, only to conform finally to a stereotype. As a school teacher, Sara becomes a surrogate mother: "My job was to teach—to feed hungry children." Guilt taints her happiness. Seeing the huddled peddlers on Hester Street, the impoverished anonymous crowd from which she has escaped, she finds happiness "hard to enjoy": "I felt like one sitting down to a meal while all the people around him were howling hungry." Altruism did not bother Faust, not Eugene Gant, that vortex of egotism; they feast while others hunger, and their unappeasable appetites have inspired poetry. In contrast, women who appease their hunger without guilt inspire childlike fantasies: they are allowed "the happy endings" they seek by the fairy-tale matrix of their story. As symbolic accounts of female development, fairy tales describe the emergence of the self as a process of transformation:[23] Cinderella changes into a princess, needless to say, and the ugly duckling into a swan. An ugly duckling, the hungry heroine escapes tyrannical demands for physical beauty which must defeat a woman as her beauty fades. In Edith Wharton's novel *The House of Mirth*, Lily Bart sees her doom etched in the incipient lines of her face; but the heroine who values her intellect more than her complexion and her person more than her personality can survive without beauty. Reversing usual standards of judgment for women, she respects brains: "When I get to college," the modern Woman Warrior shouts, "it won't matter if I'm not charming. And it doesn't matter if a person is ugly; she can still do schoolwork." Doing schoolwork, as we have noted, may be a circuitous path back to motherhood. We have yet to see a portrait of the satisfied hungry woman who transcends either social stereotypes or fairy-tale transformations. Perhaps the most we can expect now is the portrait of a woman in process, her consciousness still emerging, her self in a state of becoming as she seeks the power to *be*. We have accepted inchoateness in our portraits of the developing male. *Of Time and the River* ends with Eugene still reaching towards his identity as an artist, and Joyce's great novel tells us who Stephen Dedalus aspires to be, but does not show us unironically who he has become.

We know who Edith Wharton became, and Willa Cather, to choose two of our most celebrated women writers, both "omnivorous" readers, the hungry heroines of real life. Writing of her emergence as an artist in *A Backward Glance,* Wharton recalls on page after page the endless number of books she "devoured."[24] When she was a child, "home" and "New York" were synonymous to her with "the kingdom of my father's library." Critics can of course trace achievement to neurotic sources, but I find the persistent imputations cast upon the origins of Wharton's art ungenerous and peculiar. That she wrote out of intense personal needs has become somehow a special criticism of her work—a criticism implicit in Edmund Wilson's influential essay called (ironically, I find) "Justice to Edith Wharton."[25] A recent biography uses Erik Erikson's theories of human development (now held suspect by many feminist critics) to interpret Wharton's "hunger," her driving creative force, as "a residue of infantile emotion."[26] If Wharton suffered from "the undispelled, unmitigated rage of the hungry and unsatisfied infant," so do we all. That is why we all recognize and respond to hunger as a metaphor for desire; and desire, Willa Cather insisted, is the elemental source of art. Like Edith Wharton, Cather read "omnivorously," hungrily, her biographer tells us.[27] Whatever her emotional problems, difficult to document because many of her personal papers have been destroyed, no psychobiography can make us doubt her luminous art, an achievement that makes us expect from American women writers the great novels they have still to create.

I would like to end by demanding the novel I expect and want, one whose style and form are commensurate to the Faustian theme of a woman's healthy hunger, her desire for personal freedom. But great novels are not written because of a reader's demand, and great novelists, though nurtured by social and literary traditions, are not willed into being by an audience. Obviously, there has always been an audience responsive to heroes and heroines who express inordinate desires, aspiring like Faust to an ultimate freedom for which we contemporaries have only such vague sociological terms as *personal autonomy*.[28] The magnificent Fausts created by Goethe and Marlowe failed finally to define freedom any more clearly or to achieve it; and their inordinate desire damned them to hell. Nevertheless, they inspired the genius of poetry. The realistic novel as a genre not only avoids the heights of poetic language, but also, inherently, prohibits the portrayal of an autonomous person. For since the realistic novel predicates a society for its protagonist, it must inevitably show individual freedom to be circumscribed. How can one be free, autonomous, and still part of a society? This is the issue that Freud resolved pessimistically by stressing our inevitable discontents with civilization. As we know, the imaginative appeal of Robinson Crusoe persists to our time; we still respond with interest and delight when Crusoe appears in American fiction in the guise of modern man. But an autonomous woman living alone in the city, independent emotionally as well as economically, tests our disposition as readers, for she threatens our sense of an established order as much as she satisfies our sense of daring. She challenges the realistic novelist who wants to dramatize autonomy as an actual state of being within the constraining social world we recognize as our own. Nevertheless, we can discern the pattern that ideally her life would follow, and though any single heroine may not trace this pattern in its entirety, even when she deviates from it, she reveals its heroic intention and design.[29] Her *desire* for personal freedom places her clearly within the context of urban literature, for desire has always been the great energizing theme of the American city novel since the startling appearance in 1900 of Dreiser's *Sister Carrie*. For a woman, a writer or heroine, to express impelling desire (other than a desire for love) requires courage, for she must defy literary and social conventions. I commend the daring she shows when she avows sheer voracious hunger for knowledge, for power, for possession of her self. If this daring has not yet found its full scope, we can be encouraged by the signs we see. Recently, desire has begun to inspire American women novelists as a theme of their own. The beginnings may still be tentative, ending in abortion—or with abortion, as does *Ella Price's Journal*. Novels describing the hungry heroines may still be inchoate because they express an inchoate but emerging consciousness, establishing a precedent for heroines who are not passive, or self-starving, suicidal, or mad: rather, vigorously and healthily hungry. If some will say infantilely hungry, I look forward to growth and development and maturity. Then we might have a heroine who inspires the poetry commensurate to her Faustian aspirations. Meanwhile, with Oedipa Maas, one of my favorite heroines, I wait.

"Lives" of Women Writers:

Cather, Austin, Porter /

and Willa, Mary, Katherine Anne

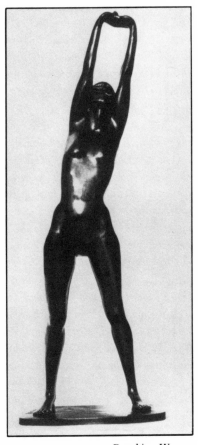

Reaching Woman

ON "LIVES" OF WOMEN WRITERS—AND READERS

Like the women I have been writing about, my "life" has been associated with pages of books, those I have been reading since my sister taught me the alphabet before I started kindergarten. One wonders, looking back, about the meaning of a life devoted to books and their imaginary worlds. Cather asserted that literature offered escape from the world; escape was its primary function, its beauty and utility. If so, then like Margaret Atwood's Lady Oracle, I can claim to have been an "escape artist." In Atwood's novel Lady Oracle, *the heroine escapes from her husband, her lover, her mother, the bonds of her childhood, from constraints that interfere with her becoming her self— or rather, her various selves. I cannot say what I have escaped from, except immediate surroundings of time and place; and I would like to think that I escaped into consciousness. Reading, I believed, should make one aware, extend the boundaries of one's limited consciousness beyond that which experience, fortuitously assigned, would offer. Actual experience, during the years I was incessantly reading, seemed to me limited. Travel was not a family activity, neither when I was a child nor when I was an adult, studying, working, and bringing up children. I traveled into the landscape of American novels, felt the wind rushing through the high grass of the Midwest prairies before I saw Nebraska, felt the clayey quality of the rich red soil between my fingertips before I saw Georgia. Now, as I review a lifetime of imaginary experience, all vivid, usurping, and time-consuming, I wonder, as Cather did late in her life, whether the imagination is fearsome and false, seducing us away from real experiences and actual relationships—making us somewhat mad as we see what is not there to be seen. The "hungry" heroine I have described believed that literature would educate her to life, not withdraw her from its activities and conflicts, its realities, whatever they might be. I shared the belief, and now I share the doubt of some troubled hungry heroines who wonder whether associating their lives with books meant displacing their energies from an actual world where they must live to one that is imaginary, unreal, and hence misleading; whether literature is a tortuous guide. These essays are not intended as a vindication of a life devoted to books. As pieces placed in juxtaposition, they create a literary collage that one can show—that is all one can make public or publish. The rest remains in the mind where the red prairie grass and the red soil, long gone, still exist.*

I

Orlando had become a woman—there is no denying it. But in every other respect, Orlando had remained precisely as he had been. The change of sex, though it altered their future, did nothing to alter their identity. Their faces remained, as their portraits prove, practically the same.

Like Virginia Woolf's fantastical biography *Orlando*, recent biographies of American literary women raise the controversial issue of sexual difference. One wonders if the story of a life, the *writer's* life, can remain, like Orlando's face, "practically the same," essentially the same, when the sex of its protagonist has changed. Modern feminist theory would lead one to assume that literary biography tells a different story and tells it differently when its central character is Willa Cather, Mary Austin, or Katherine Anne Porter rather than, say, Ernest Hemingway.[1] Indeed, a statement that gender affects genre seems platitudinous: not surprisingly, a recent study of women's autobiography concludes that it differs significantly in style as well as content from the life stories men have traditionally told.[2] Literary biography has not yet been formally examined for gender variation, though as a genre (defined persuasively by Leon Edel)[3] it might be expected to alter its mode in response to sexually altered content, to make accommodations, however subtle, in narrative method, imagery, tone. Orlando's biographer seems to have claimed otherwise, noting that Orlando's identity as writer remained inviolate even though he/she had changed sex. If such integrity of a literary life does exist, creating a self impervious to sexual (and historical) change, then the story of a woman's struggle to shape a career—the writer's paradigmatic struggle with material and métier—should fall naturally into patterns of biography formed by the traditional telling of men's lives. This inference seems validated as one looks at three recent portraits of the American woman as writer in which she appears, at first glance, "practically the same" as a man.

In 1902, when she was twenty-eight and the author of a single volume of poetry, Cather was traveling in Europe and sending back descriptive dispatches to the *Nebraska State Journal*.[4] In 1908, Austin toured Italy before leaving for London; she was forty years old and had published stories, novels, and the essay collection *The Land of Little Rain*, now considered a classic. Porter arrived in Mexico in 1920; a late starter and slow worker, at the age of thirty, she had produced only some children's fairy tales; but like Cather she was a journalist traveling on assignment. One year after Porter left for Mexico (and three years after his fateful wounding in Italy), Hemingway was returning to Europe. Younger than Porter by nine years, and two and three decades younger than Cather and Austin, he was twenty-two when he arrived in Paris. In time he would zigzag through Spain, Italy, Switzerland, through Wyoming and Montana, Tanganyika, Kenya, Havana, Bimini, Key West, and Paris again. Impelled by a love of foreign lands, by restlessness, curiosity, need for change and adventure, he desired above all experiences that could be transmuted into art.

Such motives, however modulated by their individual temperaments, also impelled Cather, Austin, and Porter to crisscross the American continent and the Atlantic Ocean. Throughout their lives, they traveled with rhythmic regularity, alternating work with wandering; home (different homes at different times) with a world elsewhere. Travel constituted an essential part of their personal lives and, more important, their creative lives. Like Hemingway, each sought and found experiences, places and people, which were to become the facts of her fiction. Porter seems to have had an instinct for being someplace at a dramatically portentous moment: in Greenwich Village at the hectic height of Prohibition; in Mexico as revolutions raged and waned; in Berlin during Hitler's rise; in Paris under the threat of invasion; and in Washington, D.C., while the country was at war. If Hemingway's travels seem more far-flung and compulsive than those of Porter, Cather, and Austin, and begun at an earlier age (war providing a means for young men to leave home), their wanderings were nonetheless wide, adventuresome, and (as the contemporaneous lives of Edith Wharton and Gertrude Stein show) not unique. All these women writers seemingly had latitude to go where they wished and as they wished. Moreover, they went not as daughters or wives or somehow kept women, but as free-lance writers. True, their wishes may have been circumscribed by a sexually determined *lack* of desire—they preferred not to shoot lions[5] or watch bulls killed and men gored—but they did not feel themselves shut out, against their will, from a world open to men only. Images of confinement or enclosure, which feminist critics have found expressive of women's experience in literature and life, seem inapplicable to these "lives," shaped though they were by Victorian mores which should not have prepared women to work and recreate in the world at large. Nevertheless, the biographies indicate, they did.

They were not excluded from the company of literary men, or of famous men. Though Cather had published only one novel at the time, she was invited (as were Austin and Ellen Glasgow) to the lavish celebration of William Dean Howells' seventy-fifth birthday, a "gathering of distinguished men," as the *New York Times* reported it, which included the president of the United States. Thirteen years later, now a novelist, she was among the distinguished literati celebrating Robert Frost's fiftieth birthday. While Sinclair Lewis praised her work and F. Scott Fitzgerald wrote her unctuously admiring letters, the list of literary men Cather associated with is shorter and less glittering than that of Austin or Porter, or of Hemingway. Cather was always more private than they, more self-contained and steady in her work, less needy; she was exclusive, rather than excluded. Austin may have been initially rejected by the artists of "San Francisco's Bohemia" because, as her biographer states, "unattractive women, however talented, were not welcome"; but in time she helped sustain the circle of Carmel artists which included Jack London, Ambrose Bierce, Joaquin Miller, John Muir, Edward Markham, the ill-fated George Sterling, and Lincoln Steffens. Austin's list of literary connections expanded in London, where she came to know George Bernard Shaw (whom she introduced to Sinclair Lewis), Conrad, Yeats, and H. G. Wells. Wells confided to Austin the intimate details of his strange sexual ménage and then threatened to sue her for reference to them in her autobiography. In London, she traveled with the Herbert Hoovers, and continued her friendship with them until she disagreed with Hoover's policies as president. Porter frequented the White House at the invitation of Jack Kennedy and of a fellow Texan, Lyndon Johnson. Just as Austin associated mainly with Western writers, Porter knew closely Southerners such as Robert Penn Warren, Alan Tate, Carleton Beals, and Cleanth Brooks; and among others, Glenway Wescott, Malcolm Cowley, and Hart Crane. Her relationships, not unlike Hemingway's, were marred by disorder and occasional violence. Here Porter's sex and sexuality enter into consideration. Porter liked to cook for and entertain her friends; she needed them about her, and she allowed herself to be drained by them of time and energy and to be drawn into sordid affairs. She quarreled seriously with the drunken Hart Crane when he tried to seduce her fourteen-year-old Mexican houseboy. She was either raped or abused by Robert Coates at a wild party; the details are not clear, but broken ribs landed her in the hospital. Her affair with Matthew Josephson, like Austin's with Lincoln Steffens, dwindled and left her humiliated, feeling hurt and rejected. This murky mixture of personal and literary relationships should not obscure the point, however, that as writers Porter and Austin had a circle of male friends who respected their work and helped them publish it, giving them advice, support, and money.

Though the individuals of their literary coterie were different, the "lives" of the women paralleled that of Hemingway as a writer among writers—so much so that he, apparently more than anyone else, resented their prestige. When Sylvia Beach introduced Porter and Hemingway to each other as "the two best modern American writers," he "hurled" himself silently into the rainy Paris night, galled, Porter said, "to have his name pronounced in the same breath as writer with someone he had never heard of, and a woman at that."[6] When Cather won the Pulitzer Prize for *One of Ours,* a novel dealing with an American soldier stationed in France during World War I, Hemingway called the war scenes "fake" and Cather a "poor woman" who had gathered her material from a movie (rather than, as he would, from life). Hemingway's aptitude for making malicious remarks—a "capacity for contempt," his biographer called it—was not limited by the sex of another writer: he demeaned, among many others, his friends Sherwood Anderson and F. Scott Fitzgerald. His casual insulting of Porter and Cather belongs in the context of his reproachable treatment of women in general, which is more pertinent to his biography than to their "lives."

Their lives as writers did not go unhonored. All received honorary degrees from prestigious universities, Cather from Columbia, California, Michigan, Yale, Smith College, Creighton, and in her home state, from Nebraska. The first woman to whom Princeton University awarded such a degree, she was seated during the graduation ceremonies alongside Charles Lindbergh and Robert Frost. Other honors were diverse and high. Besides the Pulitzer Prize, she received the Mark Twain Society silver medal for *My Ántonia,* the Howells Medal for *Death Comes for the Archbishop,* the Prix Femina Americaine for *Shadows on the Rocks;* and in 1944, the gold medal of the National Institute of Arts and Letters, a distinguished award, given to few writers, which recognized the artist's total achievement. Porter also was awarded the National Institute's gold medal and the Pulitzer Prize, and in addition the National Book Award and Guggenheim Fellowships. She too received honorary degrees; had a university library room named after her; and occupied the Chair of Poetry at the Library of Congress in Washington. Austin delivered a series of lectures at London's famous Fabian School (where her friendship with Bernard Shaw was formed) and at Yale University. In 1922, a lavish testimonial dinner was given in her honor by the National Arts Club; escorted by a Native American artist dressed in embroidered buckskin and feathered headgear, Austin swept into the New York banquet hall wearing a gown the rose color of a Southwest sunset. Among those who lauded her were Carl Van Doren and Henry Seidel Canby, canonizing critics of American literature. Honorary degrees were to follow. Of course, none of these honors compares with the Nobel Prize awarded to Hemingway in 1954 ("I should have had the damn thing long ago," he is reported to have said); but that any of the three was deprived of this highest award because she was a woman, few critics, however persuaded of sexual discrimination, would seriously argue. In 1962, Porter had come close to the prize when her name appeared on the selection committee's short list.

Like men, the women supported themselves by writing. They

all came from families without money and had to struggle for their start. Austin never ceased struggling, for though she was the most prolific of the three, her books earned little money. Several that have recently been reissued should enhance her reputation by the modernity of their ideas, a disadvantage in her own time. Cather produced several best sellers and lived comfortably on her earnings. Her lifelong companion, Edith Lewis, said that the "financial rewards" Cather received for her writing "freed her from worry about money and assured her of liberty to work with complete independence." Porter became rich through the sales of her monumental novel *Ship of Fools*, though throughout her career she always needed money, no matter how much she earned, because she was notoriously extravagant. The reasons for this extravagance cannot be separated from her ideal of a beautiful and successful woman, a culturally engendered ideal personified by the glamorous movie star whom Porter resembled, might almost have been. Here again distinctions must be made: Porter may have spent her money impulsively and foolishly because as a woman she valued (had been taught to value) clothes, jewels, furs, and lavish furnishings; but she had the power to earn money, and she did that, finally, on a scale to which any male writer would have aspired.

Obviously, no women (and few men) marched with Hemingway at the forefront of the American army to liberate Paris; and though Cather, Austin, and Porter wrote about war, their lack of experience with its actualities can in no way be construed as "practically the same" as his involvement. Nevertheless, each of them participated in public life in a manner and to a degree she wished. None presented herself as powerless or politically incompetent. Cather chose to interest herself in the timeless values of art rather than the social vicissitudes of her time, but as editor of *McClure's*, the famous muckraking journal, she could not help influencing public opinion. After six successful years, she resigned to devote herself entirely to writing. Immersion in public life seemed to her a distraction, not an impossibility. Porter's relationship with public events was as checkered and inscrutable as her personal relationships. She had early implicated herself, somewhat mysteriously, in revolutionary activities in Mexico. In 1927, when Sacco and Vanzetti were to be executed, she marched in protest (along with John Dos Passos, Dorothy Baker, and

Edna St. Vincent Millay) and was duly arrested; fifty years later she published an essay on this "never-ending wrong," as she called it, which was to prove controversial. She declared, with dubious justification, that she had alerted the world to the rise of Nazism by the scooping reports she had sent home from Germany. In 1944, she justified her "political existence" by speaking at a public rally for the reelection of Franklin Roosevelt.

Austin was always a political activist—so much so that her career as writer may have suffered because of her commitment to a variety of social causes which seem now presciently in advance of her time. Like John Muir and John Burroughs, men she came to know, she was a naturalist; she studied closely and recorded the growth of the desert flora she loved, as well as the habits of the bobcat, the elf owl, and diverse creatures of the desert wild. Inevitably, she became an environmentalist. In 1927, as a state representative to the Second Colorado River Conference, she argued cogently for Arizona's water rights on the basis of principles which ideally should govern natural resource policy. History was to side with her views, in this case as in others. Her contributions to the preservation of Native American cultures in the process of being eradicated are inestimable. Having educated herself about native life—she had an anthropologist's application and a poet's sensitivity—she helped educate the public by her widely disseminated lectures on Indian art and religion and her many books. *The American Rhythm,* a pioneering work, remains an authoritative if controversial study of the influence of indigenous motifs upon American poetry and life. She prevailed in a struggle to gain essential land and water rights for the Pueblo Indians. Indeed, her activities in their behalf are too numerous to relate here. Much as Hemingway loved Spain, she loved the American Spanish heritage she found in the Southwest. Almost single-handedly, she saved for posterity a priceless old Spanish chapel, El Santuario of Chimayo, and its treasured shrine and statues. She also helped save the old Spanish ambience of Santa Fe; travelers enchanted with muted adobe houses, gardens enclosed in courtyards, and rambling shop-lined streets owe Austin a debt of gratitude. In 1930, she served as president of the Spanish Colonial Arts Society. Contemporary attempts to preserve the nation's Spanish heritage update Austin's early support of American minority cultures. Since her exploits (unlike Hemingway's) are little known, they should be noted here, and noted for their effectiveness and for the independence of spirit with which they were undertaken. She took issue with Cather at the height of Cather's fame, reporting in her autobiography her dismay that the writer of *Death Comes for the Archbishop* "had given her alliance to the French blood of the Archbishop; she had sympathized with his desire to build a French cathedral in a Spanish town."[7] All of Austin's activities—as environmentalist, polemicist, committee organizer, Washington lobbyist—indicate her astute appraisal of her historical times and the need for individual social responsibility. Her "life" should allay any fear that the woman writer would somehow be rendered politically impotent.

In their private lives, Cather, Austin, and Porter lived through family dramas which were to prepare them for their role as writer. Cather and Austin responded ambivalently towards their willful mothers, wanting maternal approval while behaving unacceptably; both resembled their mothers in their unsubmissiveness, their sense of self which would enable them to pursue literary lives. Porter's mother died young and, the biographer opines, not inopportunely. Had she lived, this "gentle, accommodating woman" (supported by "society's expectations of women") might have "compelled" Porter "to play the traditional feminine role"—to become another "Angel in the House." As it was, "the death of her mother, while . . . a personal tragedy . . . became an asset in her [Porter's] development as an artist, the basic necessity for which was that she become a free and independent woman." Of course, independent women are not necessarily artists; the biographer's logic is questionable and blood-curdling, placing upon the woman writer's mother a formidable onus. Were a mother gentle and accommodating, the reasoning goes, she could occlude her daughter's career—at least in Porter's time. Austin's mother was cold and rejecting; clearly, that made her daughter unhappy; whether or not it helped make her a writer, the biographer can only speculate.

Grandmothers figured significantly in all three "lives." Cather's grandmothers taught her Greek and Latin and the value of literature—the beauty of stories and of storytelling. Austin admired the matriarchal pioneer women from whom she descended and whose westward trail she continued in her quest for a new life. At the age of two, Porter was given to the care of her grandmother, a woman of sixty-five who had brought up nine children and now, "aware of her Christian duty," once more assumed the responsibility of rearing. Besides "feeding,clothing, and instilling moral and religious principles," Porter's grandmother "laid the foundation for Porter's literary gifts" by her example as storyteller. Her less tangible influence "was to convey a sense of a woman's being independent, effective, and totally in control of her world." If such control was the grandmother's lesson, Porter failed egregiously to carry it out—except in her stories.

The writers' fathers were notably handsome men and, in different ways, feckless. Always the luckiest of the three, Cather had a father she loved, a refined Southern gentleman whose venial weaknesses reappear in her fiction: he was not a good provider and could not act aggressively in the world. Austin's adored father died young, leaving her with poignant memories of his love and his suffering. Porter's father roused himself from the depression he fell into after his wife's death only to express hostility and rage. He was pathologically violent and at the same time apathetic and self-pitying, providing Porter with a "powerful negative example" of a "wasted life" which may have spurred her ambition to make something of herself. He seems also to have fixated her upon handsome young men of his age to whom she became disastrously attached.

All suffered traumatic dislocations as their families moved to a new place. Each child felt she had irretrievably lost her home, a response to change which may typify them as girls, since, presumably, boys would define movement as adventure rather than as loss. Austin's childhood trip west, like Cather's, "almost killed her." In time, all found in their new homes neighbors who helped satisfy their hunger for books, for culture, a sense of an intricate world beyond their small town; some of these neighbors—the Wieners and the Schlemmers—were immigrants who welcomed the lively and curious girls to their homes, told them stories about the lands they had left, and engendered a desire to travel which they were to spend their lives fulfilling. All considered themselves unpopular, Cather because she was bold and different, Austin because she was not pretty, Porter because she was poor; and all because they were opinionated. As young women, all may have been penalized for being intelligent, perceptive, ambitious, and inadmissibly outspoken. None, however, was openly thwarted or opposed in her desire to become a writer; at worst, such desire was disregarded. If as young women they were pressured by implicit expectations to conform to preconceived gender roles, their burden as females may have been no heavier than Hemingway's as a male. Obviously, he had an obsessive need to prove his masculinity according to a strictly defined code of behavior he found inviolate and challenging.

From a "long perspective," to use Cather's famous phrase, the dislocation and drama the women experienced in their personal lives enriched the writer. If, as modern critics speculate, the need for language is engendered by absence and loss, the loss of home that each child experienced as "tragic" may have generated a desire for recovery which was symbolically fulfilled by the act of writing. Each recovered the original scene of her childhood in her fiction, Cather returning to Virginia in her last novel, *Sapphira and the Slave Girl. My Ántonia,* considered now an American classic, recapitulates Cather's childhood journey from a family home in Virginia to the void of Nebraska's prairies—a landscape immortalized by her descriptions of windswept red grass, slow sunsets, open sky, an endless flat horizon. Inescapably Midwestern no matter how far she traveled, Cather determined to become the Virgil of her region: to be like him the first to bring art to and make art from a landscape poets had ignored. Austin knew that the literary world cared little about the Southwest desert to which she had been removed; but like Cather, she created exquisitely detailed poetic descriptions of an alien land she came to love. They are still pristine in the essays of *The Land of Little Rain.* Porter's stories about southern life cannot be separated from the pain she suffered in the poverty-stricken life to which she was early inducted: "the move to Hays county began one of the most unhappy periods of her life." Out of this period, the writer was to draw the material and emotions of such consummate stories as "Noon Wine" and "Old Mortality." This is to say that women writers transmuted their personal histories into art—as all writers do, as did Hemingway. His ambivalent feelings towards his mother and father, described by his biographer, are inscribed in the first stories of *In Our Time;* and the complexities of his friendships, enmities, and marriages, the experiences that shaped his personality, the values that sustained him and places that renewed his interest and energy—all this, as the biographer can amply document, constitutes the inspiration and substance of his art.

For both men and women literary biography becomes, thus, a discovery and disclosing of sources and an attempt to penetrate the secrets of creativity. As Leon Edel pointed out almost thirty years ago, the literary biographer must be a historian and a critic—and, one might add, a detective. Like the writer, the biographer is also a magician who transforms the accessible facts of a life into the "life" of a character known as Cather, Austin, Porter—or Hemingway. Their reality—that is, their effectiveness in evoking the once-living persons to whom they refer—may be unascertainable. Nevertheless, one can attempt to judge the biographer's skill and integrity, as well as the devotion with which he or she pursues documentary evidence upon which to base a "life." Thinking of sexual difference, one wonders whether the selection of a biographer, the determination of who writes about Hemingway rather than Cather, may be influenced by sexual biases. Certainly, Hemingway was fortunate in his biographer, a patient, knowledgeable, and distinguished scholar (a scholar who earned distinction by writing as he did about Hemingway). Porter also was fortunate. Her life fell into hands which could sort out verifiable facts from the fictions which she invented as her past. Though Porter's admirers may be dismayed at revelations of her extravagances, erratic affairs, and drinking—and of the origins of the stunning final dream sequence of "Flowering Judas" in a drug-induced hallucination—they will appreciate the biographer's skill in depicting Porter's power to survive as a writer and create perfectly ordered prose in the midst of the disorder of her life. In this combination of personal chaos and artistic perfectionism, her "life" resembles Hemingway's.

Austin's biography fills out an earlier skeletal account of the writer's life, but it has to contend for interest and information with Austin's autobiography *Earth Horizon,* to which it is indebted. Slanted or self-serving as any autobiography may be, Austin's life story is also perspicacious, revealing in its tropes and figures as well as its facts, and cumulatively powerful. The sense of rush which drove Austin as she wrote produced in places a succession of apparently simple declarative sentences which become, in the manner of Gertrude Stein's sentences, hypnotic. The effect, as in Stein, is to create the impression of an immediate state of being, of presence and present-ness. The biographer gives a distanced view, describing how Austin struck others, including the biographer herself. Like Porter's biographer, and Hemingway's, she describes a persona that evolved and became in late years "arrogant and imperious," "harsh and abrasive." One finds no case here to argue sexual difference in the way all three biographies tell of weakness, idiosyncracy, meanness, and sporadic outbursts of paranoia; nor in their respect for the writer and his or her work.

On the other hand, the qualifications of Cather's biographer seem, by her own admission, ignorance and nostalgia. Although by now anyone who knows anything about Cather knows that she spent most of her life in New York, her biographer confesses astonishment at this news. She is equally astonished by the person she has discovered. Seeking for the "heroine of her childhood," a stereotypical "woman in a faded portrait," she found instead a woman who was "passionate, alive, more vivid than any of her characters." This is the kind of bosh that would have offended Cather, to fall into the conditional mood that mars this biography. Here one may well wonder about the basis for selection, since the biographer evinces little aptitude for scholarship—not to be confused with speculation, no matter how titillating—or for literary criticism. Is it because Cather was a woman that the biographer creates a pseudofamiliarity with her, setting herself upon a first-name basis? In life, one did not approach Cather so easily, as her biographer well knew, describing her as "always slightly formal," and adding that even after years of association "her publisher . . . never called her anything but Miss Cather." Who is the biographer's Willa, as opposed to the writer Cather?[8] Why the interest in "secrets" (which may not exist) of a woman who, the biographer says, "had an aversion . . . almost obsessive, to revelations of her personal life"? At this point, Orlando's biographer should be recalled, for she is now having second thoughts. "The truth is," she is discovering, "that when we write of a woman, everything is out of place. . . . The accent never falls where it does with a man."

II

Her modesty as to her writing, her vanity as to her person, her fears for her safety all seem to hint that what was said a short time ago about there being no change in Orlando the man and Orlando the woman, was ceasing to be altogether true.

Modesty, vanity, and fear—traits displayed by the woman Orlando signify to the biographer that sexual change has indeed produced difference. For she assumes these are feminine traits which would not be expected to emerge in the male writer's life. In fact, Hemingway's biography is short on modesty. Vanity and fear, however, appear saliently. Why, then, an assumption that this trio of traits differentiates women from men? More pointedly, one might ask whether certain gender-inflected characteristics belong to the woman writer or are attributed to her by the biographer in accordance with his or her assumptions and expectations. Can a contemporary biographer, aware of if not committed to feminist thought, ignore ideology? Does not the epithet "woman" concentrate attention on assumed or putatively discoverable sexual difference? Recently, a study of Ellen Glasgow cited a panoply of respected feminist critics who helped focus attention upon the "problems inherent in being female writers." Inherent in what? one wonders—in woman's "nature," a word Cather's biographer bandies about, or in engendering cultural conditions?

In any culture, problems arise when women (or men) refuse to fulfill the expectations designated for their sex by society. As their birthdates indicate—1868 for Austin, 1873 for Cather, and for Porter, 1890—the three women were to grow up in a changing society, their lives bridging a confusedly rapid transition from Victorian to modern times. As children of Victorian parents and grandparents, they faced expectations for their future which had been fashioned in a past more remote than historical dates would indicate, especially if allowance is made for an inevitable cultural gap. Obviously, young women of their time were expected to marry and mother children, to submit to their husbands' wills, and to seek their happiness, or more important, their duties, within the home. If they wrote for pleasure, they were to do so surreptitiously and without neglecting their domestic chores. If they wrote for money their family required, an acceptable motive, they were to produce sentimental novels in which women prevailed through the power of their Christian meekness and impeccable morality.

Of the three, Cather refused early and adamantly to fulfill any of these expectations. From childhood on, she assumed considerable freedom: she rode her pony where she wished through the open farmlands; she spoke her mind and was respected for her intelligence; she read promiscuously and asked incessant questions, was the terrible but indulged interrogator of neighbors and older friends who told her all she wished to know. To maintain her freedom in the future, she decided early upon renunciation of a traditional woman's role, an act made easier for her, perhaps, because she was the oldest of a large family and a natural leader of the other children. They adored her and she took care of them: in an involuted way she always had a younger family though she had denied herself the possibility of motherhood. She grew up to be a devoted aunt; she never lost her family ties, except by death. As might be expected, she described the conception of a story through images of pregnancy: "First she felt it [the story] in the front of her head, where it enlarged as a baby grows in its mother's womb. And finally, it reached the back of the head where it lay heavy and painful awaiting delivery."[9]

All this suggests a successful avoidance of a woman's expected fate. The costs to Cather were not negligible, however, as her late fiction shows. There, through protagonists who have aged along with the author, she questioned the value of a life devoted to art and devoid of the kinds of personal fulfillments she had given up—essentially a home filled with one's children and with (however she imagined it) love. Such middle-aged characters as Godfrey St. Peter in *The Professor's House* and Clement Sebastian in *Lucy Gayheart*—both successful and highly acclaimed figures, artists—view the vacuity of their middle years and project, Cather's scholars believe, her doubts that she had made the right choice by dedicating herself entirely to writing. Her biographer overlooks these well-known signs of Cather's misgivings. She plays upon Cather's lesbian "passion," though the evidence for it still remains inferential. Cather's biographer writes with a certain prurience which may make her book popular; but she obscures Cather's clear and clearheaded intention to create a design for living which would allow her solitude in which to write and yet not leave her isolated and lonely. Cather chose friends who furthered or fitted into this design. Isabelle McClung, the rich and beautiful woman whom all critics agree Cather loved, was the young writer's patroness, giving her a place to work, contacts with other artists, and constant encouragement. Edith Lewis gave her lifelong companionship. Cather's biographer believes that the liaison between Cather and Lewis was "undoubtedly a marriage in every sense." "Undoubtedly" in this biography usually signifies maximum doubt and minimal documentation. The biographer's efforts to penetrate the secrets of Cather's sexuality result in conjecture and conditional expressions (perhaps, probably, may have, might have, would have) and in assertions made in the absence of fact (it is impossible to know, *but*). Since Cather's personal papers have been destroyed, all that can be known with certainty is that Cather believed art demanded total dedication. She had formulated her aesthetic creed as a young woman in her twenties: "In the kingdom of art there is no God, but one God, and his service is so exacting that there are few men . . . strong enough to take the vows."[10] She spoke of men but meant herself, believing that as a woman she must take a vow which would preclude all others, especially marriage vows. Whether this decision reflects the secret "nature" to which her biographer often alludes remains conjectural. One wonders, speaking of conjectures, whether the biographer would have felt free to take so many liberties guessing at the sexual secrets of a man's life.

To Porter, married at the age of sixteen, a husband seemed the means of escaping a dreary, poverty-stricken, emotionally meager home. To Austin, a husband meant vindication. At last she was fulfilling the expectations of a world, and a mother, that had found her abrasive and undesirable. For both, marriage was to become synonymous with entrapment. As soon as she married, Porter "thought herself permanently trapped in a degrading, restricting situation." The thought was to recur after later marriages: "The marriage was a total and unmitigated disaster, and she knew it to be so on the day it began." Austin also had the "feeling of being trapped both by her marriage and by the narrowness of her existence." After years of incompatibility, made tolerable by frequent separations (so that she could earn money), Austin was divorced. Porter was divorced four times, exceeding Hemingway's three-time record. Husbands brought anguish into the lives of these women (which is not to say that wives may not make the same contribution). When not indifferent to their work, or magnanimously "allowing" it, the men were jealous of time and attention deflected from them. They wanted "wives," even though they were failing as husbands.[11] Austin's husband burdened her with debts she worked to pay. Once she was unceremoniously evicted from a hotel after he had gone without telling her that she was to be thrown into the street. "How would that have helped?" he reasonably asked his wife. Hemingway's biographer, on the other hand, tells of Pauline, the writer's second wife, "who seemed to be devoted entirely to caring for Bumby [Hemingway's son by his first wife] and shielding Ernest from interruption"; moreover, Pauline "had the wealth . . . that he had needed at the time." Financial and emotional support—this is what Hemingway could find in marriage, while Austin and Porter found their writing interrupted, disdained, or ignored, and their emotional life disordered by guilt over their divided loyalties and frustration over impediments to their work.

At the same time, marriage failed to give them the child each wanted. Austin, with her blighted luck, had a retarded daughter whose intermittent violence made her impossible to keep at home. She became a financial and emotional burden that Austin had to bear. Porter evinced deep "sorrow," her biographer says, over her barrenness. Apparently unable to have children, at one time she told friends that she was pregnant, as she may have been, or else was pretending, if not fantasizing. Always concerned with the presentation of her self to others, she obviously believed that her announced pregnancy would make her seem a complete and "real" woman. Childlessness was for her a public as well as personal failure. Coincidentally enough, both biographies tell how Porter and Austin declared proprietary rights to their nieces. Austin's interest became almost obsessive; she wanted to bring up her niece, a motherless child, according to her own enlightened principles. She was not entirely successful. Porter eventually appropriated a nephew who served her like a dutiful son; he came when she called, and she called frequently. Nevertheless, for all their surrogate motherhood, both women, the biographies suggest, suffered because of unfulfilled maternal desires.

This said, one must add a conclusion that the biographer describes Porter reaching, not quickly or "voluntarily" but under the compulsion of repeated failure of her marriages: "writing demanded its own discipline and was not compatible with the demands of ordinary domestic life." In her seventies, Porter was finally concurring with the view that Cather had expressed in her early twenties. Austin also concluded that for her marriage and a career were incompatible. In her autobiography she tells why she had rejected remarriage: "the men who might have married me were . . . involved in creative careers and not financially secure. One or the other of us would have to make sacrifices; and it was sufficiently plain that I should have to be the one." Ironically, to have married would have meant giving up an "activity," writing, that her biographer says, "would be husband, lover, and child to her." Finally Austin regretted, her autobiography states, "not the lack of a satisfying marriage, but the loss out of my life of the traditional protection, the certification of ladyhood." She wondered what she had missed by never having a man take care of her, but she knew what she had gained: "The experience of being competent to myself has been immensely worth while for me."

Thus, though their personal lives seemed superficially as different as their personal appearances—Porter was beautiful, Austin was not, and Cather uniquely herself—their lives as writers demanded, each concluded, a singleness of purpose which the traditional role of wife would have complicated, diverted, and finally destroyed. Each came to see her "life" as shaped, to use Austin's words, by an "immanent Pattern." This predetermined pattern, which excluded marriage and motherhood, was, they found, the woman writer's fate. Even a "life" as full of procrastination and turmoil as Porter's, as idiosyncratic, conformed to the design. As Porter herself said, "All our lives we are preparing to be somebody or something, even if we don't do it consciously." She was, she meant, preparing to be a writer—as Hemingway was always preparing. Like Cather and Austin, Porter would become a writer, "a single, a real self"—to return once again to the words of Orlando's biographer.

To uncover this single self was an enormously complicated task, Orlando's biographer had realized, since the person to be captured in words was in life protean. There were in fact a "thousand" selves, or even "two thousand and fifty-two." Underlying all, there might be one which had ultimate authenticity. For Orlando him/herself, the single, continuous, and immutable identity was that of the writer. After centuries of change, this person was still putting words on paper and still secreting a manuscript close to his/her breast. For the three women, it was Cather, Austin, and Porter. They also were writers and as such to be distinguished from girls and women—from Willa, Mary, and Katherine Anne. These three might worry about physical appearances, with which their photographs show them carefully tampering. They might be concerned with clothes, often conspicuously rich and flattering; and with husbands and lovers, their relationships with men by which the world would judge their success as women. That Willa, Mary, and Katherine Anne would be considered aberrant and arrogant if they tried to conform to an immanent pattern waiting for them angered Cather, Austin, and Porter, who desired recognition as writers and had difficulty winning it from those closest to them: parents, lovers, and husbands. Since to make accommodations which might bring social approval meant, they thought, jeopardizing their careers, Cather, Austin, and Porter inevitably adopted, whether or not they would admit it, resistant feminist positions.

For one thing, each surrounded herself with women friends who would represent her ideal of a woman artist. In this way, each reinforced the "real" self she wanted to nurture. Even abbreviated lists of the writers' women friends show a strong and significant identification with their sex. The list for Cather is shortest because of her usual exclusiveness on the one hand, and on the other her numerous relationships with women known to her since her childhood in Red Cloud. Besides these personal friends, such world-famous musicians as the pianist Myra Hess and the opera singer Olive Fremstad, and the anomalous Mabel Dodge Luhan, Cather was close with the playwright Zoë Adkins, the painter Laura Hill, and the writers Dorothy Canfield Fisher,

Margaret Deland, Elizabeth Sergeant (who has left a memoir of Cather), and late in life, Sigrid Undset. Most important to her career was Sarah Orne Jewett.

Austin's list is more audacious in including politically radical women, for Austin was an articulate feminist whose advanced ideas have by now been formalized into an ideology. Austin associated with Charlotte Perkins Gilman, Margaret Sanger, Ida Tarbell, Elizabeth Gurley Flynn, Emma Goldman, Jane Addams, Beatrice Webb (and among others, Mabel Dodge Luhan, Fanny Hurst, May Sinclair, and Willa Cather). Moreover, she marched in support of women's rights, spoke at public rallies, and infused her fiction with feminist thought, particularly her novels *A Woman of Genius* and *26 Jayne Street*. Her autobiography, *Earth Horizon*, articulates her feminist ideals and exemplifies them by the story of her life.

Porter's women friends, as reported by her biographer, were mainly literary. One intimate was the proletarian novelist Josephine Herbst, from whom she became alienated, in part over political differences. Over the years she knew the novelists Caroline Gordon and Dorothy Day, and the poets Elinor Wylie and Genevieve Taggard. In her early quest for an identity as writer, she took as role models much-traveled women journalists, one of whom became her personal friend and professional mentor. Like everything about Porter, her feminism was volatile, generated by inner needs and subject to change. Her biographer notes the rise and fall of her feminist consciousness. It emerged with early frustrations, when she was young, "strong-willed and independent and very conscious of being deprived, as a married woman, of certain rights." It waned with success and the rise of official feminism, a movement she separated herself from and publicly ridiculed, in part, her biographer believes, simply for effect. "Any man who ever did wrong to me got back better than he gave," she is quoted as saying, a remark that trivialized the women's movement and her own emotionally wrought life. More important than such facetious statements are the prevailing women characters in her fiction. Even in her early fairy tales, her biographer points out, Porter showed a "feminist bias" by featuring "a strong, resourceful female character contrasting with a weak, ineffective male." She had seen this combination in her grandmother's house, where her father had displayed irresponsibility and weakness, and an aging woman great strength.

As a child, Cather had dressed herself in boy's clothes, cropped her hair, and called herself Will. She declared her ambition to become a doctor, made up the signature Wm. Cather, M.D., and startled the audience at her high school by an "unfeminine" speech favoring animal vivisection. As an adult, she remained conspicuously silent on issues concerning women. Her expressed concerns revolved about artistic performance. In early newspaper reviews, she criticized popular women writers for being sentimental and emotional, for not producing "manly" tales. She denigrated Kate Chopin's novel *The Awakening*, now acclaimed by feminist critics, for romanticizing a woman who kills herself for lack of a man's love. In later years she wrote admiringly of the fiction of Sarah Orne Jewett and Katherine Mansfield, judging by standards untinged by sex. Yet though she did not espouse feminist ideals, she served them by creating images of strong and resourceful women upon whom the fate of a new country depended—characters like Alexandra in *O Pioneers!* and Ántonia Shimerda in *My Ántonia*. While Austin articulated feminist ideas in *A Woman of Genius*, producing a prescient tractarian novel and a lifeless heroine, Cather *created* a woman of genius in *The Song of the Lark*, not her best novel but one that dramatizes the best that she thought a woman artist could be and accomplish. Thea Kronberg has driving talent, discipline, singleness of purpose and dedication, energy, desire, and power—and great success. Her song might inspire other women artists, as Olive Fremstad's song had inspired Cather, and as Cather's own stories would energize younger writers such as Porter. Porter, who like Hemingway could defame others, praised Cather in an essay called "Reflections on Willa Cather." She placed her among the "great ones," in the company of Flaubert and Tolstoy. Porter imagined the older writer as "a curiously immovable shape, monumental, virtue itself in her art and a symbol of virtue—like certain churches . . . or exemplary women, revered and neglected." Neither as symbol nor as artist has Cather been neglected; rather, she has become increasingly a center of attention. For as an exemplary woman writer, she now serves feminist causes she refused to espouse in her lifetime.

This may be an irony of her "life" and an unexpected turn in its "immanent pattern": that by fulfilling her destiny as writer, Cather would represent a feminist ideal.

"The biographer is necessarily intrusive, a trespasser even when authorized," wrote Richard Ellmann, an authority on James Joyce's life. In order not to trespass idly, thoughtlessly, the biographer must become aware of the peculiar kind of narrative he or she is telling—of what William Gass called (in his review of a Faulkner biography) "the mechanics of its kind, the physics of its unfolding." Hemingway's life story unfolds as a catalogue of killings; only a computer could give an accurate count of the animals, fish, and fowl dead by his hand. Whether this killing was Hemingway's obsession or an artifact produced by the "mechanics" of a particular biographical narrative cannot be known. The person is inaccessible and the "life" factitious. If it contains secrets—as Cather's biographer hints, Porter's reveals, and Austin's believes disclosed—they may be probed by the sensitive reader of the writer's work. That at least is the contention of Orlando's biographer, who noted this irony: that "every secret of a writer's soul, every experience of his life, every quality of his mind is written large in his works, yet we require critics to explain the one and biographers to expound the other."

If Virginia Woolf is correct, then the secrets of sexual difference being sought here in the narrated facts of a "life" would best be found in fictions that project the writer's personal experiences and emotion—in characters such as Cather's Ántonia, Porter's Miranda, and Austin's woman of genius. No one like them can be found in the fiction of Hemingway. On the other hand, in the women's stories few hunters and fishermen appear, and few soldiers in combat. Such obvious sexual preference in choice of character merely opens the area of difference which includes narrative structure, imagery, theme, symbol, linguistic code (what "mother" signifies in Cather and in Hemingway)—all aspects of literary language and style. The clues offered by the biographer both undermine and reinforce the probabilities of such sexual difference. For the narrated lives reveal that men and women both had opportunities and obstacles, that both demonstrated loyalties and treachery, bravery and cowardice, virtues and weaknesses, love and disdain. Here, as Orlando's wise biographer noted, "we come to a dilemma. *Different though the sexes are, they intermix.*"

Whatever the mixture and whatever the differences, women and men persisted in their drive to write and to create not only stories but their very selves as storytellers. Perhaps that is why so many writers of both sexes have played with their names, as though by naming themselves they could bring into being the writer they felt destined to become. Cather changed her original name of Wilella (her biographer has it Willela), to William, Willie, and finally Willa. Porter's name was Callie May, which became Katherine Russell, K.R., and then Katherine Anne. Austin differentiated between Mary and I-Mary: the one, a girl who tried to live up to social expectations, and the other, an essential, invulnerable, inviolate self who was in touch with the cosmic forces of creativity. This I-Mary, Austin said, always "was associated with the pages of a book." Willa, Mary, and Katherine Anne—they are to be associated with mothers, fathers, lovers, husbands, friends; as women, they lived quotidian lives which were in some ways like and in others radically different from Ernest's. At the same time, these three, Willa, Mary, and Katherine Anne, contributed their lives to the consummate art of Cather, Porter, and Austin, whose names prevail because they will always be associated with the pages of their books. This is the inaccessible secret beyond that of sexual difference: how the stuff of the woman's life—and the man's—becomes transmuted into art and the person into the artist.

"Life? Literature?" Orlando's biographer cried, "One to be made into the other? But how monstrously difficult!"

Notes

Women Writing in America

[1] In an essay published elsewhere, I discuss American ethnic literature as an essential part of American literature. See "Mingling and Sharing in American Literature: Teaching Ethnic Fiction," *College English* 43 (December 1981) 8: 763–778.

The Mountain Lion Reread

[1] Jean Stafford, *The Mountain Lion* (New York: Harcourt, Brace and Company, 1947), 158.

[2] Katherine Anne Porter, "Old Mortality," *Pale Horse, Pale Rider* (New York: Random House, 1939), 81.

[3] Charlotte Brontë, *Jane Eyre* (New York: Norton, 1971), 12.

[4] In her book, *Poets in Their Youth: A Memoir* (New York: Random House, 1982), Eileen Simpson reports a conversation in which Jean Stafford claims Molly's poem as her own, written when she was six: "Want to hear my first poem? [Stafford says]. It's called 'Gravel.' I've just given it to my character Molly in *The Mountain Lion*" (123). Like Molly, Jean Stafford lived in Covina, California, her birthplace, and grew up in Boulder, Colorado. There her father wrote popular Westerns under various names; her mother ran a boardinghouse. As a girl, Stafford "resented her family's poverty," Simpson tells us, presumably repeating Stafford's confidence, "and had felt kinship only with her brother Dick, to whom she was very close" (123). Apparently, Molly enacts some of Stafford's childhood fears and rituals, particularly those related to her aquaphobia.

In 1936, Stafford received a Master of Arts degree from the University of Boulder; subsequently, she studied philosophy at Heidelberg. She has been a teacher, a literary editor, a public lecturer, and an acclaimed fiction writer, the recipient of the Pulitzer Prize in 1970 for her collected stories. Some of the vicissitudes of her adult life, particularly the break-up of her marriage with the poet Robert Lowell, are presented in Simpson's memoir. She died in March 1976 at the age of sixty-one.

Tillie Olsen's "Requa"

[1] Tillie Olsen, *Silences* (New York: Delacorte Press, 1978).

[2] *The Partisan Review* published sections of *Yonnondio* in 1934. See "The Iron Throat," *Partisan Review* 1 (April–May 1934): 3-9; and "The

Strike," *Partisan Review* 1 (September–October 1934): 3–9. The novel appeared forty years later as a still-unfinished work. See Tillie Olsen, *Yonnondio: From the Thirties* (New York: Delacorte Press, 1974).

³Tillie Olsen, *Tell Me a Riddle* (New York: Dell Publishing Co., 1961). Stories in this collection had been published earlier, the first in 1956.

⁴Tillie Olsen, "Requa," *The Iowa Review* 1 (1970): 54–74. Reprinted as "Requa I" in *Best American Short Stories*, ed., Martha Foley and David Burnett (Boston: Houghton Mifflin, 1971). "Requa I" was part of a larger work-in-progress Olsen has just completed.

A long review-essay on Olsen refers to "Requa" briefly. See Selma Burkom and Margaret Williams, "De-Riddling Tillie Olsen's Writings," *San Jose Studies* 2 (February 1976): 79–80, 81–82.

⁵Olsen's knowledge about the varieties of junk comes from her experience as an office worker in a junk yard.

⁶For a discussion of this story, see Annette Bennington McElhiney, "Alternative Responses to Life in Tillie Olsen's Work," *Frontiers* 11 (1977): 76–91. See also Joanne S. Frye, "'I Stand Here Ironing': Motherhood as Experience and Metaphor," *Studies in Short Fiction* 18 (Summer 1981): 287–92.

⁷In reaffirming the radical aesthetics of the thirties which identified the writer's voice with the voice of "the people," Olsen recovers from the past a nearly lost legacy that she values.

⁸In effect, Olsen has recovered the site of Requa as she knew and loved it, for many aspects of her setting no longer exist. The graveyard was vandalized; the salmon are few; and the town of Klamath has become a shopping center with that name. I am indebted to Tillie Olsen for this information, as well as for her plans concerning the continuation of her story.

In a letter dated July 30, 1984, Olsen has added that "Klamath (the town) was destroyed in 1964 by flood—the river had changed—the bridge 'swept away.' Two of the standing bears remain and a fragment of the old bridge—leading to land now, yards from the river."

⁹Tillie Olsen intends the landlady, Mrs. Edler, to play a larger part in Stevie's life "Requa II." Wes, apparently, will die, and Mrs. Edler will carry on his role as "mother."

¹⁰On *Yonnondio* as "class literature from a woman's point of view," see Deborah Rosenfelt, "From the Thirties: Tillie Olsen and the Radical Tradition," *Feminist Studies* 7 (Fall 1981): 371–406. Note particularly 397–405.

Meridel Le Sueur's "Indian" Poetry

¹*Rites of Ancient Ripening* (Minneapolis: Vanilla Press, 1975, reprinted in 1976). The poem "Rites of Ancient Ripening" was published originally in *Corn Village* (Sauk City, Wisc.: Stanton & Lee, 1970), 69–72.

²For an excellent selection of Le Sueur's writing, as well as information about her life, see *Ripening: Selected Work, 1927–1980*, ed. Elaine Hedges (Old Westbury, N.Y.: Feminist Press, 1982). Of interest also may

be my review of *Ripening,* "Rereading a Radical," *New York Times Book Review* (April 4, 1982), 7, 19.

[3] In a recent study of sexual difference, Carol Gilligan says she has "evidence" to show "that women perceive and construe reality differently from men" (171); consequently, she concludes, "men and women may speak different languages that they assume are the same, using similar words to encode disparate experiences of self and social relationships" (173). See *In a Different Voice: Psychological Theory and Women's Development* (Cambridge, Mass.: Harvard Univ. Press, 1981).

Modern French feminists offered theories of difference more complex and subtle than Gilligan's. See Elaine Marks, "Women and Literature in France," *Signs: Journal of Women in Culture and Society* 3 (Summer 1978): 832–42.

At issue in a quest for feminine language is an imputation of biological determinism. Le Sueur's sweeping statements about new "feminine" forms—or more precisely, the emergence of buried forms—correlate women's expression with their anatomy: women artists "structure something that isn't a cube or a square, something related to a woman's body. The round, the circular imagery." See Neala Schleuning Yount, "'America: Song We Sang Without Knowing'—Meridel Le Sueur's America" (Ph.D. diss., Univ. of Minnesota, 1978), 302. For arguments that a "woman's language" would prove inimical to women's welfare, see "Variations on Common Themes" in *New French Feminisms: An Anthology,* eds. Elaine Marks and Isabelle de Courtivron (New York: Schocken Books, 1981), 212–20. A manifesto of radical French feminists asserts, "One cannot claim 'the right to be different,' for this means in today's context 'the right to be oppressed'" (215). The manifesto rejects biological determinism or "naturalist ideology," insisting that "the social [and aesthetic] mode of being men and women is in no way linked with their nature as males and females nor with the shape of their sex organs" (215).

[4] See Le Sueur's statement that "women [writers] have to really make their own language," quoted in Yount, 300. Yount's dissertation is an important source of direct quotation from Le Sueur. Yount begins, significantly, with the problem of how to discuss Le Sueur, given her resistance to "'objective' or analytical observations" and Yount's lack of neutrality as an observer (4). Another problem, I would add, is Le Sueur's elusive manner of expression. Le Sueur often makes statements whose correctness cannot be ascertained; they are interesting and evocative but unsupported by evidence—as, for example, her assertion that "insane women reflect imagery and speech that is often female" (301).

[5] Quoted in Yount, 301.

[6] See Patricia Hampl, "Meridel Le Sueur—Voice of the Prairie," *Ms.* (August 1975): 62–66, 96. Le Sueur said, "When I was nine or ten . . . I went to where the peasants were. . . . I loved farm women especially . . . thought they were the story tellers . . . poets"; and so were "Indian girls [who] changed my life" (62). As an adult, Le Sueur read through old

newspapers filed in the Minnesota State Historical Society, looking for women's stories as told in a language she would consider their own—a quest for discovery and recovery that presages modern feminist research (Le Sueur to Hampl, 62).

[7] "Wind," *Windsor Quarterly* 1 (Fall 1933): 266–76.

[8] "Psyche," *Windsor Quarterly* 3 (Fall 1935): 17–27; "Persephone," *Dial* 82 (May 1927): 371–80.

[9] *Annunciation* (Los Angeles: Platen Press, 1935). Reprinted in *Salute to Spring* (New York: International Publishers, 1940, reprinted 1977), 75–89; and in *Ripening*, 124–32.

[10] "Annunciation" in *Ripening*, 131.

[11] I omit mention of Le Sueur's novel *The Girl* because I think it deserves close and considerable attention. I hope to discuss the novel's circular structure in detail in an essay now in progress. The novel is unusual for its urban setting, though the protagonist comes from farmlands and returns for a brief visit. See *The Girl* (Minneapolis: West End Press, 1978).

[12] "Eroded Woman," *Masses and Mainstream* 1 (September 1948): 32–39.

[13] Quoted in Yount, 4.

[14] "I Was Marching," *New Masses* (September 1934): 16–18.

[15] I discuss the theme of recovery in modern American ethnic fiction in "Mingling and Sharing in American Literature: Teaching Ethnic Fiction," *College English* 43 (December 1981): 763–772.

[16] Frances Densmore, *Papago Music,* Smithsonian Institution, Bureau of Ethnology, Bulletin 90 (Washington, D.C.: U.S. Government Printing Office, 1929), 76. The title is given as "Song of the Women by the Sea."

[17] *The Sacred Pipe: Black Elk's Account of the Seven Rites of the Oglala Sioux,* ed. Joseph Epes Brown (Norman: Univ. of Oklahoma Press, 1953), 5.

[18] *The Sacred Pipe,* 44–112 passim. Though she tampers with the sex of the participants in the original ceremony, Le Sueur often "renders" Black Elk's (translated) words exactly: compare her first line, "I am making the sacred smoke," with *The Sacred Pipe* (88). The lines "The light is upon our people / Making the earth bright" slightly vary the original: "The light of Wahan-Tanka is upon my people; It is making the whole earth bright" (91). For particular references to the grandfather, see 55 and 65.

[19] In his study of white images of natives, Robert F. Berkhofer, Jr., states, "Native Americans were and are real, but the *Indian* was a white invention . . . a white image." See *The White Man's Indian: Images of the American Indian from Columbus to the Present* (New York: Random House, 1978), 3. For a "genealogy" of the changing social and literary uses that the "Indian image" served for whites, see pages 3–111. Berkhofer describes a "paradigm of polarity": "the Indian as an image was always alien to the White" (xv). See also N. Scott Momaday, "The Morality of Indian Hating" in *Ramparts* (Summer 1964): 30–34, esp. 30. Momaday

says, "The Indian has been for a long time generalized in the imagination of the white man."

[20] *Black Elk Speaks: Being the Life Story of a Holy Man of the Oglala Sioux,* as told to John G. Neihardt (New York: William Morrow & Company, 1932), 276.

[21] Interview with Simone Wilson, "Activist poet Meridel Le Sueur talks about writing, radicalism, renewal—past and future," Sonoma County *STUMP* (1981): 1.

[22] Interview with Dorinda Hale, "Le Sueur: Living, Writing from Within," *Sojourner* (January 1982): 10. Published originally in *Sojourner* (November 1977): 9, 21.

[23] Interview with Katherine Wakeham, "Meridel Le Sueur, Novelist for a New Age," *Womannews* (December and January): no page.

[24] White scholars who have studied Amerindian myths and expression have long recognized their "communal origin," but as Mary Austin early pointed out, since these scholars "lack" an "adequate concept of group-mindedness," they have difficulty accounting for the genesis and form of communal song. Austin pointed out, too, that one's "Own Song" was peculiarly one's possession, but could be "transferred as a legacy to the tribe." See Mary Austin, *The American Rhythm: Studies and Reexpressions of Amerindian Songs* (Cambridge, Mass.: Riverside Press, 1930, published originally in 1923), esp. 3–66 and 20–22. See also Ruth Murray Underhill, *Singing for Power: The Song Magic of the Papago Indians of Southern Arizona* (Berkeley: Univ. of California Press, 1938), esp. 1–19; and *Teachings from the American Earth*, eds. Dennis Tedlock and Barbara Tedlock (New York: Liveright, 1975).

For a contemporary Native American writer's account of traditional expression which exemplifies in its own form the literature it describes, see Leslie Marmon Silko, "Language and Literature from a Pueblo Indian Perspective" in *English Literature: Opening up the Canon, Selected Papers from the English Institute, 1979* (Baltimore: Johns Hopkins Univ. Press, 1981), 54–72. Silko confronts the problem of writing an essay about literary works that define themselves as antithetical to linear writings by explaining that her "'essay' is an edited transcript of an oral presentation. The 'author' deliberately did not read from a prepared paper so that the audience could experience first-hand one dimension of the oral tradition—non-linear structure" (54, footnote).

Unlike traditional Native American song, modern lyrics are valorized by the poet's individual voice. Only a very few, the greatest poets, "invent a voice that sounds like no one else's," Helen Vendler has said, declaring that she seeks in modern lyrics "the idiosyncratic voice wonderfully different from any other." See Helen Vendler, *Part of Nature, Part of Us: Modern American Poets* (Cambridge, Mass.: Harvard Univ. Press, 1980), ix–xi.

[25] Interview in *STUMP*: 1.

[26] See Le Sueur's autobiographical essay "The Ancient People and the Newly Come" in *Growing Up in Minnesota: Ten Writers Remember Their*

Childhoods, ed. Chester G. Anderson (Minneapolis: Univ. of Minnesota Press, 1976), 17–46, esp. 17–36 for Le Sueur's description of the influences upon her of her grandmother, her mother, and the Mandan woman Zona. Zona "taught me," Le Sueur said, "that violence is linear and love spherical" (27), and that "the circle never ends" (22–28). Published within a year of *Rites of Ancient Ripening,* this essay is very much concerned with circles and visions of cyclical return—"What turns . . . returns" (25)—and with congruences between women and earth.

On going to school with Indian girls when she was a child living in Oklahoma, Le Sueur said recently, "Those Indian girls changed me. They had no guilt, no sin, no hell." Much as she admired her grandmother, she also rebelled against her "puritanism." See interview with Harriet Stix, "Feminist Radical Is a Survivor," *Los Angeles Times* V (November 6, 1981), 6; and Yount, 77–79.

[27] "The Ancient People and the Newly Come" in *Growing Up in Minnesota,* 17.

[28] See "Excerpt from the Origins of Corn," *New America: A Review* 2 (Summer–Fall 1976): 20–23.

[29] Interview in *STUMP:* 1. See also *Womannews* interview.

[30] Quoted in Yount, 296.

[31] Ibid., 166.

[32] Interview in *Womannews.* In 1982, Le Sueur said, "I want to get away from the noun. Our language is based on naming things, as if that's the whole point, a matter of winning or losing." See John F. Baker, "Meridel Le Sueur," *Publisher's Weekly* 221 (May 21, 1982): 18–19, esp. 19.

[33] "Preface," *Corn Village,* 11. See also Benjamin Lee Whorf, "The American Indian Model of the Universe" in *Teachings from the American Earth,* 121–29.

[34] Interview in *Sojourner:* 10.

[35] Ibid. and in Yount, 166.

[36] Interview in *Sojourner:* 10. On the "Hopi, with its preference for verbs, as contrasted to our own liking for nouns," see Whorf, 128.

[37] *Black Elk Speaks,* 198–99 and in passing. See also Paula Gunn Allen, "The Sacred Hoop," *The Remembered Earth: An Anthology of Contemporary Native American Literature,* ed. Geary Hobson (Albuquerque: Univ. of New Mexico Press, 1979), 222–39. For an Oglala view on the sacredness of the circle, see "Oglala Metaphysics," *Teachings from the American Earth,* 216. Le Sueur would agree with Lame Deer that the "white man's symbol is the square"—or more precisely, the white square house, which symbolized for her the white woman's (her grandmother's) puritanism. See Lame Deer (John Fire) and Richard Endoes, *Lame Deer: Seeker of Visions* (New York: Simon and Schuster, 1972), esp. 108–18 on "The Circle and the Square"; and "The Ancient People and the Newly Come" in *Growing Up in Minnesota,* esp. 18 and 31–37. The pejorative phrase "white square houses" appears in the poem "Dead in Bloody Snow."

[38] These last lines suggest the presence of a strong woman—perhaps the phallic mother whose return various feminists invite. I trace the

lines back to the myth of "The Buffalo Rock" as given by Margot Astrov
(who derived it from a series of renderings of Blackfoot myths). See
American Indian Prose and Poetry: An Anthology, ed. Margot Astrov (New
York: Capricorn Books, 1962, published originally in 1942), 81–83. In
the myth, the rock utters the words "Take me, / I am powerful!", and
when the woman obeys, she assumes power to provide food for her
husband and tribe. Le Sueur refers specifically to the buffalo rock and
its power in a published section of her *Journals,* which contains her
renderings of "Indian chants and poetry." See Patricia Hampl, "A Book
With A Lock And Key: An introduction to a selection of journal writings," *The Lamp in the Spine* 9 (Summer/Fall 1974): 49–126, esp. 115–26.
A specific reference to the buffalo rock ties together the "Indian," his
white conqueror ("carson berfield"), and the power inherent in the
buffalo, a power now destroyed but which may come again and "will
have songs" (126).

[39] *Black Elk Speaks,* 276. For a contemporary Native American (Hopi)
poetic version of a woman's experience at Wounded Knee, see Wendy
Rose's "I expected my skin and my blood to ripen" in *Lost Copper* (Ban-
ning, Calif.: Malki Museum Press, 1980), 14–15. The poem begins, "I
expected my skin / and my blood to ripen / not to be ripped from my
bones"; and its concluding lines recognize that there was "Not enough
magic / to stop the bullets."

[40] Paula Gunn Allen (Laguna Pueblo) makes this point in her essay
(yet unpublished, as far as I know) "Answering the Deer: Genocide and
Continuance in the Poetry of American Indian Woman." This essay was
the basis for Gunn's talk at the Conference of Women Writing Poetry in
America, held at the Center for Research on Women, Stanford University (Spring 1982).

[41] The straightforward statement that earth is our mother—a highly
traditional view, of course, and one frequently made—appears in various contemporary Native American poems: in Robert J. Conley's "The
Earth," for instance, which begins, "the earth is my mother"; and in a
Leslie Silko poem which begins, "The earth is your mother, / she holds
you." Conley's poem can be found in *The Remembered Earth* (72), and
Silko's in Leslie Silko, *Storyteller* (New York: Seaver Books, 1981), 51. Le
Sueur has explained that the Indian image of mother-earth "has nothing to do with the private mother. . . . In the Indian structure it [the
mother-earth image] means nitrogen, protein, nourishment" (interview
in *Sojourner:* 10). Such statements identifying the woman as mother with
woman as corn, a source of essential protein, as Le Sueur points out,
attempt to valorize ancient myths by suggesting a scientific vocabulary
in which they can be rephrased—protein or DNA substituting for corn.

[42] Le Sueur draws upon the important myth of Changing Woman who
grants long life through her power of rejuvenation. For a considered
discussion of this figure, see Keith H. Basso, "The Gift of Changing
Woman," *Anthropological Papers,* Smithsonian Institution, Bureau of
American Ethnology, Bulletin 96 (Washington, D.C.: U.S. Government

Printing Office, 1966), 119–73. A short account of Changing Woman bears retelling for its relevance to Le Sueur's themes and peripatetic lines: "When Changing Woman gets to be a certain old age, she goes walking toward the east. After a while she sees herself in the distance looking like a young girl walking toward her. They both walk until they come together and after that there is only one. She is like a young girl again" (151).

[43] Yount, 150.

[44] Jan Clausen, "Review," *Conditions* 1 (Spring 1978): 136–47.

[45] *Rites of Ancient Ripening*, xi.

[46] See Leslie Silko, "An Old-Time Indian Attack Conducted in Two Parts: Part One: Imitation 'Indian' Poems; Part Two: Gary Snyder's 'Turtle Island'" in *The Remembered Earth*, 211–16. For a concise and informative account of an historical relationship between white American poetry and native traditions, see James Ruppert, "Discovering America: Mary Austin and Imagism" in *Studies in American Indian Literature: Critical Essays and Course Designs*, ed. Paula Gunn Allen (New York: Modern Language Association of America, 1983), 243–58. Interestingly, though Ruppert gives many reasons why white poets were attracted to "Indian" forms, reasons pertinent to Le Sueur's renderings, nowhere in his essay does the issue of a "feminine" language arise. This seems to me a unique issue in Le Sueur's poems; Le Sueur consciously and persistently transformed the songs she rendered into expressions of her feminism, changing originally male figures into females, as I have pointed out, emphasizing the unity of woman (rather than man) with the earth, and relating the sacredness of the circle to the pro-creativity of the sex.

[47] Rose, *Lost Copper*, 23.

[48] *North Star Country* (New York: Duell, Sloan & Pearce, 1945), 83–111, esp. 84. The University of Nebraska is reissuing *North Star Country* as a Bison paperback, for which I have written a foreword.

[49] "Proletarian Literature and the Middle West," *American Writers' Congress*, ed. Henry Hart (New York: International Publishers, 1935), 135–38, esp. 135.

[50] "The Ancient People and the Newly Come" in *Growing Up in Minnesota*, 17.

[51] About the final set of poems in *Rites* grouped under the title "Dòan Kêt" I have said comparatively little because, though they borrow from traditional native forms, they have more in common with Le Sueur's polemical—one might say propagandistic—writing of the thirties. One can pick lines almost at random—"The sweat shops will multiply stolen wealth of her [woman's] living skin" (53)—which inveigh openly against capitalists who make war. I do not mean to dismiss the poems, but to indicate that they might be discussed most meaningfully in a context other than that of their "Indian" form.

[52] Yount quotes from a speech Le Sueur gave in 1976 entitled "The Circle and the Square," in which "quantum theory and particle theory" are adduced to support a holistic view of life: "now it's a scientific fact

that there's no outside . . . only the interrelated movement on the inside. But you can't say inside anymore. Nothing is removed or alienated" (62).

[53] Quoted in Yount, 114.

[54] "I Hear You Singing in the Barley Ripe" conflates various songs from an Arapaho sequence. See *Literature of the American Indian*, eds. Thomas E. Sanders and Walter E. Peek (Beverly Hills, Calif.: Glencoe Press, 1973), 352–56. Le Sueur's poem appropriates from the Arapaho song cycle exact lines—"I then saw the multitude plainly"; "I am humming to you"; "O my children! O my children!"; "thus I shouted"—and references to fruit, to circling round the earth, to "approaching" personages, to singing. The reference to the father as whirlwind can be traced to a song, "The Father Comes Riding the Whirlwind" from a Cheyenne sequence (ibid., 351).

*To Professor Andrew Wiget of the State University of New Mexico at Las Cruces, whose knowledge of Native American oral traditions is considerable, I owe thanks for the helpful comments he made when I was first reading Le Sueur's poetry.

Sex in *My Ántonia*

[1] Terence Martin, "The Drama of Memory in *My Ántonia*," *PMLA*, (March, 1969), 304–11.

[2] John H. Randall, III, *The Landscape and the Looking Glass: Willa Cather's Search for Value* (Boston, 1960), 149.

See Cather's remark "The best thing I've ever done is *My Ántonia*. I feel I've made a contribution to American letters with that book," in Mildred Bennett, *The World of Willa Cather* (1951; reprinted, Lincoln, Neb., 1961), 203.

[3] Bennett, 212. Cather is quoted as saying, "If you gave me a thousand dollars for every structural fault in *My Ántonia* you'd make me very rich."

[4] David Daiches, *Willa Cather: A Critical Interpretation* (Ithaca, N.Y., 1951), 43–61.

[5] Willa Cather, *O Pioneers!*, 1913; reprinted, Boston, 1941, 259. When Emil finally approaches Marie to make love, she seems asleep, then whispers, "I was dreaming this . . . don't take my dream away!" The mergence of the real lover into the dream reminds me here of Keats's *The Eve of St. Agnes*—"Into her dream he melted." Here, too, the realization of love means facing the cold wintry world from which Madeline had been protected by her castle and her fantasy.

[6] Willa Cather, *My Ántonia*, 1918; reprinted, Boston, 1946, p. 2. All italics in quotations from *My Ántonia* are in the original, and all subsequent references are to this text. I use this edition not only because it is readily available but also because the introduction by Walter Havighurst and the suggestions for reading and discussion by Bertha Handlan represent clearly the way the novel has been widely used as validating the American past.

[7] James E. Miller, *"My Ántonia:* A Frontier Drama of Time," *American Quarterly,* 10 (Winter, 1958): 481.

[8] See Bennett, 148. Cather is quoted as saying, "The world broke in two about 1920, and I belonged to the former half." The year 1922, is given in her preface (later deleted) to *Not under Forty* (renamed *Literary Encounters,* 1937).

[9] E. K. Brown and Leon Edel, *Willa Cather: A Critical Biography* (New York, 1953), 203. Italics mine.

[10] Miller, 482.

[11] Elizabeth Shepley Sergeant, *Willa Cather: A Memoir* (1953; reprinted, Lincoln, Neb., 1963), 151.

[12] Brown and Edel, 202.

[13] Bennett, 47.

[14] Daiches says, "It is a remarkable little inset story, but its relation to the novel as a whole is somewhat uncertain" (46). However, Daiches finds so many episodes and details "uncertain," "dubious," "not wholly dominated," or "not fully integrated," it might be his reading is "flawed" rather than the novel.

[15] Sergeant, 117.

[16] Martin, 311.

[17] See the "pictures from the Wm. Cather, M.D., period of Willa's life" in Bennett, especially the photograph of Cather as a child with "her first short haircut." Note Cather's vacillating taste in clothes from the clearly masculine to feminine.

It is significant that in various plays at school and at the university, Cather assumed male roles—so convincingly that spectators sometimes refused to believe the actor was not a boy. See Bennett, 175–76, 179.

[18] Willa Cather, *The Professor's House,* 1925; reprinted, Boston, 1938.

[19] Sergeant, 46.

[20] Ibid., 121.

The Disembodiment of Lucy Gayheart

[1] An essay published in 1981 notes that "more than six hundred books and articles published during the first half of this century attempt to define Romanticism" (Hans Eichner, "The Rise of Modern Science and the Genesis of Romanticism," *PMLA* 97 [January 1982] 8–30). In 1983, Jerome J. McGann proposed "to reopen the problem of defining Romanticism." See *The Romantic Ideology: A Critical Investigation* (Chicago: Univ. of Chicago Press, 1983), 20. Important as the quest for definition is, it need not be pursued here, since I am concerned with generally agreed upon aspects of Romanticism and only as they are relevant to Cather. As McGann says, "informed persons *do* generally agree on what is comprised under the terms Romantic and Romantic movement" (18, original emphasis). To distinguish the love story or popular romance from Romanticism as an aesthetic movement and mode, I capitalize the latter.

Though the essay mentions Keats, many parallels between Wordsworth and Cather could have been drawn, since both valorized childhood, joy, quiet reflection, recovery of the past through memory, and even the transformation of memory into music with which I am specifically concerned. Lines from "Tintern Abbey" might have been Cather's epigraph for *Lucy Gayheart:* "Thy memory be as a dwelling-place / For all sweet sounds and harmonies." In a brief footnote, David Stouck has suggested "the origin of Lucy's name in Wordsworth's Lucy Gray." See *Willa Cather's Imagination* (Lincoln: Univ. of Nebraska Press, 1975), 240. Geoffrey Hartman's discussion of the Lucy poems has applicability to Lucy Gayheart as I interpret her and to her effect upon Harry Gordon who, like Wordsworth's poet, remembers a "deathless" young woman. See *Wordsworth's Poetry: 1784–1817* (New Haven: Yale Univ. Press, 1964), 157–62. Frances Ferguson's discussion of the Lucy poems also provides oblique insights into Cather's Lucy. Ferguson's statement that "Wordsworth seems to move toward a poetics in which representation involves a recognition of Lucy's absence" (174) seems transposable to Cather; but the turn of this statement as it questions the "representing" of (Wordsworth's) Lucy through memory leads away from Cather's insistence upon the power of memory and the art it inspires to re-present an absent figure. See *Wordsworth: Language as Counter-Split* (New Haven: Yale Univ. Press, 1977), 173–74. An earlier work, C. M. Bowra's study *The Romantic Imagination* (Cambridge, Mass.: Harvard Univ. Press, 1949), is particularly relevant to a reading of *Lucy Gayheart.* When Bowra describes the English Romantic poets' "prevailing mood of longing for something more complete and more satisfying than the familiar world" (272), he expresses as precisely as one can Lucy's vague Romantic aspirations. Indeed, Bowra explains such vagueness by suggesting that the object of Romantic desire is, as Cather said, beyond the power of language to express: "the poets could not but be indefinite about a matter which was beyond the reach of descriptive words" (276).

[2] All page references are to the original edition of *Lucy Gayheart* (New York: Alfred A. Knopf, 1935). Conveniently, the Vintage paperback (New York: Random House, 1976) has the same pagination.

[3] An invaluable source for Cather's early formative views on art is Bernice Slote's *The Kingdom of Art: Willa Cather's First Principles and Critical Statements, 1893–1896* (Lincoln: Univ. of Nebraska Press, 1966). See especially the discussion of Cather's early Romanticism (63–65) and the quotations from Goethe and from Verlaine on the ineffability of feeling and the inexpressible in literature (65, 73).

[4] As her statement in a 1925 interview indicates, clearly Cather knew the "usual" fictional pattern she was repudiating in *My Ántonia:* "'My Ántonia' . . . is just the other side of the rug. . . . In it there is no love affair, no courtship, no marriage, no broken heart, no struggle for success. I knew I'd ruin my material if I put it in the usual fictional form." See Cather's interview with Flora Merrill in the *World* (April 19,

1925), 6. Another statement Cather made about *My Ántonia* shows how important musical analogies were to her conception of a novel. Bernice Slote quotes a 1924 *New York Times* interview in which Cather said, "I expressed a mood [in *My Ántonia*], the core of which was a folk-song, a thing Grieg might have written." See "Willa Cather as a Regional Writer," *Kansas Quarterly* 2 (1970): 15.

⁵The novel is almost obsessively crisscrossed with contradictions, statements which seem to wipe each other out. One might claim that *Lucy Gayheart* is Cather's most fashionable text in its self-deconstruction. Even Lucy, an idealized figure, cannot be trusted, for she transgresses against the code of honor she is explicitly said to represent. Sebastian knew "she would never use his name for her own advantage" (80); but shamefully, Lucy lied and "used his name in a way she could never tell" (114). If Sebastian has misjudged Lucy, then so have the other characters and the narrator.

⁶Edith Lewis describes Cather's physical incapacity while writing *Lucy Gayheart*. See *Willa Cather Living* (New York: Alfred A. Knopf, 1953), 174–75. James Woodress describes Cather's fatigue and emotional depletion, her "diminished vitality and feeling that life was really over." See *Willa Cather: Her Life and Art* (New York: Pegasus, 1970), 248–49, 282. In a recent biography, Phyllis C. Robinson claims that the novel's "melancholy note" reflects Cather's personal sense of loss at the death of her parents. See *Willa: The Life of Willa Cather* (New York: Doubleday, 1983), 268. Cather's well-known phrase, "the gift of sympathy," comes from her introduction to the collected stories of Sarah Orne Jewett, first published in 1925 and republished in two important collections of Cather's essays: *Not under Forty* (New York: Alfred A. Knopf, 1936), 80; and *Willa Cather on Writing: Critical Studies on Writing as an Art,* forward by Stephen Tennant (New York: Alfred A. Knopf, 1949), 51. Though my thesis and conclusion differ from his, Paul Comeau notes that the passage on the aging soprano implies "a critical guideline" for reading *Lucy Gayheart*. See "Willa Cather's *Lucy Gayheart*: A Long Perspective," *Prairie Schooner* 55 (1981): 199, 208.

⁷For the characters' formularized versions of Lucy's love affair, see *Lucy Gayheart*, 222, 176, 219–20, 177, 216. Almost in chorus, critics refer to the conventionality of Cather's plot, some designating it a "Hollywood" story; however, almost none notes that Cather herself draws attention to stereotypical love stories by encapsulating them in her characters' descriptions of Lucy's fate.

⁸See *The Song of the Lark* (Lincoln: Univ. of Nebraska Press, 1915, reprint 1978) 294, 303, 460.

⁹"The Novel Demeublé" (1922) defended the value of imagination in art as opposed to journalism, literalness, or enumeration, Cather's terms for realism. In 1936, one year after the publication of *Lucy Gayheart*, the essay was included in the collection *Not under Forty*, from which I quote (50).

¹⁰Ibid.

¹¹Both David Stouck and Mildred Bennett shared with me their

knowledge that Cather called Book III the best part of the novel in a letter to Zoë Akins written soon after *Lucy Gayheart* was published (the letter is in the Huntington Library). Even in her longest and most explicit novel, *The Song of the Lark*, Cather resorted to an epilogue which would express in other words, spoken by a minor character, the value of art. Though Thea denies that money can measure an artist's success, in the epilogue, her Aunt Tillie flaunts Thea's earnings, "one thousand dollars a night," as a sign of her worth. At the same time, Tillie tells herself, "Surely, people didn't for a minute think it was the money she cared about" (485). Words with a referent as exact as a sum of money mean something else, something intangible and elusive that Cather was after words to express.

[12] See J. Donald Adams, "A New Novel by Willa Cather," *New York Times Book Review* (August 4, 1935), 1; "Lucy Gayheart," *London Times Literary Supplement* (July 25, 1935), 476; Howard Mumford Jones, "Willa Cather Returns to the Middle West," *Saturday Review* (August 3, 1935), 7.

[13] "'Lucy Gayheart' is simply a maudlin book," Robert Cantwell writes in "A Season's Run," *New Republic* (December 11, 1935), 149. "Miss Cather surrenders to the temptation of facile sentimentalism," William Troy says in "Footprints in Cement," *Nation* (August 14, 1935), 193. The complaints of triteness, banality, and superciliousness appear in Newton Arvin, "Sweet Story," *New Republic* (September 11, 1935), 138. William Plomer describes "Lucy Brokenheart" in "Fiction," *Spectator* 155 (August 2, 1935): 200.

[14] See Stouck, 214; and Comeau, 199, 208.

[15] John H. Randall III, *The Landscape and the Looking Glass: Willa Cather's Search for Value* (Boston: Houghton Mifflin, 1960), 355–56.

[16] E. K. Brown says that the first part of *Lucy Gayheart* has "a heaviness, a lagging pace, for which there is no parallel in any of her [Cather's] earlier writings." See *Willa Cather: A Critical Biography*, completed by Leon Edel (New York: Alfred A. Knopf, 1953), 294. Brown considered the epilogue the novel's "finest part" (302), but David Daiches complained of its pointlessness and "excessive deliberation." See *Willa Cather: A Critical Introduction* (Ithaca, New York: Cornell Univ. Press, 1951), 131. Randall ridicules and misrepresents the epilogue when he says that "everyone mournfully loves Lucy" (354).

[17] Daiches, 132.

[18] John J. Murphy calls Lucy "silly" in "'Lucy's Case': An Interpretation of *Lucy Gayheart*," *Markham Review* 9 (1980): 28. Murphy's comparison of Lucy to Paul of Cather's famous story "Paul's Case" seems particularly invidious in light of Richard Giannone's statement that "Paul's attachment to art is false, subjective . . . insane." See *Music in Willa Cather's Fiction* (Lincoln: Univ. of Nebraska Press, 1968), 46. According to Woodress, Cather herself called her heroine "a silly young girl" (251, 248). Complaining that "Lucy never comes alive," Woodress contrasts Thea Kronberg as "a flesh-and-blood character" with Lucy as "a pallid, disembodied spirit" (252). Philip Gerber finds Lucy "a rather bloodless

cousin to Thea" (94). See *Willa Cather* (Boston: Twayne, 1975). Dorothy Tuck McFarland says that though *Lucy Gayheart* is "not a bad novel, it is curiously lifeless" (127). See *Willa Cather* (New York: Frederick Ungar, 1972). Randall dismisses Lucy as "an adolescent schoolgirl" (356).

[19] Cather said she conceived of Marion Forrester as "a thin miniature painted on ivory" (interview in the *World*, 6), the Bishop and his Vicar as the etiolated saints of medieval legend (*On Writing*, 9), and Ántonia as an "old Sicilian apothecary jar" or a "Taormina" vase viewed from various angles (Elizabeth Shepley Sergeant, *Willa Cather: A Memoir* [Lincoln: Univ. of Nebraska Press, 1963], 139). Also, Cather described *The Professor's House* as analogous in form both to a sonata and a Dutch painting (*On Writing*, 31). Her esoteric comments on *Shadows On the Rock* again draw analogies between music and her text: the novel, she says, grew out of a "feeling" that was "hard to state . . . in language; it was more like an old song. . . . The text was mainly an anacoluthon. . . . I took the incomplete air and tried to give it what would correspond to a sympathetic musical setting; tried to develop it into a prose composition" (*On Writing*, 15). I comment below on Cather's use of "composition." By noting Cather's rather recondite conceptions of her characters and the novel, I do not mean to deny that she drew, as critics well know, from real life prototypes (see note 27). I intend only to emphasize her deliberateness in transforming the human figure into an artifact. As she said, figures from life roamed in her memory like ghosts waiting for the bodies she would give them in her novels. See Cather's interview in the *World*, 6, which is quoted in Mildred Bennett, *The World of Willa Cather* (New York: Dodd, Mead, 1951), 211; and Bennett, "Willa Cather's Bodies for Ghosts," *Western American Literature* 17 (May 1982) 39–52. In *Lucy Gayheart*, Cather reversed her usual process of incarnation by depriving Lucy of a body so that she could exist as (e)motion.

[20] Susanne Langer's contention that music is "a language of feeling . . . of emotions" (221) supports Cather's view. Langer asserts that "*music articulates forms which language cannot set forth*" (233, original emphasis), and these forms are precisely "the forms of human feeling" (235). Music makes its meanings known through "*revelations*," Langer says, though "literal minds" have difficulty grasping "the idea that anything can be *known* which cannot be *named*" (233, original emphases). Here an agreement with Cather's statements in "The Novel Demeublé" is remarkable. Langer refers to Wagner's view (which assuredly Cather knew) that music can express "what is unspeakable in verbal language, and . . . may therefore be called simply the *Unspeakable*" (235, original emphasis). Langer's chapter on music expresses in philosophical terms a definition of music that is implicit in *Lucy Gayheart*, as well as the novel's unstated but assumed distinctions between verbal and musical language. See *Philosophy in a New Key: A Study in the Symbolism of Reason, Rite, and Art* (Cambridge, Mass.: Harvard Univ. Press, 1960), 204–45. In *The Mirror and the Lamp: Romantic Theory and the Critical Tradition*, Meyer Abrams points out that "music was the first of the arts to be generally regarded as non-mimetic . . . the art most immediately expressive of

spirit and emotion" (New York: Oxford Univ. Press, 1953), 50. Bowra records the aspiration of Romantic poetry "to become music" (278), a desire I find in Cather's heroine and in Cather herself.

[21] Brown describes a "chance encounter" in 1896 between Cather and a vivacious young woman named Lucy Gayhardt who provided one prototype for the novel's heroine (297–98). See also Leon Edel's interesting speculations about Cather's choice of this Lucy as her inspiration in "Willa Cather: The Paradox of Success," *Willa Cather and Her Critics*, ed. James Schroeter (Ithaca: Cornell Univ. Press, 1967), 265–66. Another prototype, mentioned by Woodress (250), was Sadie Becker of Red Cloud. Like Lucy, this young woman was an accompanist, had an unhappy love affair, and left her small town for the city. Cather also remembered Sadie's ice-skating and the color of her eyes which she gave to Lucy. Robinson refers to both prototypes as providing the "memories" upon which Cather drew (269). Still another source for Lucy is Cather's heroine in an early story called "The Joy of Nelly Deane." Bennett points out similarities in "Cather's Bodies for Ghosts," 45–46; and in the "Introduction" to *Willa Cather's Collected Short Fiction*, ed. Virginia Faulkner (Lincoln: Univ. of Nebraska Press, 1970), Bennett says that the "tragic yet joyful story [of Nelly Deane] is a sketch in miniature of Lucy's" ("Introduction," x1).

[22] Like Thea in *The Song of the Lark*, Lucy wants to prolong an ecstacy she calls "ravishing," but the very word, which suggests sexual assault or rape as well as joy, opposes the divorce between body and soul that Lucy has made crucial to her life, and Cather to her novel. Indeed, Lucy seems raped by Sebastian's songs: they leave her "tired and frightened," "shivering," and "with a feeling that some protective barrier was gone" (32). Cather's words suggest a violation, if not of Lucy's body then of her spirit, as melody exposes Lucy to the ominousness of an "outside world" which began to seem "dark and terrifying, full of fears and dangers that had never come close to her until now" (31). If Sebastian's ravishing melodies enchant and transport Lucy, they also force her to recognize the fatality of "passion."

[23] The forlorn lover of *Die Winterreise* wishes in vain for a "keepsake" of his lost love. Harry Gordon has Lucy's footprints, but the cycle's rejected lover cries out in "Erstarrung" or "Frozen Rigidity" (song 4): "In vain I seek her footprints / in the snow." See "Die Winterreise," *The Penguin Book of Lieder*, ed. and trans. by S. S. Prawer (Baltimore: Penguin, 1964), 55.

[24] In her essay "My First Novels" (1931), Cather turned, as she often did, to analogy in order to define an "element" she valued in the novel—in this essay "a very satisfying element analogous to what painters call 'composition'" (*On Writing*, 97). In the same collection, Cather describes an artist beginning a work by deciding upon "a certain composition" ("Light on Adobe Walls," 123). Composition, a term Cather borrowed sometimes from painting and other times from music, meant to her selection, simplification, premeditated design—the essential elements of her art.

[25] I am not concurring here with Giannone's claim that Lucy reenacts the role of the desolate lover in *Die Winterreise*, the transporting song cycle she hears Sebastian sing (see *Music in Willa Cather's Fiction*). Though Giannone offers valuable insights into Cather's use of music, he also invites correction, particularly in his chapter on *Die Winterreise*. Giannone errs when he says that Lucy hears of Sebastian's death while she is in Nebraska (214); he selects songs to support his thesis and omits songs 17, 18, and 20 which would question it; and he misreads various songs, particularly "Courage" (song 22) which seems to mean the opposite of what he says. I am indebted to Ulrike Rainer for her close reading of Schubert's songs and her comments on Giannone (see note below). Cather's lifelong interest in music and its pervasive and particular influences upon her work have been amply documented. See, for example, Joseph X. Brennan, "Willa Cather and Music," *University Review* 31 (March 1965): 175–183; and "Music and Willa Cather," *University Review* 31 (June 1965): 257–264. Oddly enough, Brennan says that music is so important to *Lucy Gayheart* that he cannot discuss the novel in his essays. See also Richard Giannone, "Willa Cather and the Human Voice," *Five Essays on Willa Cather: The Merrimack Symposium*, ed. John J. Murphy (North Andover, Mass.: Merrimack College, 1974), 21–49. I agree with Giannone that "a consideration of Cather's handling of music might . . . help to countervail the recurrent disapproval *Lucy Gayheart* has received even from some of the novelist's most admiring critics" (*Music in Willa Cather's Fiction*, 215).

[26] Jim Burden has "the sense of coming home to myself" when he remembers himelf and Ántonia as "wondering children" in *My Ántonia* (Boston: Houghton Mifflin, 1918, reprint 1961), 371. See also *The Professor's House* (New York: Random House, 1925, reprint 1973), 264–67. While Jim proposes to become a boy again, Godfrey resigns himself to acting his age, which means to him accepting "the bloomless side of life that he had always run away from" (280) and living "without delight . . . without joy" (282), stripped of heightened Romantic emotion.

[27] Even when Lucy possessed a body, it had never been substantial; never sensuous, strong, firm, rosy, "a cheering sight" to herself, as Thea Kronberg's body had been (427); or stalwart like Ántonia's with her brown arms and legs and cheeks the color of "big dark red plums" (153); or graceful, teasing, seductive, like Marion Forrester's in *A Lost Lady*. Lucy's body seemed of no interest to her, a means for movement, in itself slight and sexless, or rather, hermaphroditic. One can only guess whether Cather was deliberately suggesting a resemblance between Lucy and the messenger-god Hermes (father of Hermaphroditus), also known as Mercury. Both at the beginning and the end of the novel, Cather alludes to Lucy's wings (8, 227), the second time referring specifically to "the herald Mercury" and his winged feet. Earlier, Cather had described Lucy as a "mercurial, vacillating person" (18). The mercurial, as well as the hermaphroditic, aspects of Lucy's character might usefully be pursued.

[28] Lucy also indulges in reflection, recovering her happiness and re-

covering from her despair by remembering. In Chicago, "she got the greatest happiness out of each day—after it had passed" (93). In Haverford, she finds reprieve from her grief only through reflection on the past: "She could breathe only in the world she brought back through memory" (156). Perhaps the best interpretation of the psychological function of a person's reflections on lost love is given in Freud's account of the "work of recollection." See Volume III of the *Standard Edition of the Complete Psychological Works of Sigmund Freud* (London: Hogarth Press, 1955), 162–64.

[29] *A Lost Lady* (New York: Random House, 1923, reprint. 1972), 171–72. In this novel Niel Herbert demonstrates the chivalric devotion that Sebastian attributes to Lucy.

[30] When Lionel Trilling complained that in *Lucy Gayheart* "the characters are unattached to anything save their dreams" (155), he was describing a state of being to which Lucy had Romantically aspired. She felt threatened by whatever separated her from her dreams which, in effect, she would die to realize. Trilling's disapproving essay, "Willa Cather," was published originally in 1937 and republished in *Willa Cather and Her Critics*, ed. Schroeter.

[31] On the fatality of sexual union in Cather, see my essay "The Forgotten Reaping Hook: Sex in *My Ántonia*" in this book. Cather implies that Sebastian has affairs with other women—richer, older, sleeker, more sensual women than Lucy—but she offers what they lack, idealism and youth.

[32] Willa Cather, "Preface" to Gertrude Hall, *The Wagnerian Romances* (New York: Alfred A. Knopf, 1925), ix. Cather's statement about Hall's achievement describes her own aspiration for *Lucy Gayheart*, as I see it. Cather says that Hall could "reproduce the emotional effect of one art [music] through the medium of another [literature]" (viii).

[33] On Cather's "horror of mutilation," see Woodress, 249 (who draws upon Lewis, 10) and Bennett, "Introduction" to Cather's *Collected Short Fiction*, xxxviii. Robinson collates all these sources, 193. On the "interrelatedness of health, success, and goodness" in Cather, see Evelyn Hinz, "Willa Cather's Technique and the Ideology of Populism," *Western American Literature* 7 (Spring 1972) 54–55.

[34] Stouck, 219–20.

[35] Cather's discussion of the "double life" in families in her essay "Katherine Mansfield" seems immediately relevant to the Gayhearts (*On Writing*, 109–10).

[36] *Not under Forty*, v.

[37] Reflecting upon his life since Lucy's death, Harry calls it "a life sentence" (221). The phrase, suggesting imprisonment (within his body, within mundane life), has a multivalence appropriate to a novel reflecting upon the freedom or limitations inherent in its own sentences.

[38] I like Josephine Lurie Jessup's no-nonsense attitude toward Harry Gordon, whom she upbraids for stranding Lucy in the restaurant without cabfare and on the icy road that leads to her death. See *The Faith of Our Feminists: A Study in the Novels of Edith Wharton, Ellen Glasgow, Willa*

Cather (New York: Richard R. Smith, 1950), 73.

*I am indebted to Ulrike Rainer with whom I consulted during the early stages of writing this essay. Ms. Rainer drew upon her considerable knowledge of music and of German Romanticism to offer general suggestions as well as specific comments on Cather's text. Her interest was encouraging and her information useful (though not all appears in this essay). She has pointed out suggestive similarities which I could not pursue here between Cather's Mockford and various red-headed diabolical figures of Thomas Mann's fiction.

The Hidden Mines in Ethel Wilson's Landscape

[1] *Hetty Dorval* (Toronto: Macmillan, Laurentian Library, 1967), 86. *Hetty Dorval* was published originally in 1947.

[2] Ethel Wilson, "Hurry, hurry," *Mrs. Golightly and Other Stories* (Toronto: Macmillan, 1961), 106. "Then the light fades [Wilson writes]. . . , but those who have seen it will remember."

[3] *Love and Salt Water* (Toronto: Macmillan, 1956), 152.

[4] "'I don't care for fresh air myself except for the purpose of breathing. I exist here . . . and here . . .' Mrs. Severance touched her heart and her head. 'Everything of any importance happens indoors. . . ,'" *Swamp Angel* (Toronto: McClelland and Stewart, 1962), 149, original ellipses. *Swamp Angel* was published originally by Macmillan of Canada Limited in 1954.

[5] "Tuesday and Wednesday," *The Equations of Love* (Toronto: Macmillan, 1974 paperback, published originally in 1952). See pages 127–28 in which the word *caused* appears seven times, linking together an incongruous sequence of events that "life and time" effect through "manipulations . . . of circumstance and influence and spiked chance and decisions among members of the human family."

[6] "A drink with Adolphus," *Mrs. Golightly*, 79.

[7] Professor David Stouck has reported to the Ethel Wilson Conference that an alternate manuscript version of *Love and Salt Water* does show them drowning.

[8] *The Innocent Traveller* (London: Macmillan, 1949), 101.

[9] See Wilson's letter of July 2, 1953, to Desmond Pacey, quoted in his book *Ethel Wilson* (New York: Twayne, 1967), 25.

[10] The phrase comes from a famous passage in *My Ántonia* that describes young Jim Burden's first sight of Nebraska: "There was nothing but land: not a country at all, but the material out of which countries are made" (Boston: Houghton Mifflin, Sentry Edition, 1954), 7. *My Ántonia* was published originally in 1918.

[11] *A Lost Lady* (New York: Random House, Vintage, 1972), 172. *A Lost Lady* was published originally in 1923.

[12] *Love and Salt Water*, 149.

[13] "Tuesday and Wednesday," *The Equations of Love*, 68.

[14] Ibid., 77.

[15] *Swamp Angel*, 146.

[16] "Lilly's Story," *The Equations of Love,* 262.

[17] "Tuesday and Wednesday," 101.

[18] In an essay on modern American city fiction, I discuss this relationship between space and freedom. See "'Residence Underground': Recent Fictions of the Subterranean City," *Sewanee Review,* (Summer 1975): 406–38.

[19] I have discussed this thematic meaning of love in Woolf in the essay "Love and Conversion in *Mrs. Dalloway,*" *Criticism,* (Summer 1966): 229–45.

[20] *The Innocent Traveller,* 124.

[21] "Truth and Mrs. Forrester," *Mrs. Golightly,* 111.

The City's "Hungry" Woman as Heroine

[1] Thomas Wolfe, *Of Time and the River* (New York: Charles Scribner's Sons, 1935), 89. Once in the library, Eugene read "insanely, by the hundreds, the thousands, the ten thousands . . . a ravening appetite in him demanded that he read everything. . . . He pictured himself as tearing the entrails from a book as from a fowl" (91).

[2] Eugene is also Orestes, Telemachus, Jason, Antaeus, Kronos—no dearth of myths for his aggrandizement.

[3] In the last book of the novel, called "Faustus and Helen," Eugene is "impaled upon the knife of love" (911) as he meets the beautiful Helen of myth and male desire.

[4] For a discussion of madwomen and anorexics as figures of rebellion, see Sandra M. Gilbert and Susan Gubar, *The Madwoman in the Attic* (New Haven: Yale Univ. Press, 1979). Also in an essay review in the Fall 1979 edition (no. 8) of *University Publishing,* Professor Gilbert pursues the symbolic meaning of "anorexic renunciation" ("Hunger Pains," 1 and 11–12). Dr. Hilde Brucke in *The Golden Cage: The Enigma of Anorexia Nervosa* (Cambridge: Harvard Univ. Press, 1978) describes anorexics as young people engaged in a "blind search for a sense of identity and selfhood": "they would rather starve than continue a life of accommodation" (x).

In her study of "female madness" in contemporary American fiction, Mary Allen declares herself dismayed, enraged, and frustrated at the depiction of women in the novels she discusses. *The Necessary Blankness: Women in Major American Fiction of the Sixties* (Chicago: Univ. of Illinois Press, 1976), 13. See particularly the chapter on Sylvia Plath's *The Bell Jar* in which Allen views the heroine's madness and attempted suicide as her "defiance." Describing Plath's heroine, Patricia Meyer Spacks has said: "In her view, psychosis is virtually a female necessity, leaving only a choice of madness" (*The Female Imagination* [New York: Alfred A. Knopf, 1975], 147).

A tradition of happy submission to a woman's predetermined role also mitigates against the emergence of a hungry heroine. See Barbara Welter, "The Cult of True Womanhood," *American Quarterly* 18 (1966), 151–74.

We should note that from Puritan times on, women were warned of the dangerous effects of education; they could be driven mad, not through repression, but through too much learning. See Ann Stanford's essay "Images of Women in Early American Literature" in *What Manner of Woman: Essays on English and American Life and Literature* (New York: New York Univ. Press, 1977), ed. by Marlene Springer. The essay notes "the fate of Ann Hopkins" (recorded in John Winthrop's journal), who lost her wits by "giving herself wholly to reading and writing" (193). In an interesting early novel about college-educated women, the woman who earns a Ph.D. suffers a mental collapse: "I broke down, that's all. I can't stand anything now that takes thought" (172). A university professor pointed out earlier that there are "men and women—but women particularly . . . staggering under a mental load too heavy for them" (96). The novel's heroine has a bachelor's degree, a manageable load. See Elia W. Peattie, *The Precipice: A Novel* (Boston: Houghton Mifflin Company, 1914).

⁵ In her essay "The Female Faust," Ann Ronald discusses a damned heroine who sells herself to the "devil" for "love and security," giving up her *self*. See *Feminist Criticism: Essays on Theory, Prose and Poetry*, Cheryl L. Brown and Karen Olson, eds. (New Jersey and London: Scarecrow Press, 1978), 212–21. As literary figures, the "female Faust" and the "sister to Faust" whom I describe are antithetical, each representing an aspect of the Faust myth, the former his damnation, the latter his aspirations and desire.

⁶ A recent "semantic" interpretation of Hesiod's account of Prometheus presents Pandora as a "gaster" or maw, "an insatiable belly devouring the *bios* or nourishment that men procure for themselves through their labour." As a "female belly," Pandora hungers for food and sex, thus representing voracity and lasciviousness, the "bitchiness" of women. See Jean-Pierre Vernant, *Myth and Society in Ancient Greece* (New Jersey: Humanities Press, 1980), 178 ff.

Note a professor's fear of the woman "bitch" who devours books—and her professor-husband—as she studies for a Ph.D. in Saul Bellow's *Herzog* (New York: The Viking Press, 1964).

⁷ Gail Godwin, *The Odd Woman* (New York: Alfred Knopf, 1974).

⁸ Lisa Alther, *Kinflicks* (New York: Alfred Knopf, 1976).

⁹ Marilyn French, *The Women's Room* (New York: Simon & Schuster, 1977).

¹⁰ Thomas Pynchon, *The Crying of Lot 49* (Philadelphia: J. B. Lippincott, 1966).

¹¹ Anzia Yezierska, *Hungry Hearts* (Boston: Houghton Mifflin, 1920).

¹² Mary Antin, *The Promised Land* (Boston: Houghton Mifflin, 1912).

¹³ Betty Smith, *A Tree Grows in Brooklyn* (New York: Harper and Brothers, 1943). See 18, 21.

¹⁴ Dorothy Bryant, *Ella Price's Journal* (New York: New American Library, 1972), 35.

¹⁵ Paule Marshall, *Brown Girl, Brownstones* (New Jersey: The Chatham Bookseller, 1959), 240.

[16] Anzia Yezierska, *Bread Givers* (New York: Doubleday, Page and Company, 1925), 208.

[17] Louise Meriwether (New York: Pyramid Books, 1971), 173. In this novel, mothers repeatedly urge their children, sons and daughters, to go to school.

[18] Maxine Hong Kingston, *The Woman Warrior: Memoirs of a Girlhood among Ghosts* (New York: Alfred Knopf, 1976), 201.

In Sylvia Plath's *The Bell Jar* (New York: Harper and Row, 1971), Esther Greenwood also earns A's in school, but her desire for education is factitious: "All my life I'd *told* myself studying and reading and writing and working like mad was what I wanted to do, and it actually *seemed* to be true" (34). When Esther feels herself "starving," it is not for books but for caviar and crabmeat, contaminated foods that poison her. She imagines heaven as "kitchens . . . stretching into infinity"; in them are avocado pears stuffed with crabmeat. In her study of "the female imagination," Professor Patricia Spacks notes that Esther's "madness, her suffering, are [sic] offered as metaphors of normalcy"; but in expressing herself through metaphors rather than action, Esther remains stereotypically passive, though she may believe herself rebellious. In New York, Esther sees none of the possibilities for freedom that the city offers the hungry heroine. Rather, she chooses to see only the debasement of women into objects of fashion and sex. Like Maria in Joan Didion's *Play It As It Lays,* she found(ed)—and created—a city that confirmed her nihilistic views of life. See the following footnote.

[19] See *Hungry Hearts.* The multiple meanings of *found*—as an act of discovery, response, and creation (one founds a country)—apply to Shenah's quest for someone to understand the "vague, blind hunger for release that consumed" her. When her teacher understands, Shenah discovers America and also her own responsibility for creating, or founding, the land of freedom she seeks.

[20] Willa Cather, *My Ántonia* (Boston: Houghton Mifflin, 1918, reprint 1946). Note that Ántonia's father begs Jim Burden to teach Ántonia to read: "Te-e-ach, te-e-ach my Án-tonia" (27), but Ántonia has no time for study.

[21] For a discussion of the "benign" effects of urban disorder, particularly the freedom it allows, see Richard Sennett, *The Uses of Disorder: Personal Identity and City Life* (New York: Alfred Knopf, 1970).

[22] Jade Snow Wong, *Fifth Chinese Daughter* (New York: Harper and Brothers, 1950).

[23] Bruno Bettelheim, *The Uses of Enchantment: The Meaning and Importance of Fairy Tales* (New York: Alfred Knopf, 1976).

[24] Edith Wharton, *A Backward Glance* (New York: D. Appleton-Century, 1934). See Chapter III, passim. The phrase "the kingdom of my father's library" appears on 42.

[25] Edmund Wilson, "Justice to Edith Wharton," *The New Republic* 95 (June 29, 1938), 209–13.

[26] Cynthia Griffin Wolff, *A Feast of Words* (New York: Oxford Univ. Press, 1977). Chapter I, "A Portrait of the Artist as a Young Woman,"

describes Wharton's genesis as a writer in psychoanalytic terms. Ultimately, Wharton's art compensates for an "irradicable" "hunger for love" that traces back to traumatic infantile emotions, "a sense of deprivation" felt as "coldness and hunger."

[27] James Woodress, *Willa Cather: Her Life and Art* (New York: Western Publishing Company, Pegasus Book, 1970). See 40–41 for a discussion of Cather's "huge, eclectic consumption of literary material."

Gertrude Stein read so widely and eclectically that, like Eugene Gant, she feared she would exhaust the library: "when she was young she had read so much, read from the Elizabethans to the moderns, that she was terribly uneasy lest someday she would be without anything to read. For years this fear haunted her but in one way or another although she always reads and reads she seems always to find more to read." *The Autobiography of Alice B. Toklas* (New York: Harcourt, Brace and Company, 1933), 68.

In an interview in *The Paris Review* 29 (Winter–Spring 1963), 87–114, Katherine Anne Porter described her early reading of Shakespeare, Dante, Homer, Ronsard, "the old French poets in translation," Montaigne, Voltaire, Jane Austen, Turgenev, Brontë, Henry James, Hardy, Dickens, Thackeray—all this (at least) by the time she was sixteen.

George Eliot and Virginia Woolf were famously "omnivorous" readers. See Gordon Haight's *George Eliot: A Biography* (New York: Oxford Univ. Press, 1968), 23 and Chapter I, passim; and Virginia Woolf's voluminous reading notebooks. In *Three Guineas* (New York: Harcourt, Brace and Company, 1938), Woolf described woman's "desire for education" as "innate," that is, natural and inevitable, like hunger (36).

[28] For a view of Goethe's Faust as a hero on "a quest for self-realization," the essential quest, however diminished, of the hungry heroine, see Hermann Wiegand, "Goethe's *Faust:* An Introduction" in *Faust: Backgrounds and Sources* (New York: Norton, 1976), tr. by Walter Arndt, ed. by Cyrus Hamplin, 446–72. Marlowe's Faust has been considered the incarnation of desire, but in a brilliant essay, Edgar A. Snow shows both desire and the self as problematic. Faustus doubts whether he has a self that exists prior to and that wills desire, and whether he can ever create a self that would fulfill desire. The essay raises complex questions about consciousness, language, and being which help us understand, even if only by contrast, the dimensions of Faust's "sister." See "Doctor Faustus and the Ends of Desire" in *Two Renaissance Mythmakers: Christopher Marlowe and Ben Johnson,* ed. by Alvin Kernan (Baltimore: Johns Hopkins Press, 1977), 70–110.

[29] I want to suggest that we re-view our familiar books to discover in them tentative explorations of the possibility for female autonomy. Consider, for example, Jo in Louisa May Alcott's *Little Women* (1868). Jo "devoured" the books of Aunt March's library and browsed "voraciously" through Mr. Laurence's library; she insisted upon her individuality and dreamt of doing something "splendid" with her life; she leaves home, exercises her talent, achieves success—but somehow comes to capitulate to common wisdom: a woman does something "splendid"

when she marries (preferably in poverty), bears children, and runs a school for boys.

We might also look again at Helen Bober in Bernard Malamud's *The Assistant* (New York: Farrar, Straus, and Giroux, 1957). Helen longs for education, a college degree, a new life for herself, but gradually she projects her dreams upon the lover she meets night after night in the public library. She "feeds" him the books that have nourished her imagination, gradually losing her identity as a hungry heroine and falling into the convoluted reasoning of Helen Gant that allows her to appease her hunger by feeding a man.

Cather, Austin, and Porter

[1] References are to Phyllis C. Robinson, *Willa: The Life of Willa Cather* (New York: Doubleday, 1983); Augusta Fink, *I-Mary: A Biography of Mary Austin* (Tucson: Univ. of Arizona Press, 1983); Joan Givner, *Katherine Anne Porter: A Life* (New York: Simon and Schuster, 1982). Since Robinson's book is a collation made from the works of Cather's critics and the memoirs of her friends, I have gone mainly to the original sources. I have drawn also upon Austin's autobiography *Earth Horizon* (New York: The Literary Guild, 1932), which is often more detailed and revealing than the biography. References to Porter's life come from the biography, except for a quotation from a Porter essay published in *The Days Before* (New York: Harcourt, Brace, 1952).

Hemingway's "life" is used here as emblematic of the male writer. This is not to deny his individuality (or the hazards of generalization) but to permit at least tentative comparisons. The authoritative Hemingway biography referred to is Carlos Baker, *Ernest Hemingway: A Life Story* (New York: Charles Scribner's Sons, 1969).

Other references are to Virginia Woolf, *Orlando: A Biography* (New York: Harcourt, Brace, 1928).

When in quotation marks, "life" indicates the writer insofar as the person concerned with literary art and career, concentrating on pursuing both, can be distinguished from the person involved in everyday functions. A deliberate and polemic attempt to distinguish between the two can be found in William Gass's review of Joseph Blotner's biography of Faulkner. See "Mr. Blotner, Mr. Feaster, and Mr. Faulkner" in *The World Within the Word: Essays by William H. Gass* (New York: Alfred A. Knopf, 1978).

[2] Leon Edel, *Literary Biography* (Toronto: Univ. of Toronto Press, 1957).

[3] Estelle C. Jellinek, "Women's Autobiography and the Male Tradition" in *Women's Autobiography: Essays in Criticism*, ed. and intro. by Estelle C. Jellinek (Bloomington: Indiana Univ. Press, 1980).

[4] The travel articles written on this trip have been collected in a volume called *Willa Cather in Europe: Her Own Story of the First Journey*, intro. by George N. Kates (New York: Alfred A. Knopf, 1956).

⁵Or leopards, antelope, waterbuck, kudu bulls, sable cows, gazelles, buffalo, rhinoceros, zebra, mountain rams, elk, grizzly bears.

⁶The same incident is reported in the biographies of both. See Givner, 286, and Baker, 258.

⁷See the contradictory stories about Cather's writing part of *Death Comes for the Archbishop* in Austin's New Mexico house in Austin's *Earth Horizon*, 359; Elizabeth Sergeant's *Willa Cather: A Memoir* (New York: J. B. Lippincott, 1953), 226; and T. M. Pearce's *Mary Hunter Austin* (New York: Twayne, 1965), 100.

⁸This was not a quibbling question to Cather, as her biographer indicates, or to Cather's companion Edith Lewis when she discussed how Cather's "life" story should be told with Leon Edel as he was about to become the writer's biographer. See Edel, "Homage to Willa Cather" in *The Art of Willa Cather*, ed. by Bernice Slote and Virginia Faulkner (Lincoln: Univ. of Nebraska Press, 1974), 189. Lewis "did not even want the little Willa of the childhood years to be on a first-name basis to her biographer."

⁹Mildred R. Bennett, *The World of Willa Cather* (New York: Dodd, Mead, 1951), 212.

¹⁰Quoted in Bernice Slote, "First Principles: The Kingdom of Art" in *The Kingdom of Art: Willa Cather's First Principles and Critical Statements 1893–1896*, ed. Bernice Slote (Lincoln: Univ. of Nebraska Press, 1966), 43.

¹¹Interestingly enough, the same may be said of Edith Wharton's husband, whom Wharton divorced after feeling herself emotionally and financially depleted by him.

Index of Authors and Titles

This index lists writers and their works and does not include critics cited in the essays and footnotes.